W9-BGL-688

LAND-USE PLANNING
for Sustainable Development

SUSTAINABLE COMMUNITY DEVELOPMENT SERIES

Chris Maser, Editor

SUSTAINABLE COMMUNITY DEVELOPMENT SERIES

LAND-USE PLANNING
for Sustainable Development

Jane Silberstein
Chris Maser

LEWIS PUBLISHERS

Boca Raton London New York Washington, D.C.

0026248

Cover design and photograph by Rosyln Nelson, Watermark MN, Inc.

Library of Congress Cataloging-in-Publication Data

Silberstein, Jane
    Land-use planning for sustainable development / by Jane Silberstein
    and Chris Maser.
       p. cm.
    Includes bibliographical references.
    ISBN 1-56670-325-5 (alk. paper)
      1. Land use—United States—Planning. 2. Sustainable
    development—United States. I. Maser, Chris. II. Title.

HD205 .S55 2000
333.73—dc21
                                                     00-033092

Visit the CRC Press Web site at www.crcpress.com

© 2000 by CRC Press LLC
Lewis Publishers is an imprint of CRC Press LLC

No claim to original U.S. Government works
International Standard Book Number 1-56670-325-5
Library of Congress Card Number 00-033092
Printed in the United States of America   2 3 4 5 6 7 8 9 0
Printed on acid-free paper

Preface

Choice — a simple but powerful word — changes the world every day in ways both great and small. People, having appropriated choice from the dawning of humanity, value it, vie for it, and die for it. Yet, many people have little or no concept of the sense of freedom that comes with the ability to choose or the sense of responsibility that comes with the consequences of one's choices.

When altering the land to accommodate human necessities and perceived needs, we have choice. Encouraging diverse community involvement in making these choices, while not becoming frozen in conflict or indecision, is the challenge we address in this book.

To do this, we review the foundations of our current land-use practices from historical, constitutional, economic, and societal perspectives; analyze the results of these practices; and propose some possible alternative methods for guiding, directing, and controlling the ways in which we modify the landscape where the basic concept of choice is emphasized.

This book is tied to our belief that we, as humans, have the capacity for community with all life and can ultimately embrace the notion that individual well-being is wrapped up in the well-being of the whole and that social change can occur before major disasters require it.

Choice. Thurgood Marshall and Mahatma Gandhi understood it. They made no apologies for wanting it equally for themselves and for all other people. They did much to make the world see that individual choice — implied by basic human rights — has no meaning unless it is universally available to all people. The ability to choose confers upon each individual a sense of value, self-confidence, and the dignity of being human.

But, are we trying desperately to see life as a series of painless options by ignoring the hard choices about the future health of the environment and thus the health of our children, their children, and their children's children? Or, are we purposefully passing the buck into the future, so those for whom we choose but give no voice can pay the social-environmental bill when it comes due? If the outcome of a hard choice is good, then people will scarcely remember the pain. The question is whether we have the wisdom and courage to be responsible and not only make the hard choices but also live with compassion.

Because choice is both the essence of democracy and sustainable community development, no greater disservice can be rendered by those in power than to unjustly limit the people's power to choose. Limiting the people's choice in favor of the traditional short-term economic desires of those with the clout or resources to make their voices heard above others is what is happening in many places today and serves usually to diminish options for future generations. The planning process we discuss in this book will not meet the needs of readers looking for a cookbook approach; rather, we offer a perspective on land-use planning that is intended to open a range of possibilities for changing current methods. In this book, we are strongly suggesting that existing approaches to land-use planning would be greatly enhanced if they embraced the complex needs, interrelationships, and interdependencies of humans and other life forms. Understanding these needs, interrelationships, and interdependencies changes the conventional approach to land-use planning in the following ways: (1) the new approach requires a higher level of understanding with respect to the needs, interrelationships, and interdependencies of humans with one another and their environment, as well as a greater frequency and duration of interpersonal interactions; (2) it incorporates ecological principles into the process and results; and (3) it converts the planning process to a cycle in which the "plan" is only one part of an ongoing process.

We further believe that if such a "cycle" were guided by a cookbook approach, the result would be less creativity and innovation and therefore less responsibility accepted for the results. For our kind of planning to work, an essential ingredient of the process is that leaders endorse the concept of persons, which begins with recognition, understanding, and acceptance of people's diversity and intuition; their creative gifts, talents, and skills; and their individual values. These creative gifts, talents, and skills will also be necessary to design lifestyles that are in harmony with the environment, which affects the sustainability of both the community and the world as a whole.

Having said all of this, we are reminded of a thought expressed by a Chinese Mandarin to a Chinese army major in the movie *Inn of the Sixth Happiness* which is important to understand in the planning process, despite the fact that on the surface it seems contrary to planning: "A planned life, my friend, is a closed life. It can be tolerated perhaps, but it cannot be lived." To expand on this notion, we will borrow from an article by Kathy Gottberg, an ex-planner.[*]

As members of Western society, we plan in a way consistent with the Newtonian model of a world characterized by materialism and reductionism. This mechanistic world view says, in effect, that if we can control all the pieces of our lives, we can plan for and thus control the outcome of our experiences, an idea that defines us as a cog within a huge machine.

[*] Gottberg, K., Confessions of an ex-planner, *The Quest,* 9(4), 12–14, 1996.

As such, our highest goals are to plot our lives and circumstances to produce the least friction, to create a new and better operating system or a richer, more rewarding feedback loop. These ideas are dualistic, however, and not only separate us from one another but also reveal our true goal, which is to control rather than "live with" Nature.

This sense of separation creates an image of us as isolated individuals, each trying to control events and circumstances in our moment-to-moment experiences for our own self-interest, which produces an underlying feeling that life is a solitary battle we are losing. We seek security and a sense of identity in our individual accomplishments, rather than trusting an inter-connected, interactive consciousness.

We therefore replace spontaneous creativity with a checklist of things to do, thus saying that we cannot trust anyone else to look out for us, that we must look out for ourselves, which leaves us feeling alone and isolated in the universe, often with a palpable feeling of powerlessness. In addressing this lack of trust, Mahatma Gandhi once asked: "Does not the history of the world show that there would have been no romance in life if there had been no risks?" Yet, risk is what we are constantly trying to avoid or, finding that impossible, minimize or even eliminate.

Author Deepak Chopra says that every intention and desire has inherent within it the mechanics of its fulfillment. "Intention" in this sense is different than planning. Intention expresses the desire and then allows the spontane-ous, intuitive outworking of the results, whereas planning, on the other hand, is typically a linear attachment to the detail and outcome which often con-tradicts trust in the spontaneous and the intuitive, thus limiting possible outcomes pregnant with unforeseen opportunities.

If we do not trust our spontaneous creativity and our intuition, if we do not trust one another to act appropriately in an other-centered fashion, then we feel forced to "plan" an alternative, a contingency. But Nature offers another perspective.

In the Australian Savannah are 20-foot-tall termite towers, which offer a magnificent demonstration of intuitive (instinctive, in the case of termites), spontaneous creation and self-organization. These intricate engineering mas-terpieces, created from what we humans consider to be the unplanned, instinctive movements of many individual termites, are the tallest structures on Earth relative to the size of their builders.

Although termites possess little individual physical capacity, they do have a strong sense of self and are constantly tuned into one another and their environment, a characteristic that results in the termites instinctively forming into groups by being attracted one to another. They wander seem-ingly at will, bumping into one another and responding to the bump. When a critical mass of termites has gathered in a given location, their behavior shifts into an emerging action. Their limited individual capabilities merge into a collective capacity and they begin building their towers. A group on one side begins building an arch. Another group notices this and begins constructing the other side of the arch in a spontaneous action that meets in the middle *sans* engineer, boss, or planner.

When first studying these termite towers, entomologists sought a planner, a leader. But, after years of study, they have concluded that the termite towers are examples of "emergent properties," which means when a group is together it is capable of behaviors that are simply unknowable when considering an isolated individual. Put differently, for all our study of the pieces of Nature, ourselves included, we will never see the potential for the collective possibility when considering the isolated individual.

There are many examples of emergent organizations, on both the micro- and macro-scale, and they have some things in common. First, there is a very strong sense of self and purpose in each individual participating in the collective. Individuals know who they are and collectively what they want to be or where they want to go (their vision), and they are tuned into themselves and to one another. Second, they recognize the value of quality relationships and the necessity of a free flow of information within the group or system. Third, each individual may wander at will, bump into others with attractive energy, and respond, which is contrary to most traditionally organized interactions because it cannot be planned. Finally, each individual has a beginner's mind that knows not what the fixed answers "should" be and can thus see what the unrehearsed, opportunistic answers might be.

The point of this discussion is to demonstrate that each of us is capable of infinitely more than the sum of our parts, far exceeding our expertise in planning. The quantum potential of our spontaneous creativity cannot be accessed by lists, calculations, or manipulations. It can only be accessed by a willingness to let something better than a rigid plan happen and participate intuitively in the happening. It is the acting out of psychologically mature awareness, with full responsibility and participation in the dance of life.

To get the maximum benefit out of any plan, therefore, people must let creative spontaneity be part of the process. A plan must always be flexible and open to serendipitous opportunities, where the exact outcome may be uncertain, but if the direction (the vision and goals) intuitively feels right, then "trust in the result" must be the guiding principle.

We offer this book as an example of what we think can be done to plan consciously with psychological maturity for sustainable development. Granted, we are writing about an ideal in that we must assume all people have sufficient consciousness to understand that sustainable human communities of necessity require healthy landscapes to nurture them by providing the wealth of Nature's renewable energy in the form of raw materials. Without a diversity of raw materials to convert into economic energy, there can be no sustainable community. Beyond that, without the free services provided by Nature in the form of pollination, clean water, clean air, and fertile soils (all of which we take for granted and, in so doing, often ignore), the quality of human life in existing communities will gradually decline with each successive generation until it sinks into mere survival. Must such a doomsday scenario be inevitable? We think not. In the last analysis, however, the future depends upon the consciousness of the choices we make when planning for use of the land coupled with complementary urban development.

As you read this book, bear in mind that we are telling it only as we see it, and we use our personal experiences to illustrate various points. And further bear in mind that we believe, as does naturalist and writer Barry Lopez, that it is our task as writers "to be the ones who recognize the patterns that remind us of our obligations and dreams." It is not our job, Lopez adds, "to be brilliant, or to be the person who always knows."

Introduction

The last neighborhood that I (Jane) lived in was a small subdivision of three-bedroom, two-bath, pastel, horizontally sided homes arranged along a cul-de-sac in Santa Cruz, CA. It could well have been part of the town where *The Truman Show* was filmed — neat little homes, tidily planted ten feet apart, each with the required tree from a 15-gallon container, postage-stamp lawn, curbs and gutters, and 6-foot fences blocking the view to the rear of the house. There were no street trees or boulevards, and the overall design of the subdivision said nothing about the general context of Santa Cruz. This was a zero lot line development, where one wall of each home was actually on the property line of the adjacent home and the opposite, parallel wall was 10 feet from the wall of the next home and so on. The lots were small relative to the size of each home — 3300-square-foot lots and 1500-square-foot homes — a pattern common in places where land is becoming more precious. The entire development was like a silk flower on an old oak tree, surrounded as it was by an aging residential area of country lanes without curbs and gutters, of tree-lined streets, out-of-use chicken farms scattered amongst homes with front porches and orchards, and the warp and woof of a neighborhood tapestry that would be impossible for any residential developer to duplicate.

While I was reasonably comfortable on Colony Way, I had a nagging dissatisfaction with one feature — the automatic garage doors on each dwelling. This feature, with its remote control device, made it possible for residents to walk from their kitchen into their garage, get in their car, and, with a push of a button, back out and drive away as the door closed with another push of a button. Likewise, one could drive home, open the garage door, and slip back inside unseen. I never saw the people who lived directly across the street, but I think they were elderly. I knew they were small, because I could just make out their shadowy images through tinted car windows as they left home or returned. But I never talked to them and likewise rarely saw any other neighbors, although I speculated on their lives and imagined that most worked because the homes were so quiet during the weekdays. I couldn't know for sure, however. Nevertheless, I did manage to introduce myself to a few neighbors, usually through a closed front screen door, but doing so did not forge a relationship of reciprocity. Be that as it may, there was one exception — Rich Apple, a zany cul-de-sac resident.

Rich and I would joke about how weird it was living so close to other people and yet not knowing who in the world the "Others" were. We decided to make an oatmeal-box telephone and stretch the string connecting the two boxes across the street. It was a small bit of theater intended to set the neighbors wondering if at least two households on Colony Way had some kind of connection with one another.

Development patterns in America, like the one on Colony Way, are part of the disappearance of American city centers, neighborhoods, and the unweaving of our very social fabric. Yet, the patterns continue and Americans continue to put up with suburbs that have no sidewalks; with development designed to make vehicular traffic flow smoothly but with little, if any, attention given to pedestrian ways; and urban sprawl that is eating up open space, farmlands, and the sense of community and safety so vital to our survival. As a result, land and land use are becoming more topical.

It is almost impossible to pick up a current newspaper in America that does not have a story about land use. More often than not, land and its value are topics of conversation for people standing in line at the bank, at the grocery store, or just sitting around the dinner table with friends.

There are many reasons for this, not the least of which is that, in the broadest view, the world's natural resources are becoming more scarce and thus more valuable. Therefore, one's real property is becoming something of greater value as well, something to protect, defend, or just talk about. Further, the one investment that seems most predictable these days is real estate, at least in the U.S. This type of investment usually explains, in part, why both adults in a mom-and-pop household leave home each day to go to work; it merits that kind of energy output in the minds of most families in America. The other reason, of course, is that both moms and pops often have to work in order to simply afford an overpriced home.

This growing interest in land and how it is used, bought, sold, developed, harmed, and helped is one reason we are writing this book. We believe there is a need to connect current problems with contemporary practices of land-use planning in the U.S. and why they exist; these notions, in turn, must be connected with potential remedies based on principles of sustainable design.

Our current ways of regulating land use are like many of our inventions, which are tied to order, structure, predictability, and linear thinking. What we are learning rather quickly as a technological society, however, is that these linear solutions to nonlinear problems frequently create more problems, even though we are sometimes fooled by the quick-fix and illusion of control that come with such remedies. Put differently, today's solutions are increasingly becoming tomorrow's problems precisely because we, with our technological sophistication, continue to build our social order, including our dominant social-technological systems, in a way that is comparable to a house of cards.

The vulnerability of our house of cards was revealed by the wave of fear that struck with the lack of absolute certainty associated with Y2K. We are not accustomed to dealing with such massive uncertainty, where machines are in charge, because machines are designed to give us greater certainty in potential outcomes, not less.

Humans, which are far less predictable than machines, are considered desirable as components of the global economic engine. However, as we depend less and less on humans — along with human error, the inherent inefficiencies of being human, as well as human creativity, experience, and moral judgment — and replace humans with machines, we do indeed create efficiencies. These efficiencies emerge in the form of levees on rivers that move water quickly through some communities yet are responsible for massive loss of property due to floods in other communities; efficiencies such as electronic commerce removing the need for human contact and contributing to the undoing of community in the process; and efficiencies not modeled after Nature and therefore not likely to be around for the long haul.

Our rapid-response command-and-control approach to problem solving lacks, among other things, humility and too often humanity. We humans need to acknowledge that our technology is in fact feeble in comparison to Nature's technology. For example, a spider web is five times stronger than steel when one considers its diameter and flexibility, not to mention that it is waterproof, biodegradable, and made from insect parts in a room-temperature process.[1] We need greater humility as humans in the web of life, greater respect for the whole, and constant awareness of the fact that when we move just a little, the entire web vibrates, much like trying to sit on the edge of a waterbed without causing a ripple.

Regulations governing changes to the landscape, such as construction of housing subdivisions or strip malls, are thought of as rational creations, yet they are neither modeled after the biophysical laws of nature nor created with processes having characteristics that resemble those of nature. Forcing a certain relationship between humans and the Earth by way of land-use law is ultimately a little like legislating morals, in that most people balk at having any restrictions placed on what they can do with "their" land because they do not view their property from a position of trusteeship, but rather from a position of outright, inviolate ownership or possession. And, as we all know, some people are unwilling or unable to separate themselves from their possessions, so strongly is their identity linked with their "things." Land-use laws are thus viewed by these people as an invasion of privacy that is simply unrelated to the common good of public health, safety, and welfare.

In addition, we are racing with time with respect to the speed at which the world's population is doubling. This race is exacerbated by changes in the global climate and our rapidly vanishing natural wealth (soil degradation, deforestation, species extinction, and declining fisheries), which strongly suggest that we must start to do things differently and quickly with regard to Mother Earth — the biosphere that keeps us alive. Significant changes in our land-use practices would be an excellent start.

The authors

Jane Silberstein brings to this discussion her background as a city planner of roughly 17 years' experience in both Santa Barbara and Santa Cruz, CA, and then in Wisconsin, where she worked for the Northwest Regional Planning Commission as planner for the City of Ashland. Jane now has her own consulting practice as a planner which includes the City of Ashland as a client. She also works at the Sigurd Olson Environmental Institute, Northland College, in Ashland, WI, where she is an environmental education specialist, adjunct instructor, and U.S. Coordinator of the Lake Superior Binational Forum, funded by the U.S. Environmental Protection Agency and Environment Canada. Jane earned her Master's degree in journalism and mass communications from the University of Minnesota and graduated from Hamline University in St. Paul, MN.

Chris Maser spent over 25 years as a research scientist in natural history and ecology in forest, shrub steppe, subarctic, desert, and coastal settings. Trained primarily as a vertebrate zoologist, he was a research mammalogist in Nubia, Egypt (1963–1964) with the Yale University Peabody Museum Prehistoric Expedition, and was a research mammalogist in Nepal (1966–1967) for the U.S. Naval Medical Research Unit #3 based in Cairo, Egypt, where he participated in a study of tick-borne diseases. Chris conducted a three-year (1970–1973) ecological survey of the Oregon coast for the University of Puget Sound, Tacoma, WA, and was a research ecologist with the U.S. Department of the Interior Bureau of Land Management for twelve years (1975–1987), the last eight of which he spent studying old-growth forests in western Oregon. He was also a landscape ecologist with the Environmental Protection Agency for one year (1990–1991). Today, Chris is an independent author as well as an international lecturer and facilitator in resolving environmental disputes, vision statements, and sustainable community development. He is also an international consultant in forest ecology and sustainable forestry practices. He has written over 260 publications, including *Sustainable Forestry: Philosophy, Science, and Economics* (1994); *From the Forest to the Sea:*

The Ecology of Wood in Streams, Rivers, Estuaries, and Oceans (1994, with James Sedell); *Resolving Environmental Conflict: Toward Sustainable Community Development* (1996); *Sustainable Community Development: Principles and Concepts* (1997); *Setting the Stage for Sustainability: A Citizen's Handbook* (1998, with Russ Beaton and Kevin Smith); *Vision and Leadership in Sustainable Development* (1998); *Mammals of the Pacific Northwest: From the Coast to the High Cascades* (1998); *Ecological Diversity in Sustainable Development: The Vital and Forgotten Dimension* (1999); *Reuniting Economy and Ecology in Sustainable Development* (1999, with Russ Beaton); and *Forest Certification in Sustainable Development* (2000, with Walter Smith). Although he has worked in Canada, Egypt, France, Germany, Japan, Malaysia, Nepal, Slovakia, and Switzerland, he calls Corvallis, OR, home.

Acknowledgments

It is with genuine pleasure that we thank the following people, listed in alphabetical order, for reviewing the manuscript with care and diligence: Kenneth (Kim) Bro, Ph.D. (Director, Sigurd Olson Environmental Institute, Northland College, Ashland, WI); Jessica Dexter (junior, Northland College, Ashland, WI); Peter Katzlberger (planning consultant, Felton, CA); Jay Moynihan (information architect and sustainable development consultant, Ashland, WI); Alan Pinkerton (Clark County Department of Comprehensive Planning, Las Vegas, NV).

Jane: I would like to thank Tom Vosburg (Community Planning and Environmental Services, City of Fort Collins, CO) for so graciously expediting my research in Fort Collins. Also, to Eric Schubring and Roslyn Nelson, thank you for your encouragement and support. And to my co-author Chris, I offer my gratitude for believing in me and continually showing enthusiasm and excitement about this joint project.

Chris: To my wife, Zane, I offer special thanks for her patience with my many hours of working on this book.

Contents

Dedication

To the memory of Eleanor Roosevelt, who spent her life in a tireless campaign for the equality and welfare of all people in all generations.

chapter one

Foundations of debate over land use in America

All truly wise thoughts have been thought already thousands of times; but to make them truly ours, we must think them over again honestly, til they take root in our personal experience. —Goethe

Property rights and responsibilities

European immigrants came to America in the 1600s to escape oppression and other miseries of non-representative governments. Immigrants continue to come to America for similar reasons, as well as for economic gain. Individual rights comprise the cornerstone of our democracy and are also the subject of much debate. Our court system is constantly dealing with issues of rights, including the rights of private property, where, in a non-totalitarian society, shades of gray are championed over the black and white of dictatorships and other oppressive regimes. The persistent and abundant debate over the rights of private property is where we shall begin to make a case for the necessity of reforming current regulations concerning the use of land.

Ownership of land and its associated rights are the bases for much litigation in America. Balancing the rights of property owners with the needs of the community at large can typically make land-use planning a contentious process or, at the very least, problematic. This quandary is important to sort out before exploring ways in which our current practices for controlling land use might be modified to be more consistent with the principles of sustainability. (For a thorough discussion of "rights," see Chapter 7 in *Ecological Diversity in Sustainable Development*.[2])

The notion of using land in a particular way originates with the owner of the land. Initially, government land-use regulations were enacted in reaction to the impact of proposed uses. More recently, government regulations have been intended to guide land-use and private decisions. "Rights" exist for both entities: the owner of the land and the community that government regulations are intended to protect. "Right" in this context is something, such as power or privilege, to which one has a just or lawful claim. "Property" is a thing or things that can be or are owned, especially land or real estate; something that is regarded as being possessed by, or at the disposal of, a person or group of persons (common property).[4]

It is this latter definition of property that might explain why confusion and arguments persist relative to property rights. When "property" is defined as something "possessed," the problem begins. "Possession" implies belonging, which in turn implies being a part of, related to, or connected to.[4] While the many historical, social, and political roots in America explain the fervor with which Americans view their property rights, the language itself may play a role in perpetuating this fervor.

If an individual believes a piece of real property "belongs" to him or her, a strong connection exists between one's "self" and one's property (the object of ownership), usually to the exclusion of the public and the general good. Broad decision-making authority over property perceived in such a manner would be an inherent part of one's "rights" associated with such property. A distinctive and pervasive lack of separation between one's possessions and one's self in a society with an increasing sense of powerlessness may fuel the flames of the current land-use debate. Further, "rights of real property" apply not only to products (such as standing timber) or development on the surface of the ground but also to the space and air above and the soil, minerals, and water below the ground if not specifically exempted in the deed of ownership. All of these rights have "value," and the constitutional question of just how far land-use regulations can restrict the exercise of these rights and thus the value of the property sums up what most land-use debates are about.

Most of these arguments usually lead to the question, "Does this regulation constitute a 'taking?'" A "taking" occurs when a regulation would deny a landowner all or substantially all practical uses of a property. If a taking is shown, just compensation is required; however, the term "taking" is generally bandied about quite loosely, frequently by those fearing loss of some perceived right with owned land. This commonly expressed misunderstanding poses a substantial barrier to land-use planning as well as regulating land use.

The authors believe that the public often contradicts itself when defending perceived property rights. This observation is supported by a survey of Wisconsin residents that was conducted in 1998 by *Common Ground*, a conservative magazine "dedicated to public involvement in the development of rational land-use policy."[4] This *Common Ground* survey of a random sample of 600 adults revealed that nearly three quarters of those polled agreed with the notion that protecting the environment and human health is a "very good" reason to place limits on how owners can use their land.[5] When the number of respondents who said that protecting the environment and human health is a "good" reason to place limits on how owners may use their land was added to the above three quarters, agreement among the respondents reached 90%. However, when respondents were also asked to rate, on a scale from one to ten, the proportion of control they believe should rest with the property owner, given specified land-use scenarios, the respondents spoke clearly and emphatically. For allocation of land-use decisions, respondents would award, on average, 70% or more of that authority to landowners. The remaining control should be turned over to local government or neighbors, on occasion to state government, and rarely to the federal government.

In summing up the survey results, the report states that property rights appear to be based more on values — protecting the environment, public safety, and rights of property owners — than on self-interest. However, people tend to redefine property rights to some extent when land-use activities encroach on their turf.[6] Further, while most of the citizens surveyed (85%) held that it is important for government to "prevent people from using their property in a way that may not be in the public's interest," the survey also revealed that the same percentage believes that government should compensate landowners for any loss of property value resulting from land-use regulations. Both findings point to a duality within and between the greater good and personal well-being; that is, the more a matter encroaches upon a person's perceived individual rights, the more that individual seems to have a diminished sense of community. The statement, "What's good for the community may not be the best thing for me," perhaps best encapsulates this common societal attitude, a self-contradiction brought to the fore in many guises during land-use debates.

Robert Miller, professor of English at Kennesaw State University, found in a study of social change in communities experiencing rapid growth that "people like to complain about how developers are building where they used to hunt birds. Then, almost in the same breath, they talk about the advantages they can get from selling their house and how it has increased in value."[7] Thus, many may have a confused and sometimes ambivalent understanding of property rights, but what about their perception of the responsibilities of land ownership?

Responsibilities associated with property rights generally involve avoiding the creation of a nuisance. A nuisance can be either public or private. Private nuisances are primarily those visited upon neighboring properties and include a variety of conditions frequently resulting from poor property maintenance, such as the accumulation of garbage or other wastes and repugnant odors. Cutting off solar access, creating unreasonable noise, and storing junk autos in an unconcealed manner on one's property would also fall into this category. Public nuisances, on the other hand, generally affect a larger geographic area and hence more people; such nuisances include actions such as polluting the air and water and generating excessive traffic.[8]

Public and/or private nuisances can typically be part of the debate over property rights. What really *is* a nuisance? Can its effects be measured? If so, by whose yardstick? Is the nuisance avoidable? What are its long- and short-term impacts? Questions such as these are thematic of many land-use contests.

The rights and responsibilities associated with land ownership may pose a challenge with respect to reform because they remain ensconced in controversy. This controversy, which is costly, burdensome, and time consuming, may detract from efforts for reform. Such debate, however, is a hallmark of a democratic society and must be carefully and actively protected. The authors hope that this persistent debate will provide the catalyst for the discovery of new and better ways to plan land use and development rather than creating a barrier to such discovery. One thing the debate has fostered, however, is the question of how our economic model influences land-use regulation in America.

Our economic model

Our economy is market driven; that is, demand — based on real necessity as well as perceived need stimulated by advertising — drives production. The prospects for change within this social dynamic seem limited, primarily because advances have historically occurred only at the rate at which individuals could profit monetarily from the change.[9] In its simplest form, our economic model has two major components: (1) households, which supply labor, land, and capital; and (2) business and industry, which supply products and income. These entities "feed" one another. A glaring omission from this two-part model, however, is natural capital and the services provided by natural capital to households (people) and to business and industry. Natural capital is comprised of the inherent wealth of Nature that we use as resources, both renewable and nonrenewable, as well as the inherent services Nature provides.[10]

These inherent ecosystem services include the production of oxygen by plants, purification of water by the soil and soil organisms, a vast genetic library, pollination of plants by animals and wind, ozone protection against cosmic and ultraviolet radiation, and pest and disease control through parasitism and predation, to name just a few.[11] And, currently, according to Paul Hawken,[10] there are no technological substitutes for these services — a critical point for business to consider if it wants to remain profitable. The failure of Biosphere II, which was an attempt to replicate the Earth's main ecosystems in miniature to sustain only eight people, drove this point home with searing clarity.[10]

How much are the Earth's ecosystem services worth? Robert Costanza, director of the University of Maryland's Institute of Ecological Economics, led the work of 13 researchers looking into the value of ecosystems. Study results to date show that the dollar value of ecosystem services in the U.S.

range between $33 and 54 trillion annually.[10] This, of course, amounts to a subsidy to business, and when unaccounted for, paints a false picture of the health of our economy.

Further, failure to recognize the subsidy to business provided by ecosystem services essentially diminishes the value of any long-term business plan lacking this component. If the bottom line of the corporate budget were to account for the value of Nature's inherent services in the assets category, the probability that those services would be protected is drastically increased. Likewise, failure to acknowledge the significance and value of natural capital hastens its demise and puts the sustainability of life on this planet in jeopardy.

Evidence of this failure is seen in our rapacious assault on the world's natural wealth; in the sphere of ever-diminishing natural wealth, we continue to extract resources at a rate greater by far than our efforts to find ways to recycle and re-use them. In the U.S. of 100 years ago, when it seemed we would never exhaust our natural resources and there were fewer people, it was understandable that extraction proceeded at the rate and scope that it did.[10] Today, however, jobs are being lost in part to more efficient ways of extracting, harvesting, transporting, and disposing of a vast flow of resources — some 220 billion tons a year.[12] It must be noted here that such efficiency comes at the expense of the diminishing ability of Nature to effectively renew the very resources upon which we depend for survival.

Now, however, we have a reduced amount of natural wealth to convert to usable resources and have many more people vying for these self-same resources, a situation calling for a radically different way of conducting business — one that not only creates jobs but also protects Nature's wealth. This point is driven home in the paper, "A Road Map to Natural Capitalism," in which authors Amory Lovins et al. assert that "the pattern of scarcity is shifting."[12] Today, people and human labor are abundant and nature is scarce; in addition, the biological limiting factors cannot be substituted for one another as can the capital and labor of traditional industrial production whereby machinery can easily be exchanged for labor. The authors of this paper go on to point out that, "No technology or amount of money can substitute for a stable climate and a productive biosphere. Even proper pricing can't replace the priceless."[12] This thought brings us to a brief discussion of the gross domestic product, eco-efficiency, genuine progress indicators, and Nature's inherent services.

Gross domestic product, eco-efficiency, genuine progress indicators, and Nature's inherent services

According to a reductionist mechanical world view, which today is overlain with the notion of continual economic expansion, the economic process of producing and consuming material goods and services has no deleterious effects on the ecosystem. This view is based on the assumption that natural resources are limitless and that any unintended effects of the economic process, such as pollution and environmental degradation, are inconsequential. In contrast to this dominant world view, however, the paradigm of sustainability is neither mechanical nor reversible; it is entropic, which means that the Earth's wealth and its ability to absorb and cleanse the waste produced by humanity's economic activities are both finite.[13]

In addition, Industrialism, which author Wendell Berry[14] contends is the name of our modern human economy, not only "thrives by undermining its own foundation" but also is "based squarely upon the principle of violence toward everything on which it depends, and it has not mattered whether the form of industrialism was communist or capitalist or whatever; the violence toward nature, human communities, traditional agricultures, ... local economies, and land-use planning has been constant literally the world over."[14] Berry questions whether the economy can be fixed without radical change. We, the authors, think not, nor can land-use planning be changed without a radical shift in the peep-hole myopia of institutionalized economic thinking:[14]

> "The Captains [and Priests] of Industry have always counseled the rest of us to be 'realistic.' Let us, therefore, be realistic. Is it realistic to assume that the present economy would be just fine if only it would stop poisoning the air and water, or if only it would stop soil erosion, or if only it would stop degrading watersheds and forest ecosystems, or if only it would stop seducing children, or if only it would quit buying politicians, or if only it would give women and favoured minorities an equitable share of the loot? Realism, I think, is in a very limited programme, but it informs us at least that we should not look for birds' eggs in a cuckoo clock."

By tying the economic process to the entropy of the physical world, economist Georgescu-Roegen pointed out that, for Western industrialized society to survive with any semblance of dignity, there must be a shift from the old reductionist mechanical world view to a paradigm built around sustainability. In making that point, however, he posed the unspoken question of how one measures sustainability in terms of human welfare. For the sake of discussion, three potential measures will be considered: gross domestic product, eco-efficiency, and genuine progress indicators.

Before we examine the gross domestic product and eco-efficiency, let us add that, according to Berry, people who use these two measures of economic viability are so far removed from the workings of Nature that they have no understanding of, feel no gratitude toward, and exercise no responsibility toward those systems of Nature that ultimately are responsible for feeding, clothing, and sheltering them.[14] Based on years of experience in a number of industrialized countries and societies, the authors must agree with Berry's statement.

Gross domestic product

The gross domestic product, which is nothing more than a measure of total output (the dollar value of finished goods and services), tells very little in and of itself because it assumes that everything produced is by definition "goods," including people.[13] William Bennett, who was President Reagan's Secretary of Education, observed that, "Socialism treats people as a cog in a machine of the state; capitalism tends to treat people as commodities." As such, the gross domestic product is an intellectual measure of the size of the U.S. economy, the amount of money that exchanges hands in a strictly additive sense, like an adding machine that cannot subtract and thus makes no distinction between benefits and costs (credits and debits), productive and destructive activities, or sustainable and nonsustainable activities, in addition to which there is no allowance for the declining quality of human life in the face of environmental degradation.

The reason for this disregard of human welfare is simply that the gross domestic product treats everything that happens in the marketplace as a positive gain for humanity and thereby *de facto* dismisses everything that cannot be converted into money as being unimportant to social well-being — such as the logging practices that destroy habitat for salmon. In this case, both logging and commercial salmon fishing cause money to exchange hands and count as a plus in the valuation of the gross domestic product, even though the degradation of the salmon's habitat caused by logging in the mountains will eventually put the commercial salmon fisher in the ocean out of business. Politicians, however, generally see this decaying quality of human life through a well-worn ideological lens that accepts economic growth as good even as it cannibalizes the family, community, and environment that nurture and sustain us.

On a more personal note, consider a man dying slowly of cancer who needs three major operations while in the middle of a messy divorce that forces him to sell his home. This man is an asset to the economy from the gross domestic product point of view, because he is the cause of so much money exchanging hands.

In the case of commercial salmon fishermen, they are faced with a declining way of life because the logging they never see is slowly destroying their livelihood. In the case of the dying man, his quality of life could hardly get much worse. In both cases, the valuation of the gross domestic product goes up at the unmeasured expense of the commercial salmon fishermen who are losing a way of life and the dying man who is losing everything he held dear to forces other than his impending death. This scenario is somewhat analogous to adding (crediting) the amount of each check one writes against one's bank account instead of subtracting (debiting) it.

The significance of such an illogical calculation of economic activity revolves around the gross domestic product being the primary indicator of economic growth (the economic score card) from one year to the next in the U.S. As such, annual growth in the gross domestic product that exceeds 3% is usually perceived as being favorable for incumbent politicians. The danger

hidden within the calculation of the gross domestic product as a real measure
of economic growth, however, is that it creates a false sense of prosperity
and security, especially when growth is rapid, because it ignores costs (adding only the benefits) and thus ignores the major problems confronting
American society. This is like adding up all of the in-flowing cash from a
shopping mall while ignoring both short-term costs (such as physical wear
on buildings and equipment and the human labor involved in maintaining
the buildings) and long-term costs (such as replacement of computer systems, resurfacing parking lots, replacing roofs, and so on).

Money itself as a measure of success is another example of a serious
flaw in thinking and valuation with regard to sustainability, because the
bottom line in business is always promoted as being the one truly important
figure.[15] The bottom line, which shows how much profit has been made, is
used as a measure of how well a company performs. Too little profit, and
a company is deemed as being inefficient, or its management is slack, or
the full potential of its workforce has not been harnessed, or its products
are out of date, or, most damning of all, the company is not competitive in
the global economy. Are such damnations justified? Is money the only valid
measure?

Suppose a family-owned furniture company is making products that
are robust and lasting and/or selling its products to people with only a
moderate income or those who are somehow disadvantaged. It may be
paying its employees higher wages than other furniture companies in the
belief that all people deserve a living wage. It may be investing heavily in
a strategy to protect the ecological integrity of the forestland from which it
draws the wood for its furniture or, having a noisy mill in a location
becoming increasingly surrounded by people's homes, the company has
chosen to operate only one shift out of respect for people living in the
neighborhood.

In a world where money is the only acceptable measure of success,
however, all these considerations count as naught because traditional economists assure us that a linear notion of progress, which means full steam
ahead in the strictly material realm, is always the correct course of action
(ready, *fire*, aim), whereas ecology is a discipline that teaches us the folly of
speeding blindly into the future and that a strategy of ready, *aim*, fire is best.
In the scenario of full steam ahead, the quality of the products and the welfare
of the people and the environment are all irrelevant in the face of a bottom
line that is not performing as desired. The irony is that the bottom-line profit
may actually account for only the last 10% of the total income earned and
overrules and overshadows the other 90% of the income that has gone
toward earning that bottom-line profit of 10%.

This type of valuation clearly points out that market economics places
value on that which is scarce instead of placing value on the real work and
worth of people and their potential for being loving and caring and for
being honest, just, and thoughtful people and neighbors. If we are to keep
the softer social capital of mutual caring from becoming scarce, we must

reward it. Doing so, however, is one of the many areas in which the last 10% of the dollars squeezed into profit margins at the expense of the 90% along the way is simply not effective in serving human welfare because it does not build families or communities or tackle poverty or protect the environment.

Clearly, therefore, the gross domestic product, with its myopic focus on dollars and its flawed logic, cannot be a measure of sustainability as it relates to human welfare. If not gross domestic product, then what could speak for human welfare? Many industrial participants of the 1992 Earth Summit in Rio de Janeiro, Brazil, touted a strategy of "eco-efficiency" that would not only refit the machines of industry with cleaner, faster, and quieter engines but also allow unobstructed prosperity while simultaneously protecting both economic and corporate structures.[16]

Eco-efficiency

Industrialists hoped that eco-efficiency would transform the economic process from one that takes, makes, and wastes into a system that integrates economic, environmental, and ethical concerns. One might ask, at this point, what is this notion of eco-efficiency that industrialists around the world herald as their chosen strategy for change. Eco-efficiency is a term that primarily means doing more with less, a precept that Henry Ford was adamant about when he wrote in 1926, "You must get the most out of the power, out of the material, and out of the time." His lean and clean operating policies saved his company money by recycling and reusing materials, reducing the use of natural resources, minimizing packaging, and setting new standards of human labor with his timesaving assembly line.

Although eco-efficiency is a well-intentioned concept that looks good on the surface, it is still within the bowels of the reductionist mechanical world view with its current overlay of economic expansionism and thus is little more than an illusion of change. Rather than focusing on a new way of thinking, such as how to *effectively* save the environment, industrialists once again have attached their hope to *efficiency* — the swan song of the environment — with which, unconsciously perhaps, they have set themselves up to quietly, persistently, and completely commercialize the world. This is but saying that eco-efficiency, while it aspires to make the old world view less destructive, languishes from the fatal flaws hidden within the embrace of such destructive practices in the first place.

To view the fatal flaws inherent in the tenets of eco-efficiency, we will design a furniture store as a retroactive system that not only allows but also encourages people to spend the inherited forests of the world as though there were no tomorrow and to pass the bill forward to the generations of the future. Such a retroactive system would:

- Encourage clear-cutting as much timber, primarily old growth, as possible to purchase lumber as inexpensively as possible, preferably rare woods from the tropics.

- Measure prosperity by economic activity and success by automation that both eliminates people's jobs and increases the profit margin.
- Measure progress as a continual technological advancement in automation that replaces people with machines.
- Promote personal self-interest, requiring thousands of complex and often competing regulations to keep self-centered, greedy people from clear-cutting entire landscapes.
- Encourage clear-cutting the entire riparian zone right down to the stream bottom if it contained old-growth timber.
- Leave nothing as a reinvestment of biological capital in the soil.
- Erode and ultimately destroy biological, genetic, and functional diversity through centralized corporate economic competition to convert as much of the world's wealth as humanly possible into quick monetary profits.

If the above system were refitted with the current notion of eco-efficiency, it would look something like this:

- Annually clear-cuts fewer acres and purposefully hides them.
- Measures prosperity by less economic activity and success by introducing automation more slowly.
- Promotes less blatant personal self-interest by meeting or exceeding many or most of the complex and often competing regulations.
- Encourages saving a minimal buffer zone of nonmerchantable trees but only along streams deemed of political importance.
- Encourages leaving two nonmerchantable logs per acre as a reinvestment of biological capital in the soil.
- Standardizes and homogenizes biological, genetic, and functional diversity by replacing forests with cloned fiber farms for cheaper wood in the future.

Clearly, while eco-efficiency aspires to make the reductionist mechanical world view more benign through reduction, reuse, and recycling, it does not stop these economically driven processes of exploitation, needless overproduction, acquisitiveness, and pollution. The real message of eco-efficiency is to restrict industry and slow or curtail growth — to put limitations on the creative and productive capacity of humankind. This message is simplistic, however, because Nature itself is highly industrious, creative through unpredictable novelty, astonishingly productive, and even "wasteful" when viewed in the short term. The salient point is that Nature, unlike human industry, is *effective*, not efficient.

Consider the pine, which annually casts billions of pollen grains to the vagaries of the ever-shifting wind so that a few might land in just the right place at just the right time to consummate the union of male and female gametes to form a few viable seeds. The seeds, in turn, must then ripen and drop to the soil in a place conducive to their germination and growth, all the while beset by the unpredictable elements of weather and the potential for a vast array of hungry microbes, fungi, insects, birds, and mammals to find and eat them. All of this so that a few, a very few, new pines might germinate in sufficient numbers to replace those that died and thus maintain the species. There is little, if any, waste in this apparent inefficiency, however, because pollen and seed alike are sought as food by myriad organism. Effective, yes; efficient no, which brings us to the genuine progress indicators.

Genuine progress indicators

Inherent ecosystem services, which we can neither replace nor live without, are not on everyone's balance sheet and thus get inadvertently discounted and liquidated in the pursuit of resources whose value in the market place *is* recognized and accepted. Nature's inherent services, on the other hand, are effectively finite precisely because they are irreplaceable.[17] With respect to human economies, however, Amory Lovins, Director of the Rocky Mountain Institute, contends that they are "supposed to serve human ends — not the other way around. We forget at our peril that markets make a good servant, a bad master, and a worse religion." In this sense, continues Lovins, "right livelihood" is certainly conducive to more worthy and durable values, and accounting for and being responsible for the protection of Nature's inherent services tend toward right livelihood.

"We hardly know what we are doing," says Berry, with respect to Nature's inherent services, which we inevitably lose when we destroy habitat, "because we don't know what we are undoing." In other words, the health of Nature's inherent services is based on the way Nature actually works, not on the way we want it to work. "In fact," says Lovins, "you can make a good case that probably half the GDP [gross domestic product] is pure waste, spent either to pay for or to remedy the effects of waste that shouldn't have occurred in the first place. ...That's why so many people have the sense that they're running harder to stay in the same place."

The notion of a system of genuine progress indicators is therefore especially valuable because it provides an accurate way to balance our social values with our growing knowledge of how ecosystems work and the limitations that their long-term integrity impose on both the potential and actual sustainability of our activities. There is a caveat to the above statement, however, which, as always, is elegantly stated by Berry:[14] "If the effort to establish genuine progress indicators is not sufficiently broad, if it becomes a specialized movement or cause, if it is not radical enough to produce the required results, it will inevitably fail to treat the cause of the problem and thus leave intact the effects intact." This means that proponents of genuine progress indicators must lead by changing their own behavior, both privately and publicly, not just trying to force others to change policy.

The worst danger, contends Berry, may be that proponents of genuine progress indicators lose the clarity of interpretation with respect to their own language, which not only fosters its own confusion about meaning and practice but also proffers the language into the hands of opponents to genuine progress indicators, and vice versa. In either case, the language is too often relegated to the pinhole vision of institutionalized intellectuals on both sides who find it easier to snipe than to lead. Once we allow our language to mean anything that someone else wants it to, says Berry, it becomes impossible to say what we mean and mean what we say.

Consider, for example, that without a broad enough platform and semantic integrity of language, environmentalists will continue to be viewed and chided as deviant, radical, subversive, extremist, anti-business, anti-growth, and un-American by business people because environmentalists rate the ecological values embodied in saving such things as old-growth forests, wetlands, and endangered species to be greater than those of economic growth. On the other hand, environmentalists often view business people as necessarily evil, greedy, and myopic by nature.[18]

Most of the problem with the economic point of view espoused by business people, according to Thomas Gladwin, director of the University of Michigan corporate-environmental management program, is that business executives and managers often lack good cross-training in science. In fact, less than 1% of 1.2 million articles written by business professors include the words "pollution," "air," "water," or "energy."[18]

The genuine progress indicator, in contrast to both gross domestic product and eco-efficiency, is a measure of total economic activity that includes both benefits *and* costs (credits *and* debits).[19] In this way, the citizens of a community could measure the true value and economic well-being of continual growth over time by assigning an economic value to non-economic indicators, such as the environmental health of the landscape within which the community rests. By assigning either a positive or negative value (a credit or debit) to each such indicator, the indicators and their respective values can be combined into a single genuine progress indicator for the economic welfare of the community.[20] Here one might ask what assigning positive and negative values to the use of farmland might tell us about the quality of life.

Consider, for example, that 160 acres of farmland, much of it prime farmland, are consumed every hour (2.7 acres every minute) by urban sprawl in the U.S., which means that half of the cropland in California will be gone in 20 more years. The irony is that, while one fourth of the land lost will become parking lots and roads, the number of vehicles to use those parking lots and roads is growing six times faster then the number of people. What, one might ask, will growth like this mean for the quality of life in a state such as Oregon?

Consider further that the American West's human population was only 4.1 million strong in 1900, about 5.4% of the 76.1 million people living in the U.S. In 1999, however, the region had 61.2 million people, or 22.4% of the nation's total population of 272.7 million. Since 1960, people have flocked to the Pacific Northwest, attracted by its quality of life that includes a largely unspoiled environment. This influx caused the populations of Oregon, Washington, and Idaho to double, reaching 3,316,000, 5,756,000, and 1,252,000 people, respectively. In other words, the Pacific Northwest has grown as much in the past 40 years as it did in the first 157 years since Thomas Jefferson purchased the Louisiana Territory in 1803.

In Oregon alone, the population grew by 50% in the 1950s. "The conservatives who governed in the 1950s proudly ignored the costs of growth," writes columnist Russell Sadler. "Growth meant prosperity in a state that had been an economic backwater on the West Coast prior to World War II. Good government was the least government and the lowest taxes."

By the early 1960s, continues Sadler, this neo-Victorian Tory philosophy resulted in an epidemic of severely crowded schools; traffic congestion; polluted soil, water, and air; inadequate open space; and a growing public concern with population growth and urban sprawl. Growth has consequences, says Sadler: "The problems of growth will not disappear because some of the self-absorbed members of the 'Me Generation' and their equally self-absorbed offspring pretend they do not exist."

Despite the growing backlash aimed at the *laissez-faire* attitudes of the 1950s, the population of Oregon doubled between 1960 and 1990. Today, growth continues apace, with nearly 474,000 people being added to the state's population from 1990 through 1999. Not only has subsequent urban sprawl degraded the environment in both Oregon and the Pacific Northwest as a whole, but it also has brought the problems of big cities to the Northwest and threatens to further impoverish the region's environment, thus making the Northwest increasingly like the rest of the nation.

In the 1970s, 1980s, and 1990s, the droves of people who moved into the Pacific Northwest were attracted by the quality of life, which included a reasonable cost of living, low crime, decent jobs, and a clean environment. The most conservative projection for the next 25 years from the U.S. Census Bureau, however, is that Oregon's population will grow another 33%.

Barring an unmitigated disaster, population forecasters at Portland State University's Population Research Center in Oregon predict that about 1 million new people are all but guaranteed to inhabit Oregon within the next 25 years, which will raise the state's population to 4.3 million people. This would mean, according to the forecasters, that Oregon would have two more cities the size of Portland, which is the largest city in the state, and the rest of the people would be scattered across the landscape.

They also predict that the demographic makeup of Oregon will change considerably over the next quarter-century as the Baby Boom generation, those born between 1946 and 1964, reaches retirement age, which means an increase in the elderly population from 13.6% in 1995 to 24.2% by 2025. In addition, racial diversity will change in the coming decades. By 2050, the Caucasian population is expected to drop from the current 89.5% to 82%, whereas the Latino population will make up 9.8% (as opposed to the current 4.8%), Asians and Pacific Islanders will comprise 4.7% (as opposed to the current 2.8%), and African-Americans will total 2% of the population (as opposed to the current 1.7%). Although changes in demographics are inevitable, continual growth in population can be controlled if the citizens of Oregon choose to do so.

"When something keeps happening that no one much likes [such as uncontrolled growth in population and the resultant urban sprawl], and it happens in many different places," wrote Donella Meadows, adjunct professor of Environmental Studies at Dartmouth College, "it goes on happening despite all kinds of measures intended to stop it... ."[20] Then we do not have a simple problem with our policies; we have instead a dysfunctional system that can be fixed only by thinking so differently that we create a different system based on radically different values.

Meadows goes on to say that she has seen only one contribution to the discussion of urban sprawl that attacks the problem at the level of completely rethinking how we use land, which fits well the notion that the level of consciousness that causes a problem in the first place is not the level of consciousness that can fix it. Meadows is referring to a book, *Better, Not Bigger*,[26] by Eben Fodor, a city planner from Eugene, OR. Fodor begins the book with a quiz, which we have modified, to examine the notion of gross domestic product vs. a genuine progress indicator as they apply to land-use planning. Before taking the quiz, consider that the remaining fraction of relatively unspoiled land — around which swirls the controversy of urban sprawl — is not only the most precious asset of the Northwest but also one of the very things that draws most of the people to the area. Once in the area, however, the new people contribute to the urban sprawl, which continually diminishes the quality and quantity of unspoiled land that drew them to the Northwest in the first place. With this in mind, think about the following questions:

1. *How much more traffic congestion do you want in your community?* (A) There is too much already; I am losing my quality of life and that of my children. (B) I suppose I have to tolerate a little more in the name of "progress." (C) I'd love a whole lot more traffic because I'm a car salesperson and my income depends on increasing traffic.
2. *How much more pollution of the air, water, and soil do you want?* (A) There is too much already; it is negatively affecting my quality of life and that of my children. (B) I suppose I have to tolerate a little more to have artificially cheap food. (C) I don't want any restrictions because I am a salesperson for a large chemical company; or, I don't want any restrictions because I am a farmer, and I need the chemicals to boost the production of my farm to its maximum; or, I don't want any restrictions because I am a forester with a tree farm, and I want to control the unwanted vegetation so my trees can grow as quickly as possible.
3. *How much more prime farmland, timberland, and open space do you want to have developed?* (A) It is imperative to save all that we have left in order to maintain our quality of life, protect our supply of water, and have open places for my children to experience the natural world. (B) I suppose we have to sacrifice more land in the name of "progress." (C) I want to see all the land developed because I am a developer, and to me any land that is not developed to its fullest potential is just

an economic waste; or, I'm a farmer, and I want the right to sell my
land for as much money as I can get so I retire in luxury; or, I own
forestland, and I want the right to sell my land for as much money
as I can get so I, too, can retire in luxury.

4. *How much higher do you want your taxes to go?* (A) For what I am getting,
   I am paying enough already. (B) I am happy to pay more, even if I
   don't see any benefits, I disagree with how my tax dollars are spent,
   and I abhor how much is wasted unnecessarily.

5. *How much more of your local natural resources (open spaces, fresh water,
   electrical power, forests, grasslands, wildlife) do you want to consume?* (A)
   I think it is imperative that we conserve our natural resources, as they
   represent the wealth of our community, and that we use them as
   wisely as possible because not only do they benefit me by maintaining
   my quality of life but they also are part of my legacy to my children,
   who have the same right to a life of quality as I do. (B) I suppose we
   have to sacrifice our natural resources to create prosperity. (C) We
   must, of necessity, sell all of our natural resources so we can compete
   effectively in the global market.

6. *Do you want your city and county governments to continue subsidizing new
   developments, including industries that pollute your air, water, and soil, or
   should they use the money to purchase and protect open spaces, fund schools,
   offer daycare for your children at community centers, create cultural and
   recreational programs to teach people about one another and foster racial tolerance, and perhaps still have money left over for a tax cut?* (A) I'll take the
   expanded services in which I deeply believe and the tax cut, which I can
   certainly put to good use for my children's health and education. (B) I
   am one of the 25% of the people whose business depends on development; I don't want anything to dampen my ability to earn all I can.

7. *How much bigger do you want your community to get?* (A) It's already
   big enough now; if it gets any bigger, it will lose the qualities I love
   it for, such as the beautiful landscape that surrounds it and the easy
   access to uncrowded places for recreation and spiritual renewal. (B)
   I suppose we have to keep growing because our city, county, and state
   governments say we do, which means whatever happens, will happen
   — but then, that's progress. (C) While I love the surrounding landscape and all, I want the amenities that big cities offer; I don't see
   why I can't have both, but I don't really want to live in a big city —
   I just want what they offer.

Although this quiz blatantly points out the obvious negative effects of
urban sprawl, we never hear about them because doing so would constitute
a direct attack on the economic myth that for an economy to be healthy it
must be ever-expanding; thus, growth — *all* growth — is not only good for
all of us all of the time but also is the very life's blood of economic health.
If growth slows or ceases, our economy will indubitably collapse; that is the
undying message of the gross domestic product.

Now let's consider the quiz in terms of both the gross domestic product (which is strictly quantity oriented, even at the total expense of quality) and a genuine progress indicator (which is oriented toward finding a balance between quantity and quality that allows the former while protecting the latter). In all of the (A) answers, the intangible values that account for "quality of life and human welfare" would be honored and accounted for, but only when computed with a genuine progress indicator. The people who espouse these values, however, are often dismissed as being "environmentalists," "crackpots," "anti-business," "anti-progress," "undemocratic," "extremist," or some other such derogatory appellation.

On the other hand, the (B) and (C) answers either grudgingly accept continual growth, development, and degradation of environmental health, quality of life, and human welfare as the necessary price of economic prosperity or say "Full steam ahead! I'll make mine now, and the future can worry about the leftovers." Those who espouse these values talk about the "real world" of competition, global markets, profit margins, and the vital necessity of continual growth in population and economic expansion for the long-term economic health and stability of the community. Both of these attitudes subscribe to calculations of the gross domestic product which deftly hide the real and lasting costs of continual growth, development, and urban sprawl.

The level of consciousness that inspired the gross domestic product, and even eco-efficiency, does not have to reign, however. Consider Oslo, Norway, as explained by Meadows. During this discussion, consider the quality of life as a genuine progress indicator and score Oslo's probable quality of life accordingly. Meadows writes that, "Oslo rises halfway up the hills at the end of a fjord and then abruptly stops," because of a huge public park in which no private development is allowed. The park is full of trails, lakes, playgrounds, picnic tables, and scattered huts where one can enjoy a hot drink in winter or a cold one in summer. Tram lines radiate from the city to a number of locations at the edge of the park and allow a person to ride to the end of a line, or ski or hike in a loop through the park to the end of another tram line and ride home again.

The park forms a "no-nonsense urban-growth boundary" that effectively forces development inward. Consequently, there are no derelict blocks in Oslo because space that is no longer useful for one purpose is converted to another, better use. Urban renewal is everywhere, a continuous process of seeking the best and wisest use for all available space which is, after all, the essence of sustainable development. Because most streets in the shopping district are designed for pedestrian use and offer only limited space to park, cars are effectively all but eliminated. In addition, the trams are inexpensive and frequent and go everywhere. The result is a city that is quiet, clean, friendly, attractive, thriving, and surrounded by ample open space for recreation, exercise, and spiritual renewal.

Can you say this about your community, town, or city? Would you like to be able to say this about your own town? Can we make our respective towns fit a similar description? Yes, we can. There is a long list of things that can be done, which Eben Fodor has organized under two categories: (1) taking the foot off the accelerator, and (2) applying the brake, both of which come under the valuation of a genuine progress indicator but are totally absent from valuation of the gross domestic product.

The accelerator represents the widespread public subsidies to urban sprawl, which, according to Fodor, include the following:[26]

- Free or subsidized roads, sewer, and water systems, schools, and so on, *instead* of charging developers fees that are high enough to ensure that the taxes of present residents will not go up to pay for the public services provided to new residents.
- Tax breaks, grants, free consulting services, and other enticements to attract new, private businesses; here one might ask why the public should be forced to subsidize new businesses, especially when they undermine existing businesses that are paying their own way to be part of the community
- Waiving environmental or land-use regulations that will degrade the quality of life for all residents for all time.
- Federally funded road projects that not only allow but also encourage further congestion of traffic.

Accelerators of growth make current residents pay for new development through higher taxes; lower services, more noise; less open space; more pollution of the air, water, and soil; and increased traffic congestion. There is no legal or moral reason to keep a foot on the accelerators of growth, although most economists argue that a community will be healthy only if its economy keeps expanding, which means that the economists subscribe to the notion of gross domestic product. Easing up on the accelerators might at least guarantee that new development pays its own way, which in our view includes long-term protection of the environment, even at the expense of growth, because one cannot maximize both quality and quantity. One must take precedence over the other.

In contrast, applying the brakes means setting absolute, non-negotiable limits to growth and new development, which can be done in the following ways:

- Establishment of non-negotiable growth boundaries and green-belt systems of open spaces.
- Protection of farmlands, forestlands, grasslands, shorelines, and so forth through non-negotiable zoning.
- Spending restrictions on infrastructure — why should a Wal-Mart, K-Mart, or any other large chain store that sucks in traffic force the resident public to widen the road at public expense? Another option would be to let the narrow road control the traffic.
- Downzoning, which rezones the land so it can be used less intensively.

- Comprehensive public review of all aspects of new development from the very beginning through to the very end.
- Public purchase of development rights.
- Either limiting the rate of growth or placing absolute limits on the size of a community that are commensurate with the limitations of the natural resources of the community as determined by the health of its surrounding environment.

On the one hand, there are unethical and illegal reasons for wanting to apply the brakes: (1) to protect a special privilege, (2) to discriminate against certain kinds of people, and (3) to take private property for public use without fair compensation. These reasons are based on calculations of the gross domestic product that foster competition that is both socially and environmentally destructive.

On the other hand, there are ethical and legal reasons for wanting to limit growth and new development: (1) to protect water catchments, aquifers, open space, farmlands, forestlands, grasslands, shorelines, and so on over the long term; (2) to protect the quality of the environment as a whole, particularly the quality of the air and the quality and quantity of the water and soil, for all generations; (3) to slow growth by directing it into places where public services can be efficiently and effectively delivered which will allow a community to absorb growth and consider its long-term ramifications in a wise and psychologically mature way; and (4) to protect the resident community from outgrowing its land base, which means protecting all its natural resources from failure due to overdevelopment. All of these reasons argue for the evaluation of growth using genuine progress indicators.

The system of genuine progress indicators would then serve not only as a baseline for all subsequent deliberations concerning the social-environmental sustainability of the community's growth but also as a means of measuring the effectiveness of the criteria used in land-use decisions and subsequent actions based on those criteria. Another function of the genuine progress indicators would be to add value to those resources and activities that have no value in terms of the gross domestic product, such as taking real care of the community's children and elders. The genuine progress indicator is an important tool because most, if not all, activities in sustainable community development, from the long-term health of the environment to the real welfare of the citizens, are omitted from valuation within the context of traditional economic measures, which becomes readily apparent when a local government deliberates over the economic strength of a community's tax base in terms of traditional economics and as a legacy for the future. Having said this, it is imperative at this juncture to elaborate on some of Nature's services, as mentioned earlier, that are omitted from traditional economic valuation. These services equate in large measure to the long-term health of every community's environment.

Nature's inherent services

The inherent services performed by Nature constitute the invisible foundation that is not only the wealth of every human community and its society but also the supporting basis of our economies. In this sense, Nature's services are also the wealth of every owner of a furniture manufacturing company. For example, we rely on oceans to supply fish; forests to supply water, wood, and new medicines; rivers to transport the water from its source to a point where we can access it; soil to grow food, forests, and grasslands; and so on. Although we base our livelihoods on the expectation that Nature will provide these services indefinitely, despite what we do to the environment, the economic system to which we commit our unquestioning loyalty undervalues, discounts, or ignores these services when computing the gross domestic product and the real outcomes of eco-efficiency. This is but saying that Nature's services, on which we rely for everything concerning the quality of our lives, are measured poorly or not at all.

Forests, for example, are far more than merely suppliers of wood fiber. They are the main source of water for most of the people of the world, and the water they produce and store greatly exceeds the value of whatever wood fiber humans may glean from the trees — even that for manufacturing furniture. They supply habitat for insects, birds, and bats that pollinate crops and for birds and bats that eat insects considered to be harmful to people's economic interests, such as the forest trees themselves. Forests are a major source of the oxygen we breathe, which has no substitute, and all the while the trees store vast amounts of carbon within their wooden bodies, which helps to stabilize the global climate.

Because of the importance of Nature's inherent services, usually thought of as ecosystem functions, it is worth while to examine one such service in greater detail — pollination. Eighty percent of all cultivated crops (1330 varieties, including fruits, vegetables, coffee, and tea) are pollinated by wild and semi-wild pollinators. Between 120,000 and 200,000 species of animals perform this service.[21]

Bees are enormously valuable to the functioning of virtually all terrestrial ecosystems and such worldwide industries as agriculture. Pollination by naturalized European honeybees, for example, is 60 to 100 times more valuable economically than is the honey they produce. In fact, the value of wild blueberry bees is so great that farmers who raise blueberries refer to them as "flying $50 bills."[21]

While more than half of the honeybee colonies in the U.S. have been lost within the last 50 years, 25% have been lost within the last 5 years. Widespread threats to honeybees (other than viruses and mites) and other pollinators are fragmentation and outright destruction of habitat (hollow trees for colonies in the case of wild honeybees), intense exposure to pesticides, and a generalized loss of nectar plants to herbicides, as well as the gradual deterioration of "nectar corridors" that provide sources of food to migrating pollinators.

In Germany, for instance, the people are so efficient at weeding their gardens that the nation's free-flying population of honeybees is rapidly declining, according to Werner Muehlen of the Westphalia-Lippe Agricultural Office.[22] Bee populations have shrunk by 23% across Germany over the past decade, and wild honeybees are all but extinct in Central Europe. To save the bees, says Muehlen, "gardeners and farmers should leave at least a strip of weeds and wildflowers along the perimeter of their fields and properties to give bees a fighting chance in our increasingly pruned and ... [sterile] world."[22]

Besides an increasing lack of food, one fifth of all the losses of honeybees in the U.S. is due to exposure to pesticides. Wild pollinators are even more vulnerable to pesticides than honeybees because, unlike hives of domestic honeybees that can be picked up and moved prior to the application of a chemical spray, colonies of wild pollinators cannot be purposefully relocated. At least 80% of the world's major crops are serviced by wild pollinators and only 15% by domesticated honeybees, thus the latter cannot be expected to fill the gap by themselves as wild pollinators are lost.

Ironically, economic valuation of products as measured by the gross domestic product fosters many of the practices employed in modern intensive agriculture and mainstream forestry that actually curtail the productivity of crops by reducing pollination. An example is the high levels of pesticides used on cotton crops to kill bees and other insects, an action that reduces the annual yield in the U.S. by an estimated 20%, or $400 million.[21] In addition, herbicides used for a variety of reasons often kill the plants pollinators need to sustain themselves when not pollinating crops. Finally, the practice of squeezing every last penny out of a piece of ground by plowing the edges of fields to maximize the planting area can reduce yields by disturbing and/or removing nesting and rearing habitat for pollinators. With the above in mind, it seems obvious that the notions embodied in eco-efficiency are hardly going to be effective in reversing the economic rationale supporting the processes that drive environmental degradation.

Unfortunately, too many people are fueled by their unquestioning acceptance of current economic theory, which not only designs and condones but also actively encourages the above-mentioned destructive practices. Such people simply assume that the greatest value one can derive from an ecosystem, such as a forest, is that of maximizing its productive capacity for a single commodity to the exclusion of all else.

Single-commodity production, however, is usually the least profitable and least sustainable way to use a forest because single-commodity production simply cannot compete with the enormous value of non-timber services, such as the production of oxygen, capture and storage of water, holding soils in place, and maintaining habitat for organisms that are beneficial to the economic interests of people. These are all foregone when the drive is to maximize a chosen commodity in the name of a desired short-term monetary profit. Ironically, the undervalued and/or discounted and/or ignored uses of the forest are not only more valuable than wood fiber production in the short term but also are more sustainable in the long term and benefit a far greater number of people.

For example, one study of alternative strategies for managing the mangrove forests of Bintuni Bay in Indonesia (a study more in keeping with the posits of the genuine progress indicator) found that leaving the forests intact would be more productive than cutting them, according to Janet Abramovitz.[21] When the non-timber uses of the mangrove forests, such as fisheries, locally used products, and control of soil erosion, were included in the calculation, the most economically profitable strategy was to retain the forests. Maintaining healthy mangrove forests yielded $4800 per 2.5 acres annually over time, whereas cutting the forests would yield a one-time value of $3600 per 2.5 acres. Maintaining the forests would ensure continued local uses of the area worth $10 million per year and provide 70% of the local income while protecting a fishery worth $25 million a year.

We can no longer assume that the services Nature inherently performs are always going to be there because the consequences of our frequently unconscious actions affect Nature in many unforeseen and unpredictable ways. What we can be sure of, however, is that the loss of individual species and their habitats through the degradation and simplification of ecosystems can and will impair the ability of Nature to provide the services we need to survive with any semblance of human dignity and well-being. Losses are just that — irreversible and irreplaceable.

It is precisely because of the irreplaceability of the inherent services provided by Nature that we must erase the notion of obsolescence from our attitudes, our thinking, and our vocabulary. "Not only does this attitude [the notion that obsolescence is acceptable, even desired] undermine the conservation of vanishing species," writes ecologist David Ehrenfeld, "but it distorts our perception of our own place in nature."[24] Ehrenfeld goes on to say that we deem ourselves to be exempt from having to play by Nature's biophysical rules, that we are somehow above and apart from the game of life in the grand scheme of things. While we can pretend this works for a little while, we have not, contends Ehrenfeld, been given either the permission or the power to remove ourselves from the parade of life.

"To call something obsolete," says Ehrenfeld, "boasts an omniscience we do not possess, a reckless disregard for the deep currents of history and biology, and a supremely dangerous refusal to look at the lasting scars our technology is gashing across our planet and our souls."[24] Thus, to keep such things of value as Nature's inherent services, we must not only shift our thinking to a paradigm of sustainability but also calculate the full costs of what we do — genuine progress indicators.

If the reductionist mechanical world view, as refitted with the current notion of eco-efficiency, were replaced with sustainability, it would (refer back to our previous comparison):

- Eliminate clear-cutting, except where ecologically necessary to create or maintain biological sustainability.

- Measure prosperity by the choices saved and passed forward to the next generation and the richness of things from which to choose (natural capital) that accompanies those choices.
- Measure productivity in part by the ecological integrity and health of the forestland from which comes the lumber used in the manufacture of furniture.
- Measure progress by the consciousness with which one cares for the company, the health of the forest from which comes raw materials, and the employees that comprise the company's foundation as a bio-economic (biological-economic) living trust as measured by the genuine progress indicator.
- Integrate the ecological integrity of the forestland from which comes raw materials with the well-being of employees and the profit margin as part of a seamless, interactive whole.
- Eliminate the notion of waste by seeing everything in the forest as part of the recyclable, reinvestable biological capital that maintains forest integrity and productivity.
- See the need for regulation as a failure in the forestland-company trusteeship for future generations.
- Honor and protect biological, genetic, and functional diversity as the principal of the biological living trust in order to protect the productive capacity of a given forestland to provide a sustainable level of interest in terms of economic goods and services for the present and future beneficiaries as part of a legacy of the furniture manufacturing company.

To achieve the kind of revolution in consciousness that is called for by the paradigm of sustainability as measured by the genuine progress indicator, we would do well to heed an ancient Arab proverb as a point of departure. Each word we utter should have to pass through three gates before we say it. At the first gate, the keeper asks, "Is this true?" At the second gate, the keeper asks, "Is it necessary?" At the third gate, the keeper asks, "Is it kind?"

How might this way of thinking fit into caring for the furniture manufacturing company as a bio-economic living trust? Each thought and action in caring for the furniture manufacturing company and the forest from which comes the raw materials must pass through the three gates. At the first gate, the trustee asks, "Is this ecologically sound and socially friendly?" At the second gate, the trustee asks, "Is it necessary to the ecological integrity of the forest and the economic integrity of my company over time?" At the third gate, the trustee asks, "Is it ecologically kind to the forest and socially kind to the welfare of my employees?" Alas, however, we pay no heed to the three gates. So how does our economic model relate to our current land-use practices?

Our economic model and planning

The development process, as we see it in our towns and cities, is typically carried out in a way consistent with the two-part economic model previously described, where the environmental impact analysis of a proposed development is done in a cursory manner or not at all. That is, the immediate potential economic wealth to be gained by way of a proposed development is not weighed against the amount of natural wealth — hence, the potential future economic wealth — lost due to the development. Here, a point that must be remembered is that markets, left to their own devices, usually (and exceedingly efficiently) produce nonsustainable results.

Although measuring natural wealth can be presumptuous due to our limited knowledge of the way ecosystems work and the true impact of a proposed development, both long and short term, a process that at least acknowledges that potential negative effects exist puts us one step closer to living in harmony with the rest of Nature. Further, to the extent that the corporate world influences governmental decision-making worldwide, planning practices will continue to be shortsighted when it comes to predicting the future. If that future is not seven generations away — a time frame used by some indigenous cultures when making major decisions — then land-use practices and decisions will not be tied to perpetuating the natural wealth of the planet, including the services Nature provides.

The planning horizon for most businesses is short term, perhaps 5 years, for the most part. To some, this makes economic sense. Gregory Dunkel, biomedical researcher for the National Biomedical Research Foundation, for example, described in mathematical terms why it makes more business sense to overexploit a natural resource while reinvesting profits elsewhere as the resource diminishes.[25] But, according to Lovins et al.,[112] it makes far greater economic sense to dramatically increase the productivity of natural capital by reducing the wasteful and destructive flow of resources from depletion to pollution. Herein lies a major business opportunity. By changing both production design and technology, industries taking the long view are designing ways to stretch by 5, 10, and 100 times the use of natural capital, resulting in major resource savings that yield higher economic profits over time, pay for themselves, and frequently reduce the initial investment of economic capital.[12]

Our economic model is directly reflected in the patterns of land use in the U.S. Land, like other natural resources, is frequently seen as an endless commodity to be used rather than leaving it undisturbed (a proposition that many consider to be unproductive) or using it in a way that increases its value to all members of the community over the long run. If, for example, a city's boundaries are reached, those with a vested interest in "development" will push for annexation as an immediate remedy — anything to keep the community growing so they can profit. But, as zoologist and ecologist Kenneth Watt noted in a speech to the Center for the Study of Democratic

Institutions in 1969, the most unlikely recommendation to come from city planners is to do nothing — a choice that is typically excluded from the array of possible options.[23] Watt's words are proving prophetic as the costs of urban sprawl are becoming increasingly well documented, and it is becoming clearer that the "go slow" approach is more prudent with respect to the long-term health of the planet's ecosystems.

Fodor, in his book *Better, Not Bigger,* reviews the literature on the cost of urban sprawl and inventories the quantifiable and not-yet-quantified costs of growth.[26] Quantifiable capital costs for public facilities and infrastructure, says Fodor, include schools, sanitary sewers and storm drainage, transportation, water, fire protection, parks and recreation, police, open space, libraries, government facilities, electric power generation and distribution, and solid water disposal. Growth-related costs that are frequently not calculated when computing the cost/benefit analysis of a proposed development include: lost open space and environmental quality, overcrowded schools, traffic congestion, noise, higher crime rates, increased cost of living, decreased air and water quality, lost wildlife habitat, higher costs of housing and living, lost sense of community, and lost visual and other natural amenities valued by people.

Studies exploring the costs associated with the loss of community or sense of place and higher crime rates could well parallel the work of Costanza et al.[27] on the value of ecosystem services. Their studies place a dollar value on Nature's services and make a case for placing this value on the balance sheet. But Nature's services are clearly related to quality of life, as well, a reality revealed when communities lose their clean air, clean water, woodlands, and open space.

Our economic model represents a particular definition of economics that emphasizes business, finance, and market-oriented activities. According to author Thomas Power, economics developed as a specific social science "seeking to prove the social logic of an unfettered market ... to demonstrate how it was that a free market, unhindered by government and medieval guild restrictions, could transform private, profit-seeking business into the social interest ... to champion the profit-seeking behavior of the business community."[28] But, says Power, economics is not just about business and market phenomena. If that were the case, then we could not assert that primitive societies in which commercial markets and business were absent had any economic activity or economic problems. Likewise, in socialist countries, where free enterprise and commerce are constrained and/or prohibited, we cannot assert that economic problems are absent.

"Economics," as defined by Webster, is "a branch of knowledge dealing with the production, distribution, and consumption of goods and services."[3] Power, on the other hand, defines economics as "the study of the way societies develop and use the scarce resources at their disposal to pursue their diverse goals," a definition more consistent with the dictionary definition of "economy" or the thrifty management or use of resources.[28] In *For the Common Good,*[29] Daly and Cobb assert that the word "economics," like "economy," has as its root the Greek word *oikonomia*, meaning the management of the household so as to increase its value to all members of the household over the long run. The current practice of business and industry, however, is, according to Daly and Cobb, more clearly tied to the archaic word *chrematistics*, or the branch of the political economy relating to the manipulation of property and wealth so as to maximize short-term monetary exchange value to the owner.[29]

Berry, in *Home Economics*,[30] states that the problem with an industrial economy is that "it is not comprehensive enough, that moreover it tends to destroy what it does not comprehend, and that it is dependent upon much that it does not comprehend," which is similar to how Hawken sees business and industry failing to acknowledge natural capital on the balance sheet.[10]

Thomas Jefferson, who lived just long enough to witness the early development of the corporate system, saw the handwriting on the wall. In 1799, Jefferson said that, "Banking establishments [his term for corporations] are more dangerous than standing armies."[31] Jefferson warned in his last years that money and banking establishments (corporations) would destroy liberty and restore absolutism, effectively nullifying the ideals for which the American revolution was fought.[31]

Preoccupied with consumption for its own sake, economics since Jefferson's time has increasingly been confined to the shallowness of appearances. Economists remain mesmerized by the theory that more rational analysis of the material world can and will provide all the necessary answers, despite the acknowledged limitations of "objective" reasoning in the physical sciences, says Frances Hutchinson: "Economics as practiced by professionals is, indeed, the 'dismal science' from which life itself is banished."[32] She asserts that economists hide behind a "smoke-screen [they] erected ... to obscure the fact that they know nothing about the real world."[32]

When policies and practices of land-use planning and development fail to treat land as natural capital and, therefore, natural wealth in a way that "increases its value to all members of the community over the long run," these policies and practices are a direct reflection of the kind of economics co-opted by the business culture decades ago. This kind of economics is shortsighted and fails to see connections important to our continued use of the land, which brings up the specter of mass human migrations.

Human migratory patterns

As our economy becomes dangerously out of kilter with the remaining natural capital, some predict an economic collapse. Jack Lessinger, professor emeritus of Real Estate and Urban Development at the University of Washington, believes that the U.S. is "in the throes of discarding our current economic structure and defining its replacement."[33] He finds evidence for this in what he believes is an imminent mass migration to more remote and spacious rural counties, as the suburbs, which for decades embodied the "middle class American dream of security and contentment," are now becoming as blighted as cities due to traffic congestion, smog, crime, and "the numbing sameness of near-by shopping malls and fast-food chains."

A case in point is the western U.S., where states such as Oregon, Washington, and Idaho are no longer dependent on the decline of California's economy for their continued growth in population; in fact, California's economic powerhouse is on the rebound.[34] The West, according to William Frey, of the University of New York-Albany and a senior fellow at the Milken Institute of Santa Monica, CA, has become so popular that "it is somewhat immune from California's doldrums." Although many of the new arrivals in the West are college educated and hail from other regions, "there will always be a symbiotic relationship between California and the rest of the West," Frey told a seminar sponsored by the Center for the New West, a think-tank. John Cromartie, a geographer for the U.S. Department of Agriculture, confirmed this notion when he pointed out that retiring Baby Boomers from California could become a major source for the influx of population into rural areas of the West within a decade because they have visited national forests and other scenic areas, and he contends that "familiarity breeds migration." But, even before the formal retirement of Baby Boomers has begun, five of the six most recent cities to gain the status of metropolitan areas according to their individual census are in the West: Flagstaff, AZ; Grand Junction, CO; Missoula, MT; Pocatello ID; and Corvallis, OR.

Frey believes that the population of senior citizens in Wyoming, Colorado, Idaho, Nevada, and Utah will increase by more than 150% as the Baby Boomers retire. Oregon, Montana, Arizona, and New Mexico could see increases in the population of retired Baby Boomers of more than 100%. In addition, Frey observed that the majority of Californians were not born in the state so leaving it to retire somewhere else will not be too difficult.

Even with the resurgence of California's economic base, Frey contends that "we still see a steady stream of out-migration to the rest of the West [as well as Texas and Florida]," particularly among the college educated. Much of the current growth in California is comprised of immigrants from other countries and not so much from Americans leaving other places to move to California, said Frey.

Jack Lessinger has studied mass migrations throughout American history that were triggered by faltering economic strategies, where new habitats, new economic directions, and new rules with which to exploit them arose.[33] Brad Edmonson, also a senior fellow at the Milken Institute of Santa Monica, CA, along with Frey, observes that Americans are the most mobile of any citizens of the world's industrialized nations. "Within the U.S.," says Edmonson, "residents of Western states are twice as likely as those in the Northeast to changes addresses in a year. In Denver, the mobility rate is one in four residents; in New York City, it is one in eight."[43] Thus, economic strategies bear a clear and distinct relationship to land use, if, as Lessinger postulates, populations migrate in response to failing economic schemes.[33]

In the period from 1735 to 1846, East Coast residents began moving westward in response to the inflexible bias toward the privileged citizens of the centralized colonial system that favored Mother England. This system was designed to assure a continuous flow of raw materials to England that depended on large plantations, government monopolies, and a rigid social stratification. Lessinger refers to this period as the Mercantile Aristocrat. The conditions of this era gave rise to a period known as the Bantam Capitalist (1789–1900), renowned for its exaltation of the "common man," the rise of "Yankee ingenuity," and the mom-and-pop enterprise. During this era, migrants moved farther into the far reaches of the Mississippi Valley, where cheap, plentiful land became dotted with small-scale farms and prosperous small towns.[33]

When mass production swept the nation and overwhelmed the inefficiencies of small-scale entrepreneurs, cities boomed and migrants flocked to places such as Chicago and Minneapolis where jobs in factories were available; some, however, went even farther west for jobs in mines, quarries, timber camps, fisheries, and large-scale farms, thus arose the period known as the Colossus (1846–1958), which focused on production and the accompanying skyrocketing values of real estate. Overproduction, however, exceeded demand and led to the Depression of the 1930s. Following World War II, with its tremendous material demands feeding a burst of growth in industrial technology and wages, the U.S. was looking for something to stimulate domestic markets and fuel the postwar economy. The answer came with the emerging sophistication of product advertising coupled with the nearly universal availability of consumer credit. And so the period known as the Little King (1900–?) was ushered in with concomitant proliferation of housing on the outskirts of cities — the suburbs.[33]

According to Lessinger, this period of the "Little King and Little Queen" residing in America's suburbs is coming to an end: "Not only are the royal nests being fouled as the suburbs become increasingly urbanized, but the acquisitive 'buy now, pay later' formula for driving the domestic economy also drives the nation's fiscal policy."[33] Further, as the U.S. continues to borrow against the future, it finds itself facing a federal deficit that makes it the largest debtor nation in the world.

Predictably, according to Lessinger, the next migration will be to "Penturbia" — the so-called fifth wave migration to places three to four hours from metropolitan centers that are economically independent of them. This migration is in response to an economic system made weak by the excesses of overspending, which in turn is made possible by liberal credit.

Thus, economic strategies that lead to social unrest may form the catalyst for migration and shifting land-use patterns. Another look at this phenomenon is presented by Nicole Achs in an article entitled "Exurbia."[7] Unlike Lessinger, who predicted a mass flight from the suburbs to places three to four hours from metropolitan areas (which is already occurring), Achs believes that the current flight is to the exurbs — places within commuting distance of urban centers that look rural but have inadequate infrastructure, a high median income, and rising property taxes.[7] This migration is in response to the growing urbanization of the suburbs and the accompanying snail's pace rush-hour traffic, hazy air, burgeoning crime, and a nonexistent sense of place. According to the 1990 Census, 30% of the fastest growing counties between 1980 and 1990 are contiguous to metropolitan areas.[28] What also brings many to the exurbs, according to Achs, is the lower cost of housing. If a person can purchase a home in the exurbs that requires the same monthly cash output as renting a home in town, why stay in town?

These rapidly growing areas of the country are becoming sentinels for land-use planning policies and practices that seek to limit growth. Such places are growing so rapidly that local governments are struggling to meet the necessities of new residents for basic services and other infrastructure. According to William Herman, selectman of Weare, NH, a town within 20 miles of Manchester and Concord, the attitude of many residents is that "now that we're here, let's close the gates."[7] But most see growth as the only way out to meet the costs of improved services. Far from discouraging development, Londonderry, NH, is recruiting corporate manufacturing, and, according to local officials, the rural atmosphere need not be lost if the development is done right.[7] Thus, a more careful look at human nature could not only help planners to better understand the people for whom they are working but also help them frame a set of basic social-environmental principles to aid them in planning sustainably for the future.

Human nature

Most of us take tremendous license when talking about "basic human nature;" that is, we express what is true for *us*. And, because it is arguable that there is any exact science associated with understanding human nature, people's perceptions of what is true for them must, in fact, be accepted as their reality. "Reality," as Lily Tomlin once stated, "is a primitive form of crowd control that has gotten out of hand." Translation: reality is (most likely) utter chaos, which simply means that biophysical reality is far beyond our understanding, so we as humans attempt to make it otherwise — ordered, understandable, and controllable.

Thus, our perception, or that which is brought to us through words (our own thoughts) and pictures (what we choose to see and not see), is our reality. What we choose to see or not see and how we choose to see it are determined and shaped by our personal experience, which we are taught to use as discernment or judgment. The intervening variable between sensing something and perceiving it, perception being the essence of our individual truth, is therefore the behavioral standard against which we judge the "right order" of the world around us. Perception, therefore, follows judgment. This, we believe, is part of human nature.

In the context of our use of natural resources, including land, we see several aspects of human nature that appear to play a role in the ongoing debate. Our perceived necessities and desires, as well as our penchant for short-term gratification (which some people attribute to ignorance), seem to supersede the need for wise trusteeship of the vital elements that sustain life on this planet. Other people, however, attribute this short-sightedness to the human sense of self and what it takes to keep that self alive — physical survival. In the industrialized world, however, where many have the basic necessities of food, shelter, clothing met, survival becomes something else — something relative and abstract, as opposed to the concrete life-and-death situations faced daily in many non-industrialized countries.

Like survival, poverty and prosperity are defined by each of us, and our personal definitions are no doubt influenced by the general definition provided by our own culture. Where basic necessities are met, as we understand them, it seems that the perpetuation and health of such life-sustaining elements as air, water, and soil are less likely to be understood, appreciated, or actively protected. Given that most humans, in the foreseeable future, may not transcend this understanding of survival to mean that everyone is a trustee of Earth, an alternative and embraceable set of principles is required if we are to achieve any semblance of social-environmental harmony.

Manfred Max-Neef and Paul Ekins, in their book *Real Life Economics: Understanding Wealth Creation,*[35] offer a new praxis relating to human necessities. Human needs, they say, must be understood as an integrated system. With the sole exception of physical survival, no hierarchies exist within the system. "On the contrary, simultaneities, complementarities, and trade-offs are characteristics of the process of needs satisfaction."[35] They suggest that basic human necessities are the same in all cultures and in all historical periods. What varies over time and among cultures is the way necessities are satisfied.

The needs postulated by Max-Neef and Ekins are being, having, doing, interacting, subsistence, protection, affection, understanding, participation, creation, leisure, identity, and freedom.[35] Food and shelter are thus viewed not as needs but as satisfiers of the need for subsistence. Education, study, and exploration are satisfiers of the need for understanding. In such a model, satisfiers of one need may impair the satisfaction of other needs. For example, censorship as a satisfier of the perceived need of protection from unwanted ideas may impair satisfaction of the need for the freedom of personal expression, understanding, participation, creation, identity, and freedom.

Human-conceived and human-developed technology, in our opinion, provides a huge resource for "satisfiers" of specific human needs, specifically protection, freedom, subsistence, having, and doing, and thus give us the illusion of fulfillment of all of our basic needs. But, because much of our current technology was neither created nor designed by and for diverse communities and/or in full recognition of the complex tapestry of human needs, the satisfaction provided is, in some instances, faltering, which brings to the surface unsatisfied human needs, and thus arises the notion of "unintended consequences."

For example, many human inventions such as computers, presumably designed to give us more time and thus leisure and possibly more income, may not be helping us attain these desired outcomes after all. In the U.S., those who are employed, and supposedly becoming more productive, find they are working 100 to 200 hours more per year than 20 years ago. In addition, real wages have not increased for more than 20 years. Carpal tunnel syndrome and failing eyesight afflict many computer users; electronic communication substitutes for human contact; rapid access to information and easy correction of errors have heightened our expectations and lowered our tolerance for error or failing systems.

The unintended consequences of computers are numerous, and, because the full range of human necessities was not considered in their development, computers may be creating more problems than they solve. Moreover, it appears that technology typically offers solutions that give humans the illusion of control, a state of mind that has extremely limited usefulness in a sustainable society.

Thus, it may simply be a feature of our species that, at this point in our evolution, we do not sense (let alone fully understand) the means that will provide long-term, if not perpetual, satisfaction of our necessities and therefore choose instead to opt for technology that appears to offer us immediate gratification. This part of our nature may continue to keep us on "disconnect" from the rest of Nature for some time, thereby exacerbating the problems associated with depletion of natural resources and associated natural capital.

The purpose of exploring human nature and associated necessities in the context of the ongoing land-use debate in our society is to suggest the possibility that government regulation of land use in its current manifestation, while ostensibly satisfying the necessity for protection, may be impairing satisfaction of the necessity for understanding, participation, identity, and freedom. This may be why "top-down" policy or law seems to work in the short term but ultimately fails.

"Development geared to the satisfaction of fundamental human needs cannot," according to Max-Neef and Ekins, "be structured from the top downwards. It cannot be imposed either by law or by decree. It can only emanate directly from the actions, expectations, and creative and critical awareness of the protagonists themselves."[35] In such a system, where feelings and values cannot be legislated, people must take the lead in developing their communities, and the state must assume a role whereby the process, as well as the end result, reflects recognition of the full range and complexities of human requirements. The development process then becomes healthy, self-reliant, participative, and "capable of creating the foundations for a social order within which economic growth, solidarity, and the growth of all men and women as whole persons can be reconciled."[35]

The salient point here, in simple terms, is that human necessities cannot viably be thought of in a linear either/or fashion because the bio-physical system does not work that way. A human cannot survive with only food or water or shelter; we require all three. Therefore, food, water, shelter, and all the other necessities of life must be simultaneously accounted for, not just a few at the expense of others.

Suppose for the moment that this notion of highly interactive and interdependent life forces — human necessities — does in fact exist; could a greater understanding of the full range of human necessities influence the way we plan for and execute land-use decisions? Is it not possible that, if such human necessities as those described above were not seen hierarchically, a new, more integrative and participative process could emerge? If such a social evolution occurred on a broad scale, the ultimate impact on the way we use land could be phenomenal, which brings us to current attempts to modify conventional land-use practices.

chapter two

Attempts to modify conventional land-use practices

The myriad problems that have surfaced in our society related to the ways we have planned for and implemented changes to the landscape have given rise to alternative approaches to land use. These include variations on existing zoning law, New Urbanism, and Traditional Neighborhood Development.

Zoning

Land-use laws, including zoning, emerged in the U.S. primarily as a result of serious public human health problems. At the turn of the century, substandard — and sometimes deplorable — sanitary conditions created such enormous hazards to public health that the government was forced to step in. Densely developed, overcrowded tenement housing with little or no sanitary facilities and factories spewing forth waste into the air and water of cities unable to handle the resulting health problems were the conditions giving birth to land and water regulations.[10]

The adoption of a public sanitary code was followed shortly by the development of land-use laws rationalized as being in the interest of public health, safety, and welfare. Zoning, for example, was a way of protecting lower impact uses (such as housing) from higher impact uses (such as industry and commerce, with their associated noise, fumes, and traffic). It was also an attempt to protect property values and create certain efficiencies in terms of delivery of services. For example, if industry is to be served by truck, train, or ship, the location of such industry in the vicinity of its commercial transportation routes makes sense. Likewise, if residents are expecting services from fire departments and schools, it makes sense to establish districts in which each is convenient to the other.

The 1926 court case, *Village of Euclid (New York) v. Ambler Realty*, created the rational basis for what came to be known as Euclidean Zoning. In this landmark case, Ambler Realty, the plaintiff, brought suit in a federal district court to enjoin the enforcement of a comprehensive zoning ordinance that restricted a portion of Ambler Realty's land to residential development — land that Ambler Realty had intended for industrial development. Euclidean Zoning, so named after this landmark case, essentially separates one type of land use from another in order to prevent, among other things, the occurrence of a "nuisance."

It is easy to see how this type of land-use control grew out of turn-of-the-century conditions wherein the absence of control would clearly bring great public harm. It is also easy to understand how such a system could remain a fixture, as it does today, in many municipalities, where it gives developers predictability in terms of the context in which development will occur, in terms of potential nuisances, and in terms of land value over the long term. It also provides neighborhoods with similar reassurances. In addition, zoning and the resulting placement of certain types of restrictions in particular places often makes sense in terms of existing public infrastructure, such as routes of commercial and industrial transportation and concern for ecologically sensitive areas. Clearly, however, Euclidean Zoning comes with certain weaknesses, which contributed to the "unlivability" of cities and the subsequent advent of suburbs in the 1950s and 1960s.

In response to the inflexibility of Euclidean Zoning, measures for providing flexibility to zoning regulations surfaced in the 1970s. The Planned Unit Development (PUD) was one of the earliest forms of what was called Innovative Zoning.[36] It was and still is typically used for residential developments of more than five units and provides certain flexibility to development standards in exchange for some public benefit provided by the developer. For example, providing public open space may be required in exchange for an increase in allowed housing density or mixed uses on a single large site.

Planned Unit Development *zones* allow such variations to existing regulations, or a PUD *permit* may exist and be applied to any site. In either case, a simple application of the PUD concept is cluster housing, where residential dwellings are clustered on a property to preserve some natural feature of the land, such as a stand of trees or a particular view. While many advantages were foreseen for application of PUD, some people were surprised with the actual results.

Planners, for example, predicted that the PUD, with its greater complexities, would discourage "fly-by-night" developers. Although developers who use the PUD concept generally tend to be better financed and well-organized and show a greater commitment to the towns where they propose development, the extraordinary approval requirements sometimes discourage even the most committed developer.[36]

Further, planners in the Truckee area of the Sierra Nevadas in California have found that, while cluster development was initially encouraged as an acceptable way to intervene on the rural landscape of this mountainous area, it is just another form of urban sprawl. It is expensive to extend infrastructure to these developments. In addition, these outlying developments add commuters to the highways and thus pollution to the air because the developments lack the array of services and job opportunities offered by towns and cities.[37]

Another variation on standard zoning law comes under the general rubric of Incentive Zoning. Like the Planned Unit Development concept, Incentive Zoning offers specific public concessions (such as increased densities or building height, tax abatement, or street improvements) in return for specific contributions by the developer (such as public plazas, park land, beach access, affordable housing, etc.). Experience with this attempt to modify the zoning system in order to provide more flexibility to developers indicates that it seems to work only where the incentives provide distinct advantages to the developer. Further, while local government has sometimes been relieved of the cost of public infrastructure because they are assumed by the developer, these donation requirements have been challenged in the courts as forced exactions,[36] which brings us to Performance Zoning.

Performance Zoning establishes a framework within which projects are evaluated based on their projected impacts on the community. Performance standards may address such things as steep slopes, visual impact, groundwater, traffic flow, stormwater runoff, wetlands, and whatever else may be important to a community.[38] The process of evaluating a project is thus based on performance standards that establish specific concrete guidelines; for example, a development will generate traffic at a maximum of 500 trips per day, or 15% of the land will be held in common open space. Performance Zoning allows for project approval on a case-by-case basis, for which capacities and demands — water, traffic, sewer, and so on — are considered. Whereas traditional zoning ensures that all development conforms to established standards (e.g., setbacks, limits to the heights of buildings, and so on), Performance Zoning reviews new development in terms of how it will "perform." Like other tools developed to give flexibility to traditional zoning practices, Performance Zoning requires more time and greater expertise by those administering zoning regulations. Another attempt to provide alternatives to standard zoning practices includes the theory and tenets of New Urbanism.

New Urbanism

New Urbanism, a term coined in 1986, grew out of the many problems associated with conventional land-use practices discussed earlier in this book. It is a movement to reform patterns of urban growth based on the belief that current development patterns are contributing to the decline of our central cities, the loss of open space and agricultural lands to low-density suburban growth, and the problems of crime, affordable housing, and social equity.[39] Principles of New Urbanism include: (1) compact neighborhoods with diverse populations that are pedestrian friendly and have mixed uses; (2) transportation systems that efficiently serve regions; (3) a wide spectrum of housing; (4) buildings and landscapes that define streets and public spaces as areas of shared use; and (5) urban places with architecture and landscape design that celebrate local history, ecology, climate, and building practices.[39]

Fort Collins, CO, a city of approximately 100,000, offers a glimpse of New Urbanism in practice. A rapidly growing city, Fort Collins expanded by about 23,000, or about 20%, over the last 10 years. In response to pressures of growth and development, the local government responded with innovation and creativity. For years, Fort Collins relied upon traditional Euclidean Zoning, but complaints of inflexibility were the catalyst for a new performance-based point system for development. This system was in place for about 10 years before it was dropped. A hybrid system of land-use controls is now in place, and the city is being redesigned based on the principles of New Urbanism.

Euclidean Zoning, or what Fort Collins referred to as a "use-by-right" system, offered clear standards, although some were outdated and incomplete, and an easy administrative review process. The system, however, was inflexible with respect to uses and standards of development, and it allowed little or no public involvement. It also included a zoning map unrelated to any plan or vision for the future of Fort Collins.

In response to these problems, the Fort Collins City Council in 1981 adopted a Land Development Guidance System, which was tied to the notion that any development could be a Planned Unit Development. However, because the Land Development Guidance System was optional for developers, the old zoning remained in effect and a landowner could have the old system applied to his or her property and development proposal. Under the new system, development proposals were reviewed and points earned or lost depending on how well the development plan responded to stated criteria.

Citizen participation was a key feature of Land Development Guidance System. Each proposal had intensive public review, including neighborhood meetings. Although most people liked the system's flexibility with regard to land use and design and generally viewed the Land Development Guidance System as an appropriate response to market forces, complaints surfaced regarding the time required for review and approval and the up-front expenditures that were sometimes lost when a project was ultimately denied. Others complained that the standards were fuzzy and provided little predictability for developers, planners, or neighborhoods. In addition, one segment of the community claimed that the Land Development Guidance System not only failed to reflect a shared community vision but was also unrelated to any physical plan for Fort Collins. Finally, a concern about growth and its adverse effects continued to be a major one for citizens.

It was the complaint about a lack of shared vision that finally reached the ears of the elected officials. In response, the city embarked on a city planning process guided by a City Plan Advisory Committee. The plan, adopted in 1997, contains three separate documents: Community Vision and Goals, City Structure Plan, and City Plan Principles and Policies. The City Plan notes that "establishing core community values, an overall vision, and broad planning goals for the next 20 years … is essential to setting a course to be followed as the city grows, develops, and redevelops."[40] The community vision, a set of community values, and strategic goals were shaped through a city dialog process, a Visual Preference Survey™, public workshops, and several meetings between the City Plan Advisory Committee and the professional planning team. Sustainability, fulfillment, fairness, and choices emerged as the core values.

The City Structure Plan focuses on the physical form and development pattern for the city, addressing density, land conservation, infill development, direction of growth, patterns of commercial development, choices for transportation, and a system of open lands. The plan sets forth a vision of the future wherein the city is made up of four basic kinds of places: neighborhoods, districts, corridors, and edges. Peter Calthorpe, noted planner, author, and advocate for the concepts of New Urbanism, helped guide the Fort Collins community in its planning by using the following principles:[40]

- Compact development pattern: urban development directed to well-defined areas at higher densities, thus avoiding urban sprawl
- Interconnected transit system, efficient because of the city's compact form
- New activity centers in transit-served areas, where the physical environment is intended to be pedestrian and transit-oriented with a mix of uses
- Interconnected system of open lands
- Urban growth boundary
- Multiple means of travel with a greater emphasis on travel enhancements for pedestrians, bicycles, and mass transit

What is notable about the resulting overall form and function of the Fort Collins plan is that it essentially recognizes, in our opinion, the notion of *comprehensible scale*. This notion asks the question, "At what scale are we truly capable of creating functioning, long-lived, healthy patterns of land use?" The principles of New Urbanism result in what might be viewed as a pattern of interconnected "villages," or mixed-use, high-density, pedestrian-friendly, human-scale centers. These nodes of activity no doubt are simpler for a community to understand and easier to plan for, and thus are more likely to engage citizens in their design. The authors are reminded of what Bill Raffo, a friend and colleague in the City of Santa Cruz Planning

Department, used to call the "salami technique" — slice the problem into pieces thin enough to understand and by so doing create a higher probability of arriving at solutions.

In Fort Collins, drawing the community into its own design and obtaining the wisdom and understanding of citizen participants throughout the process essentially guaranteed easy passage of the plan by the city. After years of work on the City Plan, only three citizens objected at the final public hearing, where the plan was adopted unanimously by the city council.

What is further notable about the Fort Collins experience is the fact that, while developing the City Plan, the citizens also undertook a revision of the zoning ordinance (and map). In many cities, creating a comprehensive plan and simultaneously revising the city's zoning ordinance are considered too much of an undertaking. And, yet, doing so is clearly the most rational choice. Ideally, a city's zoning ordinance, which is the primary tool for implementing the plan, reflects the shared vision of its comprehensive plan, which in turn is based on the citizens' values, goals, and, objectives. Ideally, the city's zoning map reflects the city's land-use plan. Rarely, however, do we see a city undertake the development of both simultaneously.

Fort Collins' land-use code (zoning ordinance) replaces both the old zoning code and the Land Development Guidance System with a hybrid system that provides clear, updated standards; a direct link to the comprehensive plan; incentives for projects that meet standards; and a focus for public involvement. The code creates new districts for large undeveloped tracts based on the City Plan, keeps old zones for existing development, retains existing subarea plans, translates Land Development Guidance System requirements into clear, more objective language, and develops new standards to address specific issues — for example, how to deal with Wal-Mart-type development, which Fort Collins planners call "Big Box" development.

In addition to developing a land-use code consistent with the City Plan, the city simultaneously developed a Transportation Master Plan tied to a Congestion Management Plan. The nuance in the Transportation Master Plan is a notion of *level of service* that emphasizes access over mobility. Thus, an "adequate" level of service is defined for each mode of travel. The Multimodal Transportation Level of Service Manual of the Transportation Master Plan states that the level of service standards were historically applied only to roads and only in engineering. Their primary purpose was to facilitate the design of specific road improvement projects based on forecasted demand. Now, however, level of service standards also serve as a system of performance planning and measurement.[41]

Under this system, estimating future necessary levels of service for roads requires predicting future levels of traffic or forecasting future supply and demand. For each non-automobile mode of travel (pedestrians, bicycles, and public transit), levels of service standards do not require forecasts of user volume or demand; rather, they are designed to "ensure ubiquitous availability of adequate bicycle and pedestrian facilities and transit service."[41] The Transportation Master Plan level of service standards for motor vehicles are designed to reflect the type of area being served, thus allowing public investment in motor vehicle capacity and efficiency in a manner that supports the city's land-use plan.

Thus, consistent with the notion of comprehensible scale, the Fort Collins Transportation Master Plan looks at levels of service relative to the land-use plan, which presents interconnected activity centers within which multi-modal transportation facilities are emphasized.

In an effort to keep the City Plan current and responsive to citizen concerns, city planners recently (May 1999) drafted a memo to the city manager that outlined areas where issues are surfacing relative to implementation of the City Plan. Complaints listed included: higher housing densities called for by the plan will not be supported by the marketplace, the plan will drive growth to other cities, it will favor large national developers, it will increase the cost of land by limiting the supply of developable land, it will increase building costs by imposing new design standards, and it will increase project planning costs through an increased development review process that will make infill development difficult.[42]

Although each complaint was refuted in this May 1999 memo, it is interesting to note that such complaints may be seen as predictable, as they are the same complaints leveled universally by developers where land use and development are regulated. Thus, the point system (Land Development Guidance System), which essentially allowed any development anywhere in the city as long as it earned enough points, was dropped because of issues with unpredictability, whereas the new land-use code, which reflects the values and vision of the City Plan, is being criticized for being too rigid, despite its predictability.

Middleton Hills, a neighborhood in Madison, WI, has also embraced New Urbanism. In addition to narrower streets, houses built on small lots, and required front porches or stoops, Middleton Hills boasts numerous parks and public spaces, and traffic-free alleys used by children as playgrounds. Residents are also all within walking distance of grocery stores and pharmacies.[43]

Like the critics of cluster housing as a technique to somehow diminish the impact of development on rural lands, some see New Urbanist developments as "sprawl in public relations clothing." Professor emeritus Phil Lewis, of the University of Wisconsin at Madison, responds to this criticism: "For what can be done now, it is quite a step forward. But we have to think in terms of even more sustainable design."[43]

Another, though similar, attempt to alter and/or undo the effects of conventional land-use practices is Traditional Neighborhood Development.

Traditional Neighborhood Development

Traditional Neighborhood Development emphasizes two broad goals: (1) reduce the destruction of habitat (such as wetlands and farmlands) and natural resources, in general, and reduce the dependency on automobiles and their associated impacts — noise, congestion, and so on; and (2) reduce polluting emissions, excessive use of energy, and fragmentation of the landscape. While the goals of both New Urbanism and Traditional Neighborhood Development are similar, their implementation reveals wide variations, and, indeed, some developments based on Traditional Neighborhood Development or New Urbanism sometimes fall short of the goals.

Important elements found to be lacking are (1) sufficient population density necessary to provide a "critical mass" that will support commercial activities within the development as well as transportation to the larger community, while simultaneously strengthening the sense of place within the community; (2) a sufficient mix of activities; (3) proximity to existing urban activities, which will allow walking, biking, or the use of public transit to these activities; (4) well-connected pedestrian walkways; and (5) an emphasis on designs that favor walking, biking, and the use of public transit vs. auto traffic.[44]

Both New Urbanism and Traditional Neighborhood Development attempt not only to reverse the effects of traditional practices of land-use planning but also to provide patterns and forms consistent with natural systems. It is a bit too early in the process of implementing the principles of New Urbanism and Traditional Neighborhood Development to evaluate their success. Some, however, already warn of over-optimism. Jerry Kaufman, professor of Urban and Regional Planning at the University of Wisconsin, Madison, suggests that New Urbanists and others who want to promote alternatives to worn-out development practices should be aware that there is "a treacherous breach between being a real community and just acting like one." Kaufman says, "You can only go so far in using design to induce relationships. If I don't like my neighbor, a front porch isn't going to change that."[43] Suffice it to say that departure from the norm, represented by these ideas, is a strong first step, admirable in that the most difficult step is always that which represents recognition of the need for change.

chapter three

Protecting diversity through land-use planning

> *It is not the brains that matter most, but that which guides them — the character, the heart, generous qualities, progressive ideas.* —Fyodor Dostoyevski

It is not within the scope of this book to deal at length with the myriad ways a community or society can protect the diversity of Nature — the wealth of society — for the benefit of all generations. Nevertheless, we shall do our best to point out a few of the options that we think will bear fruit of sufficient quality to make their cultivation worthwhile.

The protection of habitat as part of our land-use practices will be used as the example because quality habitat is the basis of biological, genetic, and functional diversity, the sum of which is the basis of natural wealth and thus economic viability, which in turn equates to long-term community well-being. Habitat is composed of food, water, shelter, and space, and the quality of the habitat depends on the quality of these four items. Further, the environment dictates the composition of the species of plants, which creates a particular structure, which in turn allows processes and functions to occur within time and space to create the living portion of habitats for wildlife and people.

Composition, structure, and function of habitat

We perceive objects by means of their obvious structures or functions. Structure is the configuration of elements, parts, or constituents of a thing, be it simple or complex. The structure can be thought of as the organization, arrangement, or makeup of a thing. Function, on the other hand, is what a particular structure either can do or allows to be done to it or with it.

Let's consider a common object, a rocking chair. A rocking chair is a rocking chair because of its structure, which gives it a particular shape. A rocking chair can be characterized as a piece of furniture consisting of a seat, four legs, two rockers, a back, and arms; it is an object designed to accommodate a sitting person who wants to rock back and forth while resting his or her arms on suitable supports. Because of the seat, we can sit in a chair, and it is this act of sitting (the functional component allowed by the structure) that makes a chair a "chair." We can rest our own arms on those of the chair while sitting, which makes the chair an "arm chair," and because of the rockers, we can not only sit in the chair but also rock back and forth in it while resting our arms, which makes the chair a "rocking arm chair." Suppose the rockers are removed (one compositional component of the chair). Now we can sit in the chair and rest our arms while sitting, but we cannot rock back and forth; the chair, therefore, is no longer a rocking arm chair but is still an arm chair. If the arms are now removed (another compositional component of the chair), we can sit in the chair but have no place to rest our arms, which means the chair is just a chair. If the legs are removed (another compositional component of the chair), we can still sit in it, but on the ground with our legs sticking out in front or bent as when sitting in the bleachers of a ball park. Finally, suppose we leave the rockers, legs, and arms in place but remove the seat so that the supporting structure on which we sit no longer exists. To sit, then, we must sit on the ground between the legs of the "chair." By definition, when we remove a chair's seat, we no longer have a chair, because we have altered the composition of the whole (removed a compositional component), which altered the structure of the whole and thus altered the function of the whole. Thus, the structure of an object defines its function, the function of an object defines its necessary structure, and both are dependent on the composition of an object's components. How might this interrelationship of composition, structure, and function work in Nature?

Maintaining ecological functions means maintaining the characteristics of the ecosystem in such a way that its processes are sustainable. The characteristics one must be concerned with are (1) composition, (2) structure, (3) function, and (4) Nature's disturbance regimes, which periodically alter an ecosystem's composition, structure, and function.

Nature's disturbance regimes tend to be environmental constraints. True, we can tinker with them, such as suppressing fire in forests and grasslands, but in the end our tinkering catches up with us and we pay the price. We can, for example, change the composition of an ecosystem, such as the kinds and arrangement of plants within a forest, which means that composition can be manipulated to meet human desire and is thus negotiable within the context of cause and effect. In this case, composition determines structure and function in that composition is the cause rather than the effect of the structure and function.

Composition determines the structure, and structure determines the function. Thus, by negotiating the composition, one simultaneously negotiates
both the structure and function. Once the composition is in place, however,
the structure and function are set — unless, of course, the composition is
altered, at which time both the structure and function are altered accordingly.

The composition or kinds of plants and their age classes within a plant
community create a certain structure that is characteristic of the plant community at any given age. It is the structure of the plant community that in
turn creates and maintains certain functions. In addition, it is the composition, structure, and function of a plant community that determine what kinds
of animals can live there, how many, and for how long. If one changes the
composition of a forest, one changes the structure and hence the function,
and thus affects the animals. The animals, in general, then, are ultimately
constrained by the composition.

If, therefore, a community wants a particular animal or group of animals
within its forest (let's say a rich diversity of summering birds to attract tourist
dollars from bird-watchers), members of the community would have to work
backward by determining what kind of function to create, which means
knowing what kind of structure to create, which means knowing what type
of composition is necessary to produce the required habitats for the animals
the community wants. Thus, once the composition is ensconced, the structure
and its attendant functions operate as a unit in terms of the habitat required
for the animals.

People and Nature are continually changing the structure and function
of this ecosystem or that ecosystem by manipulating the composition of its
plants which subsequently changes the composition of the animals dependent on the structure and function of the resultant habitat. By altering the
composition of plants within an ecosystem, people and Nature alter its
structure, which in turn affects how it functions, which in turn determines
not only what kinds of and how many animals can live there but also what
uses humans can make out of the ecosystem. Understanding and maintaining the viability of these components are therefore key to the sustainability
of quality habitat — including ours.

If we are really serious about achieving sustainability within our communities, we must learn to understand, accept, and act upon the notion that
whether populations of indigenous plants and animals survive in a particular landscape depends on the rate of local extinctions from a patch of habitat
and the rate at which an organism can move among existing patches. Those
species living in habitats isolated as a result of fragmentation from such
things as urban sprawl are therefore less likely to persist. Fragmentation of
habitat, the most serious threat to biological, genetic, and functional diversity, is the primary cause of not only the often discussed global crisis of the
rate of biological extinctions but also the less discussed crisis regarding the
rate of local extinctions.

The effect of modifying habitat

Modifying the connectivity among patches of habitat strongly influences the abundance of species and their patterns of movement. The size, shape, and diversity of patches of habitat also influence the patterns of species abundance, and the shape of a patch may determine what species can use it as habitat. The interaction between the processes of a species' dispersal and the pattern of a landscape determines the temporal dynamics of the species' populations. Local populations of organisms that can disperse great distances may not be as strongly affected by the spatial arrangement of patches of habitat as are more sedentary species.

Our responsibility as adults is not only to make decisions about patterns across the landscape while considering the consequences of our decisions on the potential quality of life for future generations but also to teach these concepts to children in school who are that future. We are, after all, planning the environmental and social conditions of the future to which all children to come must respond, a future about which they have no choice. Although the decisions are up to us, one thing is clear: the current trend toward homogenizing the landscape — which may help maximize short-term monetary profits for one generation — progressivly degrades the long-term biological adaptability of the land and thus the long-term sustainability of society as we know it, a problem that progressively falls to the children, who have no choice but to deal with it as best they are able.

Sustainability flows from the patterns of relationships that have evolved among the various species. A culturally oriented landscape, even a very diverse one, that fails to support these co-evolved relationships has little chance of being sustainable. To create viable, culturally oriented landscapes, we must shift our focus from fragmentation to *connectivity*. Because ecological sustainability and adaptability depend on connectivity of the habitats, we must ground our culturally designed landscapes within Nature's evolved patterns and take advantage of them if we are to have a chance of creating a quality environment that is both pleasing to our cultural senses and ecologically adaptable; this equates to the possibility of a purposefully created landscape that is socially and environmentally sustainable.

We must move purposefully and consciously toward the connectivity of habitats in the form of well-planned and protected systems of open spaces if we are to have adaptable landscapes with a desirable quality of living, including for our indigenous wild neighbors, to pass to our heirs. Such a move will require that we shift our focus to six primary components of sustainability.

First, *we must consciously and purposefully integrate cyclical thinking and linear thinking in such a way that we can produce the goods and services necessary to society while simultaneously understanding and protecting the cycles of Nature as a dimension of diversity that makes adaptability to the future as painless as possible for humanity.*

What do we mean by this? People generally think in one of two ways. Linear thought focuses on producing and accumulating material products as the primary purpose of life. Linear thought has a strong belief in cause and effect and, relative to cyclical thought, provides simpler explanations of reality in addition to focusing on answers rather than the questions. Cyclical thought patterns, on the other hand, focus on being an integral part of the processes constituting the spiritual center of life's cycle. This type of thinking queries multidimensional causes and effects and rests more easily with the unknowns than does linear thinking.

Thinking in cycles ultimately causes us to see our lives as a circular dance in which certain basic and necessary patterns of use and renewal, of life and death, are repeated endlessly. This is the ethical basis of indigenous American spiritual thought, as exemplified by Black Elk, an indigenous American shaman:[45]

> "Everything the Power of the World does is done in a circle. The sky is round, and ... the earth is round like a ball, and so are all the stars. The wind, in its greatest power, whirls. Birds make their nests in circles, for theirs is the same religion as ours. The sun comes forth and goes down again in a circle. The moon does the same, and both are round. Even the seasons form a great circle in their changing, and always come back again to where they were. The life of a man is a circle from childhood to childhood, and so it is in everything where power moves."

Those who think cyclically are more likely to humbly accept the mysteries of the universe. They allow Nature to teach them, and Nature's reflective lessons about infinite universal relationships are intrinsically valuable. To use something for its own sake and then to be the source of its renewal is to see it as a "re-source." In the original sense of the word, "resource" was a reciprocal relationship between humanity and Earth, a circle of taking and giving and taking again. The very structure of the word — *re* and *source* — implies a reciprocal relationship, a cycle, to use something from the Earth and then to be the source of its renewal. "It is only in the processes of the natural world, and in analogous and related processes of human culture," said Wendell Berry, "that the new may grow usefully old, and the old be made new... ."[46]

People who see life as a great circle tend more clearly and intuitively to see everything as interdependent and understand that there is no such thing as an "independent variable" in Nature. Everything in the universe is patterned by its interdependence on everything else, and it is this pattern of interdependence and change that forms the only constant. This constant is the principle of both creation and infinite becoming.

The cyclical vision is at once realistic and generous. Those who accept it recognize that in creation lies the essential principle of return: what is here will leave and will come again; what I have, I must some day give up. They see death as an integral and indispensable part of life, for death is but another becoming, a view beyond a horizon.

Some cycles revolve frequently enough to be well known in a person's lifetime. Some are completed only in the memory of several generations; hence, the notion of the *invisible present* — that which is ongoing but not seen now but will manifest itself later. Still other cycles are so vast that their motion can only be assumed. Such is our galaxy and the Milky Way, but even they are not aloof from our humble, daily activities, for we keep in touch with the universe by just knowing they exist.

In contrast to cyclical thinking, which arises from a desire to be in a harmonious relationship with the universe, our Western linear thinking is oriented almost strictly toward the control of Nature and the conversion of natural resources into economic commodities — into money, which some view as the god of Western materialism.

Wendell Berry offers an interesting point with respect to these two patterns of thought. He believes that, while natural processes may be cyclical, "There is within nature a human domain the processes of which are linear; the other, much older, holds that human life is subject to the same cyclic patterns as all other life."[46] If the two are contradictory, says Berry, it is not so much because one is wrong and the other is right, but because one is only partial and the other is complete.

Berry goes on to say that the concept of linearity is the doctrine of progress, which is supposed to bring us into a human-made material paradise. Within this concept, society discards old experiences as new ones are encountered. Although in our minds we never "repeat" the old ways or the old mistakes, in reality we repeat them constantly. We deny it, however, in our blind drive for material progress. We therefore rarely learn from history. In Berry's vision there is but one definition of progress: onward and upward forever, an endless cross-country voyage of discovery. To return is merely to come back to the used, because progress means exploiting the new and the innocent.

Characteristic of linear vision is the notion that anything is justifiable as long as and insofar as it is immediately and obviously good for something else. Linear thinkers require everything to proceed directly, immediately, and obviously to its perceived value. What, we ask, is it good for? It is only when something proves to be immediately good for something are we ready to raise the question of its value. How much is it worth? By this we mean how much money is it worth, because if it can only be good for something else, then obviously it can only be worth something other than its intrinsic value. An excellent example of this type of thinking is portrayed by Clyde Martin, of the Western Pine Association, who wrote in the *Journal of Forestry* in 1940: "Without more complete and profitable utilization we cannot have intensive forest management. ...When thinnings can be sold as a profit and every limb and twig of the tree has value, forest management will come as a matter of course."[47] Martin's notion still predominates. Anything without monetary value has no value, and anything with immediate monetary value is wasted if left unused by humans. Short-term economic profitability of resources always seems to be the bottom line.

Current dictionaries define "resource" in a strictly linear sense, as the collective wealth of a country or its means of producing wealth, or any property that can be converted into money. Linear thinkers are therefore more likely to discount intrinsic value in everything, including humans. It is not surprising, therefore, that in our own culture the intrinsic value of Nature is still largely discounted. The same can be said of the intrinsic value of human beings when our military capacity for the destruction of the "foreign enemy" assumes magnitudes of precedence over the domestic welfare and tranquility of our citizenry. Where does this kind of thinking lead us when we consider ourselves and one another only as "human resources?" Once we accept so specific a notion of utility, all life becomes subservient to its use; its value is drained of everything except its "specialized use," and imagination is relegated to the scrap heap. In turn, these patterns of thought determine the core of a society's culture.

Jules Henry, a psychiatrist, has said that we Americans are a driven people and all our activities are related to our sense of being driven. The linear pattern of human thought produces a culture like ours, of European heritage, in which the economics of acquisition is the force that drives the society, determines its mode of institutions, and relegates religion to the bottom rung of the social ladder. On the other hand, the cyclical pattern of human thought produces cultures like those of the Australian Aborigines prior to the invasion by Europeans and indigenous peoples of the Americas prior to the invasion by Europeans, in which spirituality is the force that drives the society and determines the mode of its economics and institutions.

Culture is based on and organized by the dominant patterns of human thought. Through the cultural dynamics of human-land interactions, these patterns of thought determine the care a given society takes of its land and the patterns it designs on the landscape. Assuming that a society's culture is the product of its dominant mode of thinking and given two identical pieces of land, each type of culture would, within a century, produce a different design on the landscape as a result of the pattern of its thinking, which is the template of individual values expressed in the collective mirror — the land. Because the land and the people are inseparably one, people unite with the land through their culture.

As the social values determine the culture, so the culture is an expression of those values. The care taken of the land by the people is therefore the mirror image of the hidden forces in their social psyche. These secret thoughts ultimately express themselves and determine whether a particular society survives or becomes a closed chapter in the history books. And history books are replete with such closed chapters as the great empires of Mesopotamia, Babylonia, Egypt, Greece, and Rome, all of which destroyed their forests and the fertility of their topsoil with their linear thinking, insatiable drive for material wealth, and warlike nature. In view of this catalog of extinct civilizations, one might ask where contemporary society in the "New World" of the Americas is headed.

Second, *we must consciously and purposefully accord women absolute equality with men because women are, after all, half of the diversity that comprises the whole of humanity.* Women are also psychologically more oriented toward the cyclical nature of relationships than are men, who are more oriented toward the linear nature of production. This helps to balance the two basic ways humans seem to think and thus brings humanity toward greater wholeness. Further, women who are afforded their birthright of equality tend to have fewer children and to have them later in life, which is the only way the world's human population will ever be voluntarily controlled.

Third, *we must consciously and purposefully connect, or reconnect, people with a variety of habitats through a well-integrated system of open spaces that includes educational features about the critical importance of quality habitat.*

Fourth, *we must consciously and purposefully protect existing biological, genetic, and functional diversity, which is the irreplaceable wealth forming the foundation of human dignity as it equates to the quality of one's life within any given environment.*

Fifth, *we must consciously account for the sustainable connectivity of habitats, in the form of open spaces and biological richness, which is the price we must pay for the long-term sustainability and ecological wholeness of the patterns we create across the landscape.*

Sixth, *we must focus on "cultural capacity" (the quality of life) as opposed to "carrying capacity" (the maximum number of humans the world can support), because we cannot maximize both quality (life with dignity) and quantity (mere existence) simultaneously — we must choose.*

Why are these six focal points important? Their importance can be summed up in one word — "connexity" — which, according to Geoff Mulgan, a policy adviser to British Prime Minister Tony Blair, is an old English word that better describes the quality of human relationships to one another and their environment than either interdependence (which captures the effect, but not the cause) or globalization (which drains the moral content from relationships).[48]

It is, writes Mulgan, sometimes easy to forget that in the recent past of a few generations, people seldom came across strangers because human relationships were close, intimate, demanding, and generally face to face. There was little one could do that would materially change other people's lives, except for those close at hand. As far as people from neighboring towns or countries were concerned, they might as well have been on separate continents.

Today, however, we affect one another through the global commons of air and water because everything we do that affects either of these affects all people in one way or another. People are also increasingly interconnected through the global economy and computer technology. Coming after centuries and millennia of oppressive hierarchies, says Mulgan, it is not surprising that freedom is valued so highly. But, he asks, is the achievement of new freedoms really compatible with growing interdependence, or is a world that devotes its energy to the pursuit of individual desires necessarily condemned to neglect or destroy the shared environment on which its well-being depends? He answers, "If we cannot cultivate people who are able to bear responsibilities, to recognize their impact on the world, then freedom soon becomes a pathology," a statement that brings us to the ecological notions of cumulative effects, thresholds, and lag periods.

Cumulative effects, thresholds, and lag periods

The cumulative effects of human activities compound in secret to a point that something in the environment shifts dramatically enough for people to see it. Put differently, cumulative effects are simply perpetual changes that seem subliminal to our awareness.

With this notion of perpetual change in mind, consider that all of us can sense change — the growing light at sunrise, the gathering wind before a thunderstorm, or the changing seasons, with spring's new leaves, summer's swaying blossoms, autumn's golden harvest, and winter's stark, naked trees and chilling winds. Some of us can see longer term events and remember that there was more or less snow last winter compared to other winters or that spring seemed early in coming this year. But it is an unusual person who can sense, with any degree of precision, the changes that occur over the decades of his or her life. At this scale of time, we tend to think of the world in some sort of "steady state," and we typically underestimate the degree to which change has occurred. We are unable to directly sense slow changes, and we are even more limited in our abilities to interpret their relationships to long-term cause and effect. This being the case, the subtle processes that act quietly and unobtrusively over decades are hidden and reside in the "invisible present."

The invisible present is the scale of time within which our responsibilities for planet Earth are most evident. Within this scale of time, ecosystems change during our lifetimes and the lifetimes of our children and our grandchildren. The progressive change that occurs is defined by a threshold of tolerance in the ecosystem beyond which the system as people know it suddenly, visibly becomes something else, something undesirable. Once the ecosystem shifts, however, the effect of that shift is, more often than not, irreversible.

The approaching danger goes undetected until it is too late because ecosystems operate on the basis of lag periods, which simply means there is a lag in time between when the cause of a fundamental change in an ecosystem is introduced and its visible outcome is apparent. This is somewhat analogous to the incubation period in the human body between initial infection with a disease and manifestation of the symptoms, an example which brings us to the concept of constraints, which, in turn, are somewhat analogous to techniques of disease prevention if wisely chosen.

Constraints: the building blocks of sustainable planning

To design and protect social-environmental diversity, which is the very foundation of social-environmental sustainability, one must first understand and
create a vision of the desired outcome. (For a discussion on how to create a
vision, see *Vision and Leadership in Sustainable Development*.[49]) The purpose of
a vision is to determine not only what you want but also its feasibility
because a vision is based on a series of behavioral constraints.

Constraints are limitations of freedom, which many people in our society
view as unnecessarily restrictive to human "rights," however "rights" are
defined. What must be understood, though, is that complete freedom does
not and cannot exist, because everything is defined by its relationship to
everything else, and that very relationship, within itself, is a constraint on
one's absolute freedom. In addition, all relationships are constantly changing, which means one is and must be constantly responding to changes that
are induced outside of oneself and therefore out of one's control; these are
nonnegotiable constraints. Nevertheless, by understanding constraints and
constructively using those that are negotiable, such as one's behavior in
response to circumstances, one can acquire a measure of desired freedom.

The constraints imposed by Nature, such as climate, are for all practical
purposes nonnegotiable. Nature's constraints are the ecological circumstances we are given to work with, such as the effects of a volcanic eruption
such as Mount St. Helens in the state of Washington, over which we have
little or no control. The constraints imposed by society on itself, either consciously or unconsciously, are all negotiable, however, and include trading
freedoms, accountability for outcomes, and accountability for the rate of
change:

1. Any time a community creates a vision for its future, it is trading
   freedoms. For example, to have more open space, one must limit
   growth in the human population because one cannot simultaneously
   have unlimited growth and a viable system of open spaces. One must
   choose, and in so doing one gains more freedom in a particular area
   by giving up some freedom in another area. Here, it is important to
   understand that not making a choice is still making a choice, but most
   likely not a wise one.
2. By imposing voluntary constraints on some freedoms and relaxing
   constraints on others, a vision simultaneously becomes something
   against which an outcome can be measured and a tool for holding
   the creators of the vision accountable for that outcome.
3. Because local people, through the crafting of a vision, empower themselves to guide the destiny of their future, they simultaneously become accountable for the rate of change in their own population and
   thus the rate of change they exert on their community and its immediate landscape.

The further into the future a community plans, the more diversity it can save, protect, and pass forward to the next generation. However, an important fundamental consideration that one must address at this juncture is the notion of *cultural capacity* (the quality of lifestyle) vs. *carrying capacity* (the absolute number of individuals a habitat can support).

Cultural capacity was naturally built into the indigenous people's nomadic way of life; when conditions of livability became unfavorable, the people moved to an area with favorable conditions or split into groups. When their life became more sedentary, however, with the advent of agriculture, cultural capacity had to become a conscious choice, if for no other reason than the rising problem of what to do with the accumulation of human offal, garbage, and diseases that are part and parcel of a sedentary culture. Cultural capacity as a conscious choice, however, did not materialize immediately. It was forcibly interjected into human culture by the previously mentioned ecological notions of cumulative effects, thresholds, and lag periods, which became increasingly clear through alteration of habitat — also part and parcel of a sedentary way of life.

People in society today spend much time arguing whether an ecosystem is natural or unnatural ecologically, right or wrong morally, good or bad economically. We, however, do not think of ecosystems or habitats as natural or unnatural in the sense of either/or, but rather as a continuum of naturalness. Consider, for example, that a mountaintop untouched by human alterations constitutes the most natural end of the continuum, while a shopping mall constitutes the most cultural end. Such a continuum can easily be symbolized as follows: N <—> C, where N represents the most natural end of the continuum and C the most cultural end. Everything in between, depending on where along the continuum it falls, represents a degree of naturalness and/or a degree of culturalness.

The question for us today is where along this continuum we must of necessity maintain a piece of land if the whole of the landscape, in the collective of our individual choices, is to be sustainable, both environmentally and socially. To examine this notion in terms of social constraints, we will discuss three scenarios: open space, transportation, and human population. Each scenario in its turn will be considered as the socially derived, nonnegotiable constraint at the core of a community vision. The order of presentation is important because it will lead us from a vision based on cultural capacity to one based on carrying capacity.

Open space

Open space, like water, is available in a fixed amount and thus is also a constraint. Unlike water, however, open space is visibly disappearing at an exponential rate. Once gone, it is gone, unless, of course, rural communities, and perhaps even cities, are torn down to reclaim it — an unlikely event.

Space was once sacred to indigenous peoples, but today it all seems to have a price and to be coveted for that price. Whether it is "outer space, inner space, sacred space, forbidden space, your space, or my space, the more removed we are from original participation with space [which includes the sanctity of all space], the more *all* space will continue to be desecrated," wrote poet Geoffrey Hill.[50]

Consider, for example, the forested areas around Puget Sound in western Washington State, where the forests have been thinned so dramatically in recent years that "this land of towering evergreens is now relatively tree-less."[51] Using satellite imagery, researchers from American Forests, one of the nation's oldest conservation organizations, based in Washington, D.C., found that nearly one third of the most heavily forested land around Puget Sound has disappeared since the early 1970s.

Satellite photographs from 1972, 1986, and 1996 and computer-mapping software were used to study a 700-square-mile area that stretched across King, Pierce, Snohomish, Thurston, and Kitsap counties. Overall, the heavily forested areas, those where trees covered more than half of the land, fell from 49% of the region to 31%, a loss of about 600,000 acres. According to the study, places where trees covered 20% of the landscape or less grew simultaneously from 25% of the study area to 57%, an increase of more than one million acres. Why? Because subdivisions, driven by growth in the human population around Seattle and other suburban cities, have gobbled up the available open-space land.

"If people want to know why we are having so many more landslides, if people want to know why it seems to be getting hotter and why rainstorms are more intense, well, this [deforestation] is part of the answer," according to Clement Hamilton, director of the Center for Urban Horticulture at the University of Washington in Seattle. But how do fewer trees make it rain harder?

Trees provide shade, which lowers the temperature of the air. As areas are deforested, they create a phenomenon called "heat islands," where temperatures can increase 5 to 10 degrees or more. Then, because warm air holds more moisture, heavier rains are triggered when the warm, moisture-laden air rises and cools in the atmosphere, which increases precipitation in the form of storm water.

Forested areas typically slow and absorb water from storms, allowing it to infiltrate deep into the soil instead of flowing overland or gushing into gutters, storm drains, and water-treatment plants. According to the study, it would cost about $2.4 billion to build a stormwater system that would be equivalent to the one provided inherently by the trees lost since 1972. In addition, those trees would have annually absorbed, free of charge, 35 million pounds of pollutants, such as carbon monoxide, ozone, and sulfur dioxide. With the loss of trees, however, those pollutants, circulating freely in the air, have translated into approximately $95 million in healthcare costs and other social impacts.

Thus, while there are multiple reasons why a community might want to save open space, its irreplaceability and value added to community life are critical ones because in the plurality of options saved and passed forward lies the kernel of diversity and choice. Open space, as the nonnegotiable constraint around which a community chooses to develop, places the primacy of development on quality of human relationships to both people and Nature. The ability and commitment to maintain a matrix of open spaces within and surrounding a community are critical to the sustainability of its quality of life (its cultural capacity, which is based on protecting its natural wealth) and ultimately the economic viability of the community, especially a small community in a non-urban setting. A well-designed open-space system determines where both urban development and the transportation system will be located and helps prevent a scenario such as we now see in Atlanta, GA. Atlanta has become an "urban heat island," experiencing temperatures up to 10°F higher than surrounding areas, creating its own weather, and causing thunderstorms, according to a NASA study.[52]

Communal open space

Open space for communal use not only is central to the notion of community but is also increasingly becoming a premium of a community's continued livability and the stability of the value of its real estate. It can also become a focal point around which to organize communities, such as the ecological restoration project in Iowa that became a community project.[53] Of course, continual economic growth, at the expense of open space, will line the pockets of a few people in the present, but it will ultimately pick the pockets of everyone in the future. Can an ordinary citizen do something about saving open space? Yes. Bill McDonald did.[54]

Bill McDonald, a fifth-generation rancher in southeastern Arizona, has used his skills of forging consensus among fellow ranchers, some conservationists, and others, known as the Malpai Borderlands Group, to help save 800,000 acres of open space and with it a way of life. McDonald's aim is to help ranchers become progressive trustees of an area larger than Grand Canyon National Park by keeping the connectivity of its open space intact. The parcel of land is a combination of land owned by 32 ranchers, who collectively own about half the area, and public lands the ranchers lease from the U.S. Forest Service and Bureau of Land Management, plus state trust lands belonging to Arizona and New Mexico. The ranchers' common ground — their vision, if you will — is their love of open space, the way of life it affords, and a deep desire to protect both, which means they must accept personal accountability for their own behavior.

Their achievements to date are as follows:

- Incorporating as a nonprofit organization focused on reducing polarization between the interests of ranchers and conservationists, in particular by limiting the effect of grazing livestock on public lands and in riparian zones.
- Creating a "grassbank" and "conservation easements" intended to help ensure that the ranchers can keep their lands open and that they and their children can continue ranching without having to sell or subdivide parts of their acreages.

- Emphasizing sound scientific study to discern the best approach to restoring ecologically fragile areas that will help endangered and threatened species through a "rancher's endangered species program." A working example of the program is one area ranching family trucking a thousand gallons of water to stock ponds during a prolonged drought to keep alive one of the last populations of Chiricahua leopard frogs.
- Getting federal bureaucrats and officials from two states to agree to reduce fir trees in the ecosystem through prescribed burns to help restore the area's native grasslands.
- Improving the upland areas, including the forage on hillsides, which promises not only to increase the infiltration of water and thereby reduce soil erosion but also to improve the condition of riparian zones.

For his part, McDonald knows that the extremists, who just want to fight, are still there, but, he says, "My hope is that what we're doing will encourage other people to step toward the middle and find solutions and that the extreme positions will be marginalized over time."[54]

For such communal open space to have maximum value over time, a community, like the ranchers, must have a clear and compelling vision of what it wants so that the following questions can be answered in a responsible and accountable way: (1) What parcels of land are wanted for the communal system of open space? (2) Why are they wanted? (3) What is their functional value: capture and storage of water, habitat for native plants and animals, local educational opportunities, recreation, aesthetics? (4) How much land is necessary to satisfy the first three questions? (5) Can one project the value added to the quality of life and/or the consequential value of real estate in the future?[49]

Although it is not possible in this book to discuss all the possibilities of an open-space system, we will consider some of the more critical and perhaps commonly overlooked components, such as the source and storage of water.

Water

Seventy-five percent of the surface of the Earth is covered with water, but more than 97% of it is the saltwater that makes up the oceans. Another 2% is frozen in glaciers and the polar ice caps, which means that only 1% of the water is available in usable form for life outside of the oceans. In fact, without freshwater from precipitation, even the oceans would become so salty that life in them as we know it would either have to change or become extinct.

More than 70% of the human body consists of water.[55] A 1% deficiency of water in your body will make you thirsty, a 5% deficit will cause a slight fever, and an 8% shortage will cause your glands to stop producing saliva and your skin to turn blue; you cannot walk with a 10% deficiency, and you will die with a 12% deficiency. Today, according to authorities at the United Nations, 9500 children die every day from a lack of water or, more frequently, from diseases that are carried in polluted water, so why would the U.S.

Environmental Protection Agency even consider polluting water? The answer is expediency, as the following example illustrates.

Plans for what amounts to an underwater landfill at the mouth of the Hylebos Waterway of Tacoma, WA, have infuriated local residents.[56] The waterway is one of three proposed sites chosen by the U.S. Environmental Protection Agency to dispose of a mountain of contaminated muck to be dredged over the next few years from Tacoma's Commencement Bay. The Superfund cleanup calls for extensive dredging in several of the bay's industrial waterways to remove toxic chemicals produced by the Port of Tacoma, Kaiser Aluminum, Occidental Chemical Corp., General Metals, Elf Atochem, and Asarco, among others.

Most of the estimated 2 million cubic yards of sludge will be used as fill in two small waterways that will subsequently be diked, capped with clean sediment, and paved to keep the toxic chemicals from leaking out, a proposal that will ostensibly improve the habitat for salmon, birds, and other wildlife. But not so the underwater landfill proposed for Hylebos Waterway, which calls for the dumping of an estimated 300,000 cubic yards of toxic mud about 300 yards from the shore because, according to Allison Hiltner, the project manager for the U.S. Environmental Protection Agency, the area is big enough to hold all the mud, and the underwater slope is gentle enough to be stable; also, the $17 million is a reasonable cost.

But maps belonging to Department of Natural Resources, which owns the submerged tidal flats on behalf of all residents of the state of Washington, indicate the area may be prone to underwater mudslides, which according to Maria Peeler, manager of the aquatic resources division for the Department of Natural Resources, could break open the landfill. "It really doesn't make sense," says Peeler, "to be spending all of that money removing contaminated sediments from an area and then just shoving it somewhere else. It's like taking a broom and sweeping the dirt under a rug."

Costs of the Superfund project are supposed to be paid by the industries responsible for polluting the sediments in the first place. Although the sediments could be shipped to a specialized landfill in eastern Washington, the U.S. Environmental Protection Agency rejected the idea based on logistics and the extra $7 million price tag. "They're [industry] so concerned about their costs," says Barb Bernsten, who lives along the Hylebos. "Well, I'm sorry. They're the ones who did it. Now they have to pay for it."

"Why are they dumping toxic sediments in a clean area in the first place?" asks David Adams, whose family is one of some 20 families that live along the shoreline of the Hylebos in houses perched on stilts. "It just strikes us as being ridiculous." What do you, the reader, think?

Water is a nonsubstitutable requirement of life, and its source and storage capacity are finite in any given landscape. The availability of water throughout the year will thus determine both the quality of life in a community and consequently the value of real estate. It behooves a community, therefore, to take any measure possible to maximize and stabilize both the quality and quantity of its local supply of water.

Local supply refers to water catchments in the local area under local control, as opposed to water catchments in the local area under the control of an absentee owner with no vested interest in the community's supply of water. Such absentee ownership could be a person, corporation, governing body, or agency beyond local jurisdiction.

Fresh, usable water, once thought to be inexhaustible in supply, is now becoming scarce in many parts of the world, in addition to which worldwide use of water doubled between 1940 and 1980. The per-capita consumption of water is currently rising twice as quickly as the human population of the world is growing. Until recently, 70% of all water used has been devoted to agriculture, which uses water inefficiently at best, but forecasters predicted that an additional 25 to 30% more would be needed by the year 2000 to keep pace with increases in irrigated agricultural land.

In the western U.S., for example, water pumped from deep underground aquifers is today such a valuable commodity that it is often referred to as "sandstone champagne." Much of North Africa is suffering from droughts that have forced hundreds of thousands of people to flee rural areas for low-paying jobs in cities. In Cherrapunji, a town in northern India that receives 1000 inches of rain annually — the most precipitation in the world — the people walk long distances to get drinking water, limit bathing to once a week, and have trouble irrigating their crops.

Water, not oil, will be the next resource over which nations and factions within nations will go to war. Twenty-two countries are already dependent on a flow of water that is supplied from sources in other nations. India, Pakistan, Bangladesh, the Middle East, Egypt, and Ethiopia are among the areas with the potential for armed conflict over water. There are even serious disagreements over issues concerning the sharing of water between nations on the best of terms, such as Canada and the U.S. In addition, China and the western U.S. may well have factions that are willing to compete for water in armed conflict. Wally N'Dow of Gambia, whom the *Los Angeles Times* describes as "the world's foremost specialist on cities," says bluntly: "The crisis point [over the battle for water] is going to be 15 to 20 years from now."

According to Paul Simon, former senator from Illinois, "It is no exaggeration to say that the conflict between humanity's growing thirst and the projected supply of usable, potable water could result in the most devastating natural disaster since history has been recorded accurately, unless something happens to stop it." That "something" would have to be far wiser leadership at home and abroad than we have thus far seen in our lifetimes.

With this in mind, it is wise to use the storage of water for present and future generations as one of the cornerstones in any open-space system. If outright purchase of a water catchment is not possible, a community could conceivably enter into a long-term lease or contract to rent a catchment, with control over what is done on it. Then it might be possible to accrue monthly or annual payments toward the price of purchasing the land at a later date.

Such an arrangement could benefit the owner in terms of a steady income at reasonable tax rates while allowing some acceptable use of the land.

Another alternative might be a tax credit payable to the landowner if the community could work in conjunction with the owner to protect the inherent value of the water catchment to the community itself. There are probably other options, such as reintroduction of treated water into a known aquifer, but the important consideration is to secure the purchase of local water catchments in community ownership as part of the open-space program to maintain and protect the quality of life and the local value of real estate. An added value may be that such water catchments in an open-space system can act as islands of quiet amidst the daily bustle of town life.

Quiet

Quiet, like water and open space, can now be seen as a disappearing resource and thus another constraint. The past quiet of the hometown of one of the authors is but a memory. Today, there is an increasingly noticeable din from cars, buses, and trucks, which seem to be in perpetual motion at all hours, as well as the rumblings of trains that whistle at the numerous road crossings. If a community designs its system of open spaces to dampen the constant stimulation of urban background noise, people could, for many years to come, find a peaceful quiet in which to relax and hear the songs of birds and the stories of faraway places told by the wind.

The relaxation experienced in a quiet place can be consciously enhanced in an open-space system by including farm- and forestlands, riparian areas, and floodplains as buffers against city noise. We know this is possible because one of the author's has experienced it in the beautiful Shinto shrine in downtown Tokyo, Japan, an exceedingly busy city.

Surrounding landscape

The land surrounding a community's municipal limits gives the community its contextual setting, its ambiance, if you will. The wise acquisition of open spaces in the various components of the surrounding landscape, whether Nature's ecosystem or culture's, protects, to some extent at least, the uniqueness of a community's setting and hence the uniqueness of the community itself. And the value added, both spiritual and economic, will accrue as the years pass.

Agricultural cropland.   A community could purchase open space in the form of fencerows along which to allow fencerow habitat to recreate itself. Then, in addition to mini-habitats in and of themselves, the few uncultivated yards along each fence could once again act as longitudinal corridors for the passage of wildlife from one area to another. Living fencerows would also make the landscape more interesting and more appealing to the human eye, and would add once again the songs of birds and the colors of flowers and leaves to the passing seasons.

The point is to find out what worked sustainably in the past, to begin recreating it in the present, and, where problems arise (as they will), to work together to resolve them. The only way to create, maintain, and pass forward the sense of community is by working together, because the friendliness of a community is founded on the quality of its interpersonal relationships, of which small family farmers can be an integral part.

Forestland.   If a community is in a forest setting, the forest more likely than not is a major contributor to the community's image of itself, in addition to which it may comprise an important water catchment. Furthermore, if the community is, or has been, a "timber town," then most of the forest may well have been converted into economic tree farms; therefore, maintaining an area of native forest may be of even greater value. If some old-growth trees are included in the area, its spiritual value may well be heightened and its value as habitat for some plants and animals greatly enhanced.

On the other hand, if what surrounds a community is no longer forest but rather an economic tree farm, a purchased area could be allowed to evolve once again toward a forest. As such, its aesthetic and spiritual values will increase, as will its potential value as habitat and for educational purposes. Much can be learned by comparing a relatively sterile tree farm with a real forest.[57,58] One will find, for instance, that a forest harbors a far greater diversity of species of both plants and animals than does a tree farm, even one near the age of cutting.

Although we have used the forest as an example because one of the authors (Chris) grew up in one, the same concepts can be applied anywhere. Outside of Denver, CO, for example, is a wonderful open space that represents a vestige of native shortgrass prairie that once covered the eastern part of the state. It is beautiful! And it is inspirational, creating, as it does, a tangible tie to a now intangible past and an unknowable future.

Riparian areas and floodplains.   Riparian areas and floodplains are coming under increasing pressures of urban development because of the misguided notion that we humans can unilaterally entrain streams and rivers with impunity, despite much and growing evidence to the contrary. When a levee fails, the response seems always to be to build more levees and, if need be, more dams. We have yet to understand that a problem caused on one level of human consciousness cannot be fixed on the same level of consciousness.

If we are willing to risk moving to a higher level of consciousness, we can either prevent or repair much of the damage our shortsighted human activities cause. Take, for example, the Snake River near Jackson, WY, where engineers, people from the Jackson Hole Conservation Alliance, the Wyoming Department of Fish and Game, and local officials are planning to restore part of the Snake River to a more natural condition.[59] For nearly 40 years, levees that line about 23 miles of the Snake River near Jackson have entrained high water from the melting snows of spring in the Teton Mountains and allowed lavish homes to invade the cottonwood forest of the river's floodplain.

Although researchers have known for some time the ecological havoc wreaked by dams, only recently have they begun to recognize the ecologically destructive nature of levees and their "free-form cousin," riprap, which is piles of rock and earth dumped by landowners along streams and rivers to guard against erosion.

It is not surprising, therefore, that the 15-foot-high serpentine piles of rock created by the U.S. Army Corps of Engineers to protect farmers' fields and hay meadows from flooding and erosion have caused serious and unexpected problems along one of the world's most scenic stretches of river. The river had for centuries been true to its rhythm of flooding and receding in a fluid motion that constantly redesigned its five or six channels or braids as it dissipated the energy of its floodwaters each spring. But now, squeezed into one or two rigid channels, the upper Snake River has lost its ability to flood during the spring runoff. This lost ability has increased the velocity of the water from spring runoffs within the levee straitjacket, which in turn has caused the destruction by raging spring torrents of many of the large islands in the remaining channels that were at one time occupied by willows and cottonwood trees. The luxuriant forests of cottonwood that once lined the river's banks are fading into a past era for lack of young trees to replace the dying old ones because cottonwoods require periodic flooding to reproduce successfully. And Snake River cutthroat trout, which must have clean gravel in which to spawn, have suffered from the channelization because floodwaters no longer flush and rejuvenate their spawning gravels.

In the autumn of 1998, the Teton County Natural Resource District and the U.S. Army Corps of Engineers began testing methods of breathing old life back into the river by restoring its rhythms of flooding. They hope to begin the full restoration project in the year 2000. The project will require a different level of consciousness, as Rik Gay, manager of the restoration project for Teton County, pointed out when he said, "Rivers don't just go downstream. We need to think in three dimensions. Rivers also move laterally and below the ground."

There is a sober reminder in all of this, however. The levees along the upper Snake River have not only narrowed and denuded the river over the last four decades but have also allowed million-dollar housing developments to flourish, which caused Bill MacDonald, manager of the Snake River project for the U.S. Army Corps of Engineers, to observe that restoring the natural flow of the river was "not feasible" because "behind those levees are millions, if not billions, of dollars in real estate." What might an alternative for the future be?

According to Scott Faber, a floodplain expert with the conservation group American Rivers, what really needs to be done to protect the ecological integrity of rivers is to cease building in the floodplains. One way to accomplish that, he contends, is to terminate the federal subsidy for repairing levees and make local governments pay the cost. In the meantime, however, many communities still have riparian areas that are important to understand and protect.

Riparian areas can be identified by the presence of vegetation that requires free or unbound water and conditions more moist than normal. These areas may vary considerably in size and the complexity of their vegetative cover because of the many combinations that can be created between the source of water and the physical characteristics of the site. Such characteristics include gradient, aspect of slope, topography, soil, type of stream bottom, quantity and quality of the water, elevation, and the kind of plant community.

Riparian areas have the following things in common: (1) they create well-defined habitats within much drier surrounding areas, (2) they make up a minor portion of the overall area, (3) they are generally more productive than the remainder of the area in terms of the biomass of plants and animals, (4) wildlife uses riparian areas disproportionately more than any other type of habitat, and (5) they are a critical source of diversity within an ecosystem.

There are many reasons why riparian areas are so important to wildlife, but not all can be applied to every area. Each particular combination of water source and attributes of the site must be considered separately. In addition, riparian areas supply organic material in the form of leaves and twigs, which become an important component of the aquatic food chain. Riparian areas also supply large woody debris in the form of fallen trees, which form a critical part of the land/water interface, add to the stability of banks along streams and rivers, and provide instream habitat for a complex of aquatic plants as well as aquatic invertebrate and vertebrate organisms.[60]

Setting aside riparian areas as undeveloped open space or repairing them through ecological restoration[61] means saving the most diverse, and often the most heavily used, habitat for wildlife in proximity to a community. Riparian areas are also an important source of large woody debris for the stream or river whose banks they protect from erosion.[48] Furthermore, riparian areas are periodically flooded in winter, which, along with floodplains, is how a stream or river dissipates part of its energy. It is important that streams and rivers be allowed to dissipate their energy; otherwise, floodwaters would cause considerably more damage than they already do in settled areas.

A floodplain is a plain that borders a stream or river that is subject to flooding. Like riparian areas, floodplains are critical to maintain as open areas because, as the name implies, they frequently flood. These are areas where storm-swollen streams and rivers spread out, decentralizing the velocity of their flow by encountering friction caused by the increased surface area of their temporary bottoms, which dissipates much of the floodwater's energy.

It is wise to include floodplains within the matrix of open spaces for several other reasons: (1) they will inevitably flood, which puts any human development at risk, regardless of efforts to steal the floodplain from the stream or river for human use (witness the Mississippi River); (2) they are critical winter habitat for fish;[60] (3) they form important habitat in spring, summer, and autumn for a number of invertebrate and vertebrate wildlife that frequent the water's edge;[60] and (4) they can have important recreational value.

If all these kinds of areas are incorporated into a system of well-designed, well-connected open spaces, a community would be wealthy indeed. In addition, the community would have done much to maximize the quality of life (its cultural capacity), not only in the present but also for the future.

Consider, for example, that a well-implemented system of open spaces helps to ameliorate the cumulative effects of a concentrated human population on its immediate surroundings. It also ensures that some areas are protected from the intrusion of artificial structures to clutter and fragment the space, which allows the seeming "emptiness" to be filled with wildflowers, grasses, trees, butterflies, bird song, and glimpses of wildlife in an area where they need not compete with such human endeavors as agriculture and transportation. Open space also connects people with the land and its variety of habitats and life-forms. Most importantly, open space, as the nonnegotiable constraint around which a community plans and carries out its development, allows both roads and people to be placed in the best locations from a sustainable point of view, both environmentally and socially.

Transportation

When the system of transportation becomes the center of a community's vision for its future, the community is placing the primacy of its vision on the human relationship to mass movement from one place to another, which in turn determines where and how the population and open spaces will be situated. Here, a fundamental question might be posed: Does building more and more roads really relieve congestion, which, after all, seems to be what drives the design of a transportation system? According to Bill Bishop, editorial page columnist for the *Herald-Leader* in Lexington, KY, building more roads does not relieve congestion — it *adds* to it.[62] We think he has a good point because there is a parallel in buying houses.

We have often heard people say they have so much stuff that they need a larger house. This statement seems reasonable enough on the surface, but in practice, most people we know who have actually bought a larger house immediately begin filling it to capacity. Why? Our American compulsion to fill every nook and cranny is in part a product of not having been taught how to live with empty space, or at least space that is not crammed full all the time.

Is the same true with roads? If our cities' roads are congested and we build more roads to relieve the congestion, will we not just fill the new roads again to the point of congestion, like our houses? It seems to us that one could logically say, "Like our houses, so our roads." This is also the contention of columnist Bill Bishop. "Trying to pave your way out of traffic congestion," writes Bishop, "is like trying to eat your way back into your high school jeans. Cars fill in the new pavement just like middle age created the market for Dockers."[62] Although it seems counter-intuitive, says Bishop, building more roads actually leads to more traffic. On the other hand, he continues, closing roads, or even narrowing streets, does not create more congestion — it tends to cut the volume of traffic, especially in cities.

"Lord knows," says Bishop, "the evidence of this phenomenon is stalled in full view of most citizens. As soon as roads are built, they're filled. And to relieve the new traffic, we build new roads. You'd think somebody would connect the dots." What dots? The dots pointing to the fact that the level of consciousness that caused the problem in the first place, such as the levees along the Snake River near Jackson, WY, which largely destroyed the river, is not the level of consciousness that can solve it. A higher level of consciousness is required — recognizing, accepting, and acting on the evidence under our noses, which is connecting the dots.

Some people have connected the dots, says Bishop. "Adding new roadways and widening older ones were seen as the way to solve the problem," observed the Texas Transportation Institute in a study of city traffic. "In most cities, this new roadway capacity was quickly filled with additional traffic, and the old problems of congestion returned."

On the other hand, researchers at the University College of London, England, examined 60 cases from around the world in which roads had been closed. They found that a goodly portion of the traffic that once used the roads simply "evaporated." The cars and trucks were not simply rerouted on nearby streets, but disappeared altogether. On average, one fifth of the vehicular use, and in some cases as much as 60%, went away once a road was closed, and the full volume of vehicles did not reappear once a road was reopened. The Tower Bridge in London, for example, was temporarily closed in 1994, and the traffic dispersed. Three years after the bridge was reopened, traffic still had not returned to its former level.

Writer James Howard Kunstler argued in the online magazine *Slate* that, "We have transformed the human ecology of America from sea to shinning sea into a national automobile slum."[62] "Do we get what we get," muses Bishop, "just because we can't remember any other way to live?" That is a good question because — while transportation may be the center of a community's vision for its future which increases the artificial structures of urbanization, light, and noise pollution and simultaneously precludes much of Nature through fragmentation of habitats — a community has two options when planning its transportation system: ecological constraints (greater emphasis on cultural capacity) or economic constraints (greater emphasis on carrying capacity).

If a community chooses to design its transportation system around ecological constraints, it may still be able to have a relatively good system of open spaces, but the system will suffer far greater fragmentation with a focus on transportation than if the open-space system itself had driven the vision and its implementation. On the other hand, if a community chooses to design its transportation system around economic constraints, open space as a viable system is all but foregone because fragmentation of habitat is inevitably maximized, as are noise and light pollution. There is also a greater likelihood (as opposed to a community where a system of open spaces has primacy) that both exotic and naturalized species would take over remaining parts of the landscape as habitat fragmentation created by growth in the human population accommodated by the transportation system puts ever-more outside pressure on the survival of indigenous species. All of these things operate synergistically as cumulative effects that exhibit a lag period before fully manifesting themselves.

Population

When a community uses growth as the primary nonnegotiable constraint around which development will revolve, it is most likely, in our experience, to view the size of the proposed population in terms of continual economic growth (carrying capacity) as opposed to ecological sustainability (cultural capacity). Thus, a vision based on the human population as the nonnegotiable constraint usually, but not always, places its primacy on pushing the biological carrying capacity to the perceived limit, especially when money is involved.

A case in point is Corvallis, OR, where increased population means increased money through federal block grants, which in turn means increased growth that once again is seen as a means to garner more money. (For a discussion of the "growth/no-growth" tug of war, see Chapter 5 in *Setting the Stage for Sustainability*.[63]) At a recent public forum, the Business Advocacy Committee of the Corvallis Area Chamber of Commerce made public the results of its research into the management of municipal growth.[64] According to Patricia Mulder, the executive director of the Chamber, the people of Corvallis have been diligent and "perhaps" too successful in preventing rampant growth in the town's population, which had declined 3% in the previous year, along with a work force that had shrunk by 5%. "These declines have occurred," says Mulder, "while surrounding communities continue to grow."[64]

The crux of Mulder's concern is that the loss of 1500 citizens leaves the population of Corvallis below 50,000 inhabitants and thus threatens the classification of Corvallis as an "entitlement" city following the next census. Why the concern? If Corvallis were to reach a population of 50,000, with some additional requirements, it would be "entitled" to community development block grants from the federal government — in a word, "money."

No need to worry, however. The latest U.S. Census Bureau's estimate puts the population at 50,202 people, a figure that "entitles" Corvallis to receive about $400,000 a year, beginning next fiscal year, from the U.S. Department of Housing and Urban Development for housing programs to help low- and moderate-income residents. This is deemed important because the state oversees the money, and cities with less than 50,000 inhabitants must compete for it; whereas, cities with populations over 50,000 are entitled to the money without competition. In other words, the city gets its own money without intercession by the state.

Coupled with the Corvallis Area Chamber's notion of the need to "grow" the population (which, incidentally, fits precisely the notions of many other area chambers of commerce) is the perceived need for waste in order to keep people busy and expand the economy, so says author Barry Brooks. Here, the concept is that durability (which is a perceived economic threat to business leaders because it slows sales) equates over time to sustainability, whereas built-in obsolescence (which stimulates repeated sales and equates to waste) is good for the economy as we define it, despite the regrettable fact that planned obsolescence is counter-productive to social-environmental sustainability. This is but one more example of the misleading notion of economic well-being fostered by the flawed calculation of the gross domestic product as opposed to accounting for both credits and debits according to the genuine progress indicator.

As is often the case, the desire for more and more money drives a community's population growth — as its nonnegotiable planning constraint — to such a point that the quality of life begins an almost invisible but irreversible decline. Thus, a community that chooses to move ever closer to the perceived biological carrying capacity of its human population being the nonnegotiable constraint usually sees the placement of its people dictated by the desirability of available private property based on individual tastes, precluding a connected system of open spaces with any integrity of habitat. This, in turn, usually determines where the transportation system will be located, which works to maximize the fragmentation of habitat. In addition, the community maximizes the cumulative effects of light and noise pollution, artificial structures, and declines in and extinctions of local populations and species of indigenous plants and animals.

All these effects are not only hidden for some time in the ecological lag period but also work synergistically in shifting the landscape from the more natural end of the continuum to the more cultural end. Beyond some point, these effects upset the ecological integrity and ultimately affect the quality of life, almost inevitably in the negative. So, where do we go from here?

Economics may continue to shift populations around the country, but changes in the way we use and treat the land could perhaps bring an end to this cycle. If, for example, the process of land-use planning and development was one that in and of itself helped to create a sense of place within a community, then wealth and prosperity might begin to be redefined. The natural wealth of "community" might begin to meet deeper human needs, thus diminishing the material needs met by material wealth. A case in point is the coastal community of Seaside, OR.[65]

People getting away from such metropolitan areas as Portland is a regular occurrence during the summer, and the Oregon coast is a place of choice to visit. That choice, however, has resulted in towns built around tourism that fueled development, which in turn brought traffic, strip malls, and sprawl, where people go from beachside hotels to downtown hotdog stands and video arcades.

While other coastal towns stretch highway sprawl farther and farther along U.S. Highway 101 in the name of economic growth and vitality, Seaside is taking the opposite tack. With the idea in mind to help save salmon habitat, give local residents a place to play, and reverse a century of tourist-seeking development, a farsighted, reform-minded group in City Hall of Seaside is purchasing mudflats, marshes, and mill ponds to save what is left of Nature in Seaside. Their plans even specify the tearing down of a few buildings along U.S. Highway 101 to let rivers and wetlands greet visitors instead of the proverbial gift shops and sundry tourist traps.

"Originally, we thought visitors were our treasure," says Neal Maine, the resource manager for the North Coast Land Conservancy. "And then we realized that we were standing on it [meaning the land and its diversity as the community's natural wealth]."[65] "We are trying to do it for ourselves," says city manager Gene Miles. "And the truth of the matter is, it will probably be a bonanza."[65] To realize the bonanza of which Miles speaks, however, one must not only consider but also account for the cultural capacity of a community.

Cultural capacity

Although we may think ourselves wise in our own eyes, we are too often blind to the truth that we neither govern nor manage Nature. We treat Nature wisely or unwisely for good or for ill, but we do not control Nature. We do something to Nature, and Nature responds, and in the response lies the lessons we are loathe to learn — lessons about lifestyle.

Lifestyle is commonly defined as an internally consistent way of life or style of living that reflects the values and attitudes of an individual or a culture. Many in Western society have made lifestyle synonymous with "standard of living," which we practice as a search for ever-increasing material prosperity. If, however, we are to have a viable, sustainable environment as we know it and value it, we must reach beyond the strictly material and see lifestyle as a sense of inner wholeness and harmony derived by living in such a way that the spiritual, environmental, and material aspects of our lives are in balance with the capacity of the land to produce the necessities for that lifestyle.

Whether a given lifestyle is even possible depends on cultural capacity, the notion used to describe, in qualitative terms, the kind of lifestyle a community wants to enjoy measured against the ability of the community's surrounding environment to sustain that lifestyle. Carrying capacity, on the other hand, is strictly quantitative in that it represents the maximum number of animals — or people — that can live in and use a particular area without destroying its ability to function in an ecologically specific way. Where cultural capacity deals with the quality of life per individual, carrying capacity deals strictly with maximizing the number of individuals to the threshold of habitat destruction, beyond which the population will collapse. If we want human society to survive the 21st century in any sort of dignified manner, we must have the humility to view our own population in terms of local, regional, national, and global carrying capacities, because the quality of life declines in direct proportion to the degree to which the habitat is overpopulated.

If we substitute the idea of cultural capacity for carrying capacity, we have a workable proposition for sustainable community. Cultural capacity is a chosen quality of life that is sustainable without endangering the productive capacity of the environment. The more materially oriented the desired lifestyle of an individual or a community, for example, the more resources are needed to sustain it and the smaller the human population must be per unit area of landscape. Cultural capacity, then, is a balance among the way we want to live, the real quality of our lifestyle and our community, and the number of people an area can support in that lifestyle on a sustainable basis.

Cultural capacity (= quality) of any area will be less than its carrying capacity (= quantity) in the biological sense. Cultural capacity has built into it the prudence of limitations as a margin of safety in the event of such long-term phenomena as global climate change. Carrying capacity, on the other hand, uses the environment to its maximum and lacks a margin of safety for difficult years or unforeseen environmental changes, which, when they occur, as they always do at some point in time, wreak havoc on the population. The long-term environmental risks hidden in the momentary notion of an area's carrying capacity, when exploited to the maximum, have doomed more than one civilization to collapse by destroying the biological sustainability of the surrounding landscape.

David Skrbina, a graduate student at the University of Bath in England, states the problem a little differently.[66] The problem with most human populations, as Skrbina sees it, is one of scale. In order to sustain itself, a given human population must maintain a size that is both compatible with a concept of community and consistent with a human scale, which not only means a community of a size that fosters people actually knowing one another but also means a community of a size that fits with ecological comfort into its immediate landscape.

The problem of human population has two dimensions, according to Skrbina: the *size* of the population and the *density* of the population. While a large population can be a problem, "it is a *different* problem if those people are packed onto a small island than if they are spread across a large prairie."[66] Population has two factors that must be simultaneously accounted for: the number of people and the area of land available to support them sustainably in order to make cultural capacity a workable idea.

We can, for example, predetermine local and bioregional cultural capacity and adjust our population growth accordingly. (The term "bioregion" refers to a geographically definable area of biological similarities which is largely self-contained when it comes to a supply of water.) If we choose *not* to balance our desires with the land's capabilities, the depletion of the land will determine the quality of our cultural/community/social experience —

our lifestyle. If, however, we choose to balance our desires with the land's capabilities, then we will model our planning after the biophysical relationships of Nature, which means humanity would leave a much lighter imprint on the Earth.

chapter four

Modeling the planning process after nature

"Compassion is not an individual character trait ... but a way of living together." —Henri Nouowen

In community planning, the process which creates, implements, and revisits plans is ideally modeled after natural patterns, systems, and cycles. Such a process is conducted by people for their future in an ecosystem of which they are a part. Therefore, the modeling of a planning process must consider the needs and multidimensionality of both the people and the ecosystem.

The framework of sustainability for community development rests, in part, on the definition of sustain, which is "to support or hold up from below ... to keep a person's mind and spirit from giving way."[3] This framework recognizes the importance of meeting the complex needs of humans while maintaining the integrity of natural systems that support all life. Sustainable development is intended to make it possible for future generations to have as many, if not more, options than the current generation — options for the nurturance of body, mind, and spirit.

Recognizing the complex needs of people will most likely accompany a more sensitive multidimensional approach to the landscape on the part of social leaders because the well-being of body, mind, and spirit is inextricably linked to their context in the natural world. If a social/legal system, such as municipal government, is concerned only with the minds and intellects of its constituents, while failing to recognize the full range of human necessities and the way in which they are imbedded in the rest of Nature, the usefulness or functionality of that social or legal system will ultimately terminate. Chaos and the worldwide collapse of governments and social systems may be evidence of the failure on the part of leaders to understand how essential it is to not only recognize but also accommodate the health and inner growth of the whole human being. Failing and/or deteriorating ecosystems also signal failure of governments to recognize and adequately address the exceedingly complex, multidimensional nature of the ecosystem on which humans, as inseparable components, rely for physical survival.

In sustainable communities, being accountable for the integrity of the environment, the health of the economy, and the equity of human relationships characterizes the decision-making process. Such a multidimensional process can be seen as modeled after the biophysical principles that govern Nature.

Within such a framework, where process is guided by biophysical principles, land-use decisions respect several ecological dimensions associated with time, interrelationships of species, natural disturbances, and the connectivity of habitats.[67] The previous chapter elaborated on this type of land-use management by emphasizing the importance of moving purposefully and consciously toward the connectivity of habitats in the form of well-planned and protected systems of open space. Habitat, kept in tact, provides the shelter and food for other creatures; provides ecosystem services, including water catchment, purification, and groundwater recharge; and assists in the maintenance of biological and genetic diversity. Planning for change in a sustainable community includes the protection of habitats through the protection of open spaces. For sustainable community to exist, however, this action must be linked with other actions that also lead toward sustainability.

In modeling our planning process after Nature, a fluid, nonlinear, diverse (multidimensional), self-organizing, waste-free paradigm will emerge that recognizes the interdependence of all the parts. What, you might ask, would such a paradigm look like?

From observing Nature and from a basic understanding of certain ecological principles, the following ideas emerge as guides for creating a planning process.

Fluidity

For communication to take place, four elements must be present: the source of the message, the message itself, the receiver of the message, and the medium through which the message is disseminated. In such a model, there is the possibility of "noise" between the source and the recipient which alters the original message.

In healthy systems, communication and the flow of information (in whatever form it is perceived) are constant and unobstructed. Interruption or distortion of the message can block necessary, built-in feedback loops, which reduces or stops the flow of information. When communication is interrupted, all components of a system are affected. The healthy pulse of a human heart exemplifies a steady source of information to the organism. Blocking one of the arteries in this process can have widespread and sometimes lethal results.

Communication is constantly taking place in healthy ecosystems. The film *Shimmer*, directed by John Hanson, tells the story of two young boys in a juvenile hall during the 1940s in Iowa. Because of the restrictions placed on their freedom to talk to one another, they modeled a means of communicating based on their observations and belief that "everything [in Nature] talks to everything else."[68]

Human communication is comprised of motives, attitudes, thoughts, words, and actions. Thus, a planning process communicates to the public how the entity initiating the process (be it the mayor or the state legislature) feels toward the public. It reflects an attitude that can say more than words, which brings to mind a statement by Ralph Waldo Emerson: "Your attitude thunders so loudly I can't hear what you say."

Historically, many city plans have been brought to the public for approval *after* their development, a procedure that communicates a number of things to the citizens, including: (1) the planning staff is already attached to and committed to the plan, (2) negotiation of the plans has already taken place, (3) the entity that initiated the plan only wants the citizens to approve it as written, (4) the experts recognized by the entity that initiated the plan are the only ones with valid answers, and (5) the public is neither thought to nor expected to have good ideas.[69]

Such top-down structure negates lasting citizen involvement in the planning process, reduces emotional investment in the product, and results in plans that have limited meaning or strength of focus to guide a community through change. Without a shared community vision for a shared sustainable future, which can only come from the bottom up, plans are relegated to shelves, where they collect dust.

Building trust with and among the citizenry is an essential ingredient in any planning process, and with it comes a necessity for abundant, free-flowing communication. A high-profile, highly visible, open process maintains confidence within the community. To achieve such confidence, however, one must make absolutely clear what the various stages of the planning process are; what delineates the transition from stage to stage; who makes decisions and how; what meetings will occur and when, as well as their purpose; and, of major importance, what will happen with the information provided by the public. Press releases, an interactive website, radio and television public service announcements, and newsletters all work to keep the public educated, informed, and involved.

The conscious use of language is a critical element in the free flow of communication. Whose language is one using throughout this process? It is important for planners and other technical professionals involved in the planning process to eliminate the use of professional jargon, technical terms, and agency lingo when conversing with the public. Such cliquish language serves as a means of establishing power and thus threatens or alienates the public or simply makes willing participants feel inadequate or incompetent. This "break" in communication can, and most often does, have drastic effects on the outcome largely because it stifles self-confidence and thus the willingness or courage of participants to offer creative ideas. It is the responsibility of the planners to learn the language of the public — not vice versa.

Ground rules and obtaining agreement on them are critical — for example, deciding how decisions will be made (consensus vs. voting or some combination thereof), requiring all to state possible solutions to problems raised, showing up for meetings on time, refraining from personal attack and instead seeing the discussion as one of potential differences among ideas rather than personalities.

Creating a "safe" place for people to offer themselves and their ideas is critical to maintaining a free flow of communication. So-called "ice-breakers" sometimes work to obtain a level of comfort by creating a certain equality among participants. Ice-breakers usually get people to laugh about themselves and therefore create a kind of collective humility that evens the playing field.

Ice-breakers have ancient roots. In early tribal gatherings, for example, pounding two stones together by each person in the circle was intended to create equality at the beginning of each council meeting. Saying a prayer as a group at mealtimes strikes us as being another example of creating equality. Most prayers offered before a meal convey the message that no one at the table is really in charge, especially when such prayers imply a power greater than any of those gathered.

Simply starting a meeting with a "check-in" process, where participants describe how they are doing by coming up with a number from one to ten, a color, an animal, or a weather pattern is another way of creating a kind of equality from the outset. Some ice-breakers are really simple. For example, as people are entering the meeting room, ask them to pair off with someone they do not know and find out about the other person. Ask each person in the pair to introduce the other. A more fanciful ice-breaker is to ask each person to introduce themselves by stating why they are at the meeting and then have them state their hidden "soap opera" name — their middle name plus the name of the street they grew up on. Or, alternatively, and depending on the audience, each person can be asked to add their hidden "country-western" name, which is the name of their first pet plus their mother's maiden name.

Another aspect of keeping communication free-flowing is recognition of the diversity and multidimensionality of the participants. In the context of the planning process, it is important to remember that emotional data are as valid and legitimate as factual data. Feelings, whether translated into data by those who can afford the time, energy, or dollars to do so or those simply expressed openly and willingly, translate into political clout and must be respected equally. Feelings are critical fuel for a planning process and must be acknowledged and used if the planning process is to succeed over the long term.

Sometimes, participants cannot get beyond their feelings. This can stymie their own ability to communicate. In cases such as this, a facilitator might ask a participant for clarification; that is, the facilitator can state what he or she believes he or she has heard and then ask if that is correct. Also, the person can be encouraged to offer a possible solution to the problem they perceive that has given rise to the strong feelings, which sometimes helps to bring out possible solutions.

Above all, the public should be involved in the planning process from the very beginning. A well-designed planning process keeps citizens involved in civic life long after the plan is created, which is essentially saying that the process becomes more important in some respects than the plan itself because continued positive, productive engagement by the citizens of a community in creating their future and the future possibilities for their children and their children's children is a true characteristic of sustainable community development. The above ideal does not always work, however, as illustrated by an example from the hometown of one of the authors.[70]

As you read the following account, keep in mind that when we attempt to redesign Nature (increasingly through the technology of bioengineering) to fit our desires of a risk-free system, we build in two hazards. One, we build rigidity into the system that it will one day reject — to our peril, and, two, we design the system to mirror our own human limitations, including our limited understanding of the biophysical relationships that govern Nature.

This drive to remove all risk essentially sets the stage for greater risk. Aldo Leopold once said that, "Too much safety seems to yield only danger in the long run." We are not, after all, masters of the tools and technology that we invent. They affect our lives — and those of our children and their children and their children's children — in ways we most often do not understand and too often cannot control.

Bioengineering vs. natural processes

"The dream that technology serves for us," writes John Gray, professor of European Thought at the London, England, School of Economics, "is a dream of complete control. It's the dream that we can cease to be mortal, earthbound creatures subject to fate and chance."[71] Gray goes on to say that the use of technology to remake the world according to our human will is not so much a product of science, but rather of magic, and is the fantasy by which industrialized nations have been ruled for much of the 20th century. What, specifically, you might ask, is this fantasy? It is the notion of progress without risk or instability.

"When we look to technology to deliver us from accidents, from choice, and even from mortality, we are asking from it something it cannot give: a deliverance from the conditions that make us human." Gray contends that what we once looked for in political ideologies, and before that sought in religion, we are today seeking from technology: "salvation from ourselves."[71] In this sense, says Gray, "the world today is a vast, unsupervised laboratory in which a multitude of experiments are simultaneously under way."

The restoration of the riverbank that borders downtown Corvallis is one of these experiments.[70] Downtown Corvallis is situated on the west bank of the Willamette River. The waterfront portion of the downtown area is to be renovated and 2750 feet of the riverbank restored to greater ecological health at a cost of $4 million, which is the issue of this discussion. The riverbank "restoration" work is part of a massive project to renovate the riverfront by constructing a new Riverfront Commemorative Park and to meet federal requirements to stop the overflow of sewage into the Willamette River that occurs during heavy rains.

The city council opted to convene a meeting after a proposed change in the plans to "stabilize" the riverbank prompted outrage among Corvallis residents. The proposed change was the cutting of 400 trees. The city council originally approved a plan that sought to save as many of the existing trees along the upper part of the riverbank as possible, but the consultants hired by the city said their data showed that saving those trees posed a threat to the stability of the bank. Some residents, including a team of 21 scientists from Oregon State University, opposed the consultant's recommendations.

The team of consultants included Gordon Nicholson, riverfront project manager for the engineering firm CH2M Hill, and Robbin Sotir, an expert in soil bioengineering from Marietta, GA. According to the consultants, a computer analysis of soil tests showed that "deep weaknesses" and "significant threats of slides" occur in the riverbank. Problems contributing to the crumbling riverbank were said to include seepage, leaning and top-heavy trees, cracking along the upper bank, and debris of metal and concrete in the upper bank. "These [taken] all together," asserted Nicholson, "are saying this is a bank with symptoms of stress."

In short, and grossly simplified, the bioengineering approach to stabilizing the riverbank would include: (1) removing about 400 live trees, (2) cutting the riverbank into a series of terraces and reinforcing it with packs of soil wrapped in a geotextile material, (3) piling layers of boulders (called riprap) on the bank to protect it from being washed away by flood waters, and (4) planting new trees.

"I think everyone would like a low or no-risk option," Nicholson said, "and those were our marching orders." Such thinking implies a disaster mentality that conjures the worst possible case scenario, one that requires changing the world in an attempt to prevent it from happening.

Nicholson went on to justify the bioengineering approach to stabilize the riverbank by indicating that the number of trees, including tall trees, would be increased over the number of trees that occupied the bank during the 1970s. Sotir added that the same bioengineering technology being proposed for the riverbank in Corvallis has been used in 30 other countries and along the Mississippi River.

Saying that the same bioengineering technology has been use elsewhere in no way indicates whether the technology is appropriate, whether it has worked, how well it has worked, how long it has been in place, whether it has been evaluated, and what ecological problems, if any, have arisen and/or been created. Bioengineering, at least in our experience over many years, focuses on the engineering in response to a perceived disaster with precious little understanding of the ecosystem involved or its processes. Bioengineering is too often viewed and practiced as a quick fix that puts engineered rigidity, which is presumed to build predictability or certainty, into a fluid problem governed by ecological processes, which often spawns disastrous results — such as the predictable, rigid levees placed along the banks to control the unpredictable, fluid, and uncontrollable Mississippi River.

On the other side of the coin, scientists from the Department of Fisheries and Wildlife at Oregon State University in Corvallis disputed the consultants' conclusion, which, as it turns out, was never subjected to a disinterested third-party review. The scientists, particularly Boone Kauffman, a riparian plant ecologist, and Stan Gregory, a stream ecologist, carried the argument that the consultants overstated the threat of the bank crumbling into the river. Their counterpoints to the consultants' report are as follows.

I. Riverbank instability and its risk of failure

- The Corvallis riverfront is composed of geologic materials associated with Missoula Terraces formed more than 10,000 years ago. The material forming the Missoula Terraces is much more resistant to erosion than are alluvial gravels, which are characteristic of other locations. Alluvial gravels are those that have been deposited by flowing water, such as a river.
- The Corvallis riverfront is among the most stable sections of the Willamette River from Corvallis to Eugene, a town about 50 miles to the south. It has changed very little in the last 150 years, according to historical maps and historical survey data.
- The Corvallis riverfront has experienced 20 floods since 1860 that were larger than the one of 1996 and has survived all of them with no evidence that the river has cut into its bank more than a few tens of feet.
- The consultants' estimation that the riverbank has been eroding at the rate of 1 foot every 3 years is a gross overstatement. A cursory review of the riverfront will confirm that the majority of the bank is well vegetated. If the rates of erosion were as stated by the consultants, there would be few trees left on the riverbank, whereas now there are many.
- There is no evidence of tension cracks to indicate that major planes of failure extend back from the riverbank, just as there is no evidence of slumps or bank erosion that extend back more than 10 to 25 feet from the riverbank over the last 150 years.
- Cracks along the riverfront bike path are similar in structure and frequency to those that occur throughout the bike paths of Corvallis, even those well away from creeks and rivers.

- Only two slumps are clearly related to the 1996 flood, which was severe. Others, which have occurred historically, were likely exacerbated by problems associated with drainage of the city's stormwater.
- It is difficult to assess and/or predict the risks of bank failure without analyzing the multitude of natural processes that govern the floodplains of the Willamette River in both time and space. It is therefore necessary to take a larger view of the processes that affect the riverbank, rather than conducting a microstudy of those characteristics that affect only the site in question.
- There is no evidence to support the belief that the proposed bioengineered geotextile structures will perform better than, or even as well as, the existing bank structure and accompanying vegetation, which is already well established. Commitment to this extensively engineered and unproven design may well be ecologically unsound and thus an unwise financial risk for the community, as the bioengineered design requires stripping most of the existing natural structure and vegetation from the already long-stable riverbank in favor of a largely artificial approach to preventing a potential and unlikely erosional disaster somewhere in the unforeseeable future.

II. Riverfront forest

- Tree composition of the riverfront is today a largely uneven-aged mosaic of healthy indigenous riparian hardwood trees. The majority of the trees are young and vigorous, and the arborist, who was contracted by the consultant to examine the trees, found that 80% of them were in the highest class of health and vigor.
- The overall good health of the trees along the riverbank appears to be the norm for the forest that borders the Willamette River. The current richness of species is high, with over 40 different species of plants identified, and the structural diversity of the riverfront is continuing to increase and will do so for decades to come — provided it is not stripped in the name of bioengineering.
- Given the present health and vigor of the trees, there is no accelerated risk of trees falling into the river when compared to any other riparian forest along the Willamette River of similar age and composition.
- Scientists throughout the world recognize and acknowledge the role of vegetation in providing soil stability because plant roots bind soils together. The root mass of the riparian zone is equal to or greater than the mass of trees that are seen above ground.
- A survey conducted by the scientists showed that the natural falling of trees not only appeared to be an extremely rare event along the town's riverfront but also is not associated with bank failure.
- The density of tree stems dissipates the erosive energy of high water during floods; also, the increased number of trees over the last 50 years indicates that the stand is becoming ever more stable and increasing in its ability to dissipate the energy of flood waters.

- The pistol-butt growth pattern of trees along the riverbank may be caused by conditions that are unrelated to bank instability, such as stems that sprout laterally from the butt. Straight stems above the pistol butts, on the other hand, indicate long periods of bank stability.

III. Outcome of the proposed project is uncertain

- Most projects similar to that proposed by the consultants have been conducted where erosion is severe and banks are largely unvegetated, which is not the case for the Corvallis riverfront.
- If the consultant's plan were to be implemented, the current structure of the forest would not only be destroyed but would also take many decades to regain its prominence. The use of geotextile fabric under the soil would result in a soil depth of two feet, which would limit the establishment of indigenous trees and depress the growth of both trees and shrubs.
- Projects, such as that proposed by the consultant, have not been conducted in Oregon's climate, where patterns of winter precipitation and summer drought are typical. Drainage within the project may prevent the survival of planted vegetation due to water stress during the summer, a common problem for riparian plantings even in the best of soils.
- The trees at the base of the project covered by riprap will not likely survive as depicted in the drawings presented by the consultant. The placement of large boulders would damage the trunks of existing trees, which subjects them to disease and rot. In addition, the riprap surrounding the trees would act like a choke collar by restricting the ability of the trees to grow in diameter.
- Finally, based on author Chris' own experience, the large rock riprap that is being used to form a layer of "protection" over the riverbank will most likely become an ideal place in summer for the breeding of Norway rats, something the city of Corvallis already has enough of.

The Oregon State University scientists recommended integrating the existing conditions of the healthy riparian forest into the plan for the riverfront to maintain the current and vital ecological functions and the aesthetic qualities. Their basic recommendation is simple: work with Nature — not *against* Nature.

The above admonition was reiterated by Gordon Grant, a research scientist and expert on rivers and how they flow, who said there is little evidence that the downtown reach of the Willamette riverbank is unstable. He further contends that the CH2M Hill consultants that the city hired did not clearly establish a problem with the riverbank before moving ahead with plans to "stabilize" it. "At this stage, I don't think the documents support the claim of a bank stability problem," Grant said. "If this is what the [need to stabilize the riverbank] is pinned to, [it's] on thin air. Everything they [the consultants] did was to rectify a bank stabilization problem that was never documented."

Grant feels the consultants represented a "...rush to judgment," because, he muses, "if you have a hammer, everything looks like a nail."

Dick Gamble, a civil engineer with the U.S. Army Corps of Engineers, is familiar with the riverbank in question and agrees. While the Corps had not studied that particular stretch of riverbank, said Gamble, the Corps had studied, as part of its job of controlling floods and maintaining waterways, the banks just north and just south of the downtown area which have needed little attention, Gamble said, because "historically, that reach of the river has been pretty stable."

Dick Bell, also a civil engineer living in Corvallis, is retired from Oregon State University, where he taught for 30 years. Bell is a noted expert in the mechanics of soil, foundation engineering, and the use of geotextiles, which the consultants recommended using to stabilize the riverbank. "I haven't been aware of any problems," said Bell. "You don't see a lot of trees falling down," Bell continued, and "the fact that it has been stable — common sense says it will remain stable."

Bob Beschta, a professor of Forest Hydrology with Oregon State University, said the consultant had mistakenly blamed the river for eroding the bank and used damage inflicted by the 1996 flood as an example of what could be expected in the future when viewing the riverbank with a disaster mentality. Instead of the river being at fault, said Beschta, the intensity of the rainfall and the speed with which it moved along pavement were to blame for the 1996 landslide. This meant, Beschta continued, that the city must find a way of collecting the stormwater runoff and lessen its effect on the riverbank.

Gordon Nicholson, of CH2M Hill, on the other hand, said they, the consultants, "were to come up with solutions to protect the city's investment in the riverfront" and that "*doing nothing was not seen as a solution* [emphasis added]." But, many citizens wonder where the problem requiring a solution is. Has anyone considered, one might therefore ask (as Chris did at an October 1999 meeting), what is right with the riverbank as it is, from an engineering point of view? No reply was forthcoming.

Perhaps the problem has more to do with minds predisposed to finding a "no-risk" way of protecting economic investments within the framework of a disaster mentality than it does deriving an ecological understanding of riverbank processes and the real potential of soil erosion. In other words, the mayor, city council, and consultants failed to differentiate between *possibility* and *probability*, which are two vastly different dynamics.

Listening, really listening, to the citizens

Listening, really listening, to the citizens requires an open mind, which has not been the case in Corvallis. "The riverbank plan has exploded and debris is falling around our ears," wrote Corvallis columnist Wendy Madar. She went on to say, "As a regular at Corvallis public meeting for many years, I've had the uneasy sense that public comment is not always as welcome in fact as it is in name." Madar said her unease was crystallized during a recent meeting of the city council in which a councilor told a member of the community that he had forfeited his chance to contribute to the riverfront plan because he had failed to attend the original planning meeting. "It's too late now. I'm sorry!" the councilor said in startlingly harsh tones.

The city staff also used the phrase "eleventh-hour stakeholders" to characterize citizens who did not speak out earlier about the riverfront plan. The implication is either that these citizens failed to contribute to earlier meetings and thus had no right to speak now, or they were coming forward to "get what they didn't get the first time around."

Although city leaders have repeatedly stated that the process leading to the riverfront plan would be both long and exhaustive and, therefore, must represent a consensus of the citizenry, many members of the community tell a different story. They say that while they did indeed attend the meetings and presented their concerns, the results did not reflect their testimony.

At this October public meeting on the riverfront project, the author got the distinct feeling, especially from the mayor, that the public was a nuisance to be endured, albeit grudgingly. One of his neighbors came to him the next day and told him that he and his wife had both attended the meeting and also had experienced the exact same feeling. In fact, of the 42 people who spoke at the October meeting, most opposed the consultant's plan, the author among them.

This discrepancy points to a real and continuing problem with communication between citizens and city officials, particularly when new or unwelcome issues are raised. Consider the following example of miscommunication at Corvallis: A botanist, testifying before the city council, said that the work of putting the layers of rock (riprap) along the riverbank should be stopped because it was not needed, given that the bank has been historically stable and that the rock was destroying the healthy riparian plant community. When he finished, an official thanked him for speaking out in favor of the city's plan for the placement of an underwater structure for fish habitat.

Kauffman, the riparian plant ecologist, said that people were looking for and expecting restoration of the riverbank and improving the beauty of the riverfront park when they voted. "People voted for restoration and now we're getting stabilization."

"I keep listening for a voice in the community arguing for an engineering approach [to the riverbank restoration]," said stream ecologist Gregory, "and I haven't heard it." Well, there may be one — Tom Peterson, who wrote the following in the local newspaper:[70]

> I write this after having walked the length of the river-
> bank from Harrison Boulevard to Washington Avenue.
> The view to the east is little different than walking
> through any undeveloped forest area. Yet, I know that
> there is a beautiful river on the other side of the trees
> on the riverbank that begs to be viewed.

> The current view of the river is occluded with trees and brambles. What a mess. It seems to me that hacking down the 400 trees and doing what's necessary to eliminate erosion of the riverbank will afford us a greater view of the river and give us an opportunity to landscape the riverbank so that it is an asset to the community rather [than] the jungle that it currently is. For those that prefer the view of the trees, there will still be plenty on the east bank of the river.
>
> Start the chain saws.

Although miscommunication may not be a deliberate move to limit public debate on an issue, it often has that effect. Saying that a process is public is therefore not enough; citizens not only must be allowed to speak freely and safely but also must be listened to with respect and heard with patience and accuracy. "There is no such thing as an eleventh-hour stakeholder," said Madar, and there must be time in a democratic process to listen to informed citizens.

Or only pretending to really listen

As it turns out, stabilization of the riverbank is not the central issue, but rather a two-way street with parking that would encroach right up to the functional edge of the riverbank, where there was supposed to be a park with open space for people to enjoy walking and biking along the river bank itself, a plan that would leave only room enough for the existing one-way street without parking. But, apparently, the city council had made its mind up months before to please the business people who wanted the two-way street and its attendant parking spaces to be a nonnegotiable centerpiece of the entire riverfront plan. The citizens, however, were not openly informed about this part of the plan in the beginning, and even when the two-way street became common knowledge, raising the ire of many citizens — as evidenced by comments in public meetings and many letters to the editor in the local paper vehemently opposing the two-way street — the city council simply ignored the comments.

In addition, the scientists from Oregon State University, who were appointed by the city council to be members of a peer-review team to check on the ecological accuracy and accountability of the stabilization plan developed by CH2M Hill, expressed their dismay when the main point of their review was never discussed at the January 6, 2000, public meeting in which the city council voted on the various elements of the plan for the riverfront park and bank stabilization. The scientists' point was that much expensive bank stabilization could be avoided simply by moving the park and street improvements some distance back from the edge of the river, but that would mean giving up the two-way street in the narrowest part of the proposed renovation.

As might be expected, the scientists were charged by the city council to be neutral in presenting their findings. Beschta said that "essentially, no comments were made" about the report by the city council at its January 6 meeting. Although the review team disbanded after handing its report to the city council, some members wanted to ensure that the public fully understood the implications of their report, because, said Beschta, our "report was basically short-circuited ... [and] we wanted to keep this process public." They thus decided to hold a public forum, which took place on January 19.

Dave Bella, professor of Civil, Construction, and Environmental Engineering at Oregon State University, said that it was up to the city council if they wanted to spend the money in the narrow area to shore up the riverbank as planned. But, he continued, a second option, outlined in the report, did not even get a hearing. That option was to save the money slated for stabilization of the riverbank and move the park improvements away from the river or eliminate them, which would leave more open space and cost less. "If you never look at this option," said Bella, "the cost gets hidden. To not have [all the options in the report] laid out — that makes me uncomfortable because people are liable to say that [the city council] had to [follow the heavily contested original plan] because of your report."

Gregory said that the Willamette River should drive the discussion, which means city officials should plan developments so they would not be affected by the river and would thereby respect its dynamics, rather than continually attempting to subjugate the river. But the river's dynamics have to date been ignored by the city council in favor of a two-way street. There is yet a more egregious problem concerning information about the riverbank, one internal to the city.

Eliminating unwelcome voices within

"If I were to tell you," wrote Corvallis columnist Wendy Madar, "that, nearly a year ago, the engineer in charge of the city's riverfront sewer project [Greg Peterson] raised many of the same concerns now being raised by the citizens [about the riverbank stabilization project] and soon afterward was fired, you'd very likely say, 'Not in Corvallis.'"[70] That is exactly what happened, though, says Madar, as indicated by papers given to her (by someone other than Greg Peterson) that included letters in which Peterson, who had overseen hundreds of complex environmental projects in his 24 years with CH2M Hill prior to accepting his job with the city, raised his concerns. Although the city officials say Peterson's dismissal had nothing to do with the questions he raised, the fact that he raised them so early casts "a strange light on what we're now being told."

Peterson, who was the city's overall manager for the multiple sewer and riverbank projects, soon became uneasy with several aspects of the work on the riverbank, including inadequate information being given to the citizens and discrepancies between what voters had approved and the developing bioengineering design. Peterson wrote letters to Gordon Nicholson, who you will remember is the riverfront project manager for the engineering firm CH2M Hill, city manager Jon Nelson, and others regarding the plan for the riverbank.

Peterson's questions were striking, wrote Madar, in that they echoed issues raised at recent public meetings, such as the necessity of removing vegetation and soil, the wisdom of destroying existing soil-holding root structure, the environmental soundness of the geotextile technology as proposed, the potential for bank failures during construction, the thousands of loads of debris that would have to be trucked through downtown Corvallis.

Peterson had been scheduled to address the Downtown Corvallis Association on December 16, 1998. Joan Wessell, director of the Downtown Corvallis Association, told Madar: "We were delighted to work with him. He's an excellent communicator." The presentation never took place, however, because Peterson was fired at 4:00 p.m. on December 15.

Peterson told Madar that, "It was the most incredible thing that has ever happened to me." He said that city officials had told him not to raise difficult issues with business owners concerning construction along the riverbank, especially the specter of 50,000 dumptruck loads of soil being moved through downtown Corvallis "because it will confuse the situation." Peterson, on the other hand, saw communication with the citizenry as the most important part of his job.

Why, wonders Peterson still, did the city officials not consider a wide range of options and/or have a peer review conducted on Robbin Sotir's geogrid design before deciding what to do, but he speculates that the lure of a "risk-free" riverbank diverted the process away from the ecologically oriented approach that the community both voted for and expected. Sotir's design, says Peterson, ironically had significant risks associated with it, risks Peterson detailed in his letters.

Now that the citizens are raising the same question, said Madar, "[city] officials are telling us these are new concerns that surfaced as a result of recent soil tests... ." How, one might wonder, can these be construed as new concerns when Peterson raised them a year ago?

A major point used by city officials in persuading voters to approve a $9.5 million bond for the riverfront restoration project was wrong, according to city records and to Nicholson, the lead consultant, who now says that the rate of erosion cited in the city's documents and reports by CH2M Hill was incorrect, an error that the city is blaming on CH2M Hill. Nevertheless, voters approved the bond to fund restoration of the riverbank and construct a riverfront park because city officials said that the riverbank was unstable and that, without several million dollars of engineering work, the park and nearby businesses, as well as power, sewer, and utility lines could be threatened by the eroding bank.

But this sorry saga does not end here. Those in charge of the city of Corvallis did not follow their own rules for competitive bidding when they awarded to CH2M Hill the contract to restore the riverbank, the most controversial part of the riverfront project. "The city decided CH2M Hill was the only company that could do the job — a $147,325 contract to develop preliminary designs for restoring the downtown riverbank," wrote Aaron Corvin of the *Corvallis Gazette-Times*.[70]

Although there is a "sole-source" exemption that allows a city contract to be awarded to a company without inviting bids in a public process if the goods or services are available from only one company, the city's own rules require it to document why CH2M Hill was the only company that could do the job, but this was not done, according to Nancy Brewer, finance director for the city. The city apparently awarded the contract for the initial restoration design to CH2M Hill in September 1998 and received a draft of the design in October of that same year — about a month before the voters approved the $9.5 million, 20-year bond measure to help fund the project, at which time the design draft not only failed to show how the trees would be saved along the riverbank but also stated that most of them were in poor health.

On top of all this, Nicholson, riverfront project manager for CH2M Hill, is quoted as saying: "I'd have to say the city's procedures appear to be consistent with the norm, realizing that there's a fair amount of variation from one agency to another."[70] Be that as it may, the city officials of Corvallis lost credibility by hiring CH2M Hill to begin designing the riverfront without competitive bidding. Although the officials listed logical reasons for their actions, their decision may well remain open to question because they broke their own city rules when hiring CH2M Hill as a "sole-source" contractor without the required competitive bidding.

Does this in any way sound familiar? It would not be surprising if it does, as this kind of saga is replayed in city after city, where people use the linearity of their thinking to try to control in a predictable, risk-free manner the often risky, unpredictable cyclical processes and systems that govern the lives of all living things, including us. Thus, we move on to another ecological principle we suggest be used to guide the planning process: nonlinearity.

Nonlinearity

Cyclical systems are everywhere. Even when we believe a process appears to be linear, the "waste" produced will ultimately be recycled and become part of production. A good example of this is a poor law. Let's say, for the sake of discussion, that Prohibition in the 1920s was a "poor law" because it ultimately spawned crime and was very costly in terms of enforcement and lost lives. The "waste" in terms of dollars, lives, and time incurred by Prohibition was translated into experience in the creation of new laws pertaining to drugs and alcohol, which means that the knowledge gained during Prohibition was used, rather than wasted.

Attempts to model after the cyclical, nonlinear qualities of Nature are seen in modern theories of organizational development. *Thriving on Chaos*, a book about organizational development and techniques of management,[72] recognizes that conventional means of designing linear organizations for predicting failure and success may be very limited because what appears to us to be a random or disorderly event has in fact an underlying pattern that will allow greater understanding if we humans can deal with the scale of time necessary to uncover it.[72] Chaos, after all, is simply the limit of our understanding.

The cyclical approach to human organization is more fluid than the linear approach and thus has greater flexibility when it comes to the range of possible decisions. The dynamic nature of the cyclical approach to human organization is more consistent with human behavior and thus more consistent with Nature.

Nonlinearity, therefore, does not necessarily imply unpredictability. It implies that subtle patterns exist in Nature, patterns that challenge our willingness to accept them as regular and understandable. To view people in this manner is a starting point for more enlightened styles of management — flat vs. hierarchical — and thus generates greater recognition of the complex necessities of human beings, which results in stronger, more resilient organizations. To view communities (people and the ecosystem of which they are a part) in this manner is essential to both the creation and the implementation of a healthy, productive planning process.

The real challenge comes in designing a process that is nonlinear. Recently, one of the authors was engaged in a planning process created through "Open Space" technology developed by Harrison Owen.[73] It is an innovative meeting process "that taps into the dynamics of self-management, collective leadership, self-directed work teams, and genuine community. It works best in times of accelerated change with high levels of complexity, diversity, potential conflict, and time pressures."[73] Basic premises of Open Space are that whoever is there is who needs to be there; whatever is discussed is what needs to be discussed; and when it's over, it's over.

The purpose of the Open Space planning session the author attended was to envision various futures for the Sigurd Olson Environmental Institute of Northland College in Ashland, WI, where the author is currently employed. A diverse group of participants attended this day-long event — members of the faculty, administration, and staff of Northland College; members of the Board of Trustees and the Institute Advisory Board; students; and people from the Ashland community.

The meeting was held in a church that offered a number of rooms for the group's use, one for the larger gathering and others for breakout sessions. After a brief introduction addressing the purpose of the gathering — in this case, to determine how best to perpetuate the legacy of Sigurd Olson — anyone who wished could enter the center of the circle and write on a large sheet of paper a topic they would like discussed. After topic sheets were created by all who wished to do so, the sheets were posted about the room. At that point, those who wished to join in a discussion of a particular posted topic signed their names on the topic sheets. A participant could, of course, sign up for more that one topic. Time periods for discussion were added to each sheet.

In one such Open Space gathering, described to the author by the organizational development consultant guiding this process, a secretary of a large corporation entered the circle and created a topic sheet that posed the question: "What's really going on in this place?" This question drew the largest discussion group and resulted in significant changes in the organization.

Open Space technology provides the format for gatherings without agendas; all who wish to join in may. The results that emerge from the hearts and minds of the participants in an atmosphere of equality and openness are far reaching in terms of follow-up actions. The form is nonlinear and self-designed. Human creativity is the core function and the driving force of this event. The results of the session the author attended continue to penetrate the decision-making process of the Sigurd Olson Environmental Institute and have a kind of unique durability.

Another means for bringing nonlinearity to a planning process is Study Circles. The Study Circles Resource Center was established in 1990 in Pomfret, CT, to promote the use of Study Circles to address critical social and political issues. The Topsfield Foundation sponsors this project. Its mission is "to advance deliberative democracy and improve the quality of public life in the United States."[74]

Study Circles are usually comprised of 8 to 12 people who meet regularly over a period of weeks or months to focus on critical issues in a democratic and collaborative fashion. The circle is facilitated by a neutral person who keeps the discussion focused, helps the group consider a variety of views, and asks difficult but necessary questions. The Study Circle examines an issue from as many points of view as possible and seeks to find common ground. A Study Circle progresses from an initial session on personal experience (how does the matter under discussion affect me personally?) to sessions providing the opportunity for a broader perspective (how does this issue affect our community and what are others saying about it?). Finally, a session is held on actions to be taken.[74]

The Congressional Exchange, which promotes the use of Study Circles, is now encouraging communities that are experiencing rapid growth and development to create Study Circles in order to deal with the emerging issues. The Congressional Exchange calls the program "Smart Talk for Growing Communities." In its promotional brochure, it asks if citizens in a community are experiencing any or all of the following: "Stuck in traffic? Worried about how the community will pay for new schools and sewer systems? Watching fields being turned into subdivisions? Questioning whether [you] can afford [your] own home? Afraid to open [your] property tax bill? Puzzled by new strips of commercial and housing development? Wondering what's happening to the way of life [you] cherish?"[74] It goes on to note the positive aspects of change, including such things as a more vital economy, a new infusion of energy to civic and cultural activities, improved lifestyle afforded

by new homes and housing developments, heightened land and home values, enhanced choices, and greater convenience.

It is clear from the resurgence of methodologies for building a sense of
community (some no doubt ancient in form such as Open Space and Study
Circles), that something more democratic, participatory, and multidimensional is needed, rather than the predominant linear, top-down, hierarchical
manner of doing business, whether by governments, corporations, or institutions of learning. And, perhaps this need is a reflection of the innate desire
in all of us to return to a more "natural" way of conducting business. Could
it be that we have just forgotten the old ways that worked in the past and
are now remembering ways more consistent with natural patterns, cycles,
shapes, and forms that will produce longer lasting results and possibly a life
described as thriving, rather than one of mere survival? This question brings
us to a discussion of diversity and self-organization within systems.

Diversity and self-organization

A basic ecological principle is that diversity is directly related to stability. To
the extent that diversity is diminished, so is the stability, integrity, strength,
resiliency, or durability of any system diminished.[2] Business and industry
are learning this principle as evidenced by the ever-increasing number of
corporations diversifying their interests and activities. Built-in redundancy
is part of diversity — if one part fails, another is available to serve the same
function. The importance of protecting biodiversity in land-use planning
was discussed in Chapter 2.

This dimension of Nature's model is part and parcel of re-interpreting
waste and recognizing interdependency. Diversity of opinion, background,
skills, and abilities of people involved in the planning process for sustainable
community development is critical to the outcome. The municipal planning
process, as conducted in many places in this country, begins with the selec-
tion of a committee — usually representative and diverse. When the process
welcomes this type of diversity with the inherent potential for the clash of
differences and conflicts, the value of self-organization is understood.

Diversity and self-organization can also be seen in the creation of redundancy in the planning process. For example, using a variety of techniques
for educating and informing the public throughout the process is an attempt
to reach the broadest audience. One needs to ask, "What messages and what
array of media will be most likely to reach all segments of the community?"

Self-organization is inherent in all living systems. In biological systems,
it is called evolution. In human economic systems, it takes the form of
technological advance or social revolution. Self-organization means changing any given aspect of a system, such as adding or deleting new physical
structures, or adding or deleting negative or positive feedback loops, or flows
of information, or rules. The ability to self-organize is the strongest form of
resilience in a system; it is the ability to survive change by changing.[75]

Change is a constant in all systems, and the evolutionary process of life is a response to change. Evolution is therefore change in response to change and is a part of an ever-illusive state of balance.

On the other hand, imbalance is perceived when human-made materials, which are not easily recycled, accumulate at a faster rate than they can break down and assimilate into the Earth's crust. The result is an ever-mounting "stockpile," so to speak, of accumulating materials, some of which are hazardous to the health of the planet. Since World War II, for example, humans have produced more than 70,000 chemicals, such as DDT and PCBs. A considerable number of these substances not only spread but also accumulate in Nature, such as in the fat cells of animals and humans which cannot handle significant amounts of these chemicals. This inability of bodily cells to deal with such chemicals often results in cancer, hormonal disruptions, improper development, birth defects, and long-term genetic changes.[76]

One might therefore ask what the proverbial balance of Nature looks like. One might also ask whether we humans necessarily possess all the knowledge and skills necessary to fully judge an ecosystem to be in or out of balance. We say this because, from an ecological point of view, the balance of Nature is a constant becoming — that is, constantly being approached but never achieved. And, as earlier referenced,[1] newspaper columnist Jay Moynihan says, "Balance only exists momentarily as a set of questions that is a subset of all possible questions."

Consider, for example, that ecosystems move inevitably toward a critical state in which a minor event sooner or later leads to a catastrophic event, one that alters the ecosystem in some dramatic way. In this sense, ecosystems as portions of landscapes are dissipative structures in that energy is built up through time only to be released in a disturbance of some kind, such as a fire, flood, or landslide, in some scale ranging from a freshet in a stream to the eruption of a volcano, after which energy begins building again toward the next release of pent-up energy somewhere in time on the landscape.

Such disturbances, as ecologists think of these events, can be long term and chronic, such as large movements of soil that take place over hundreds of years (termed an earth flow), or acute, such as the crescendo of a volcanic eruption that sends a pyroclastic flow speeding down its side. (A pyroclastic flow is a turbulent mixture of hot gas and fragments of rock, such as pumice, that is violently ejected from a fissure and moves with great speed down the side of a volcano. *Pyroclastic* is Greek for "fire-broken.")

Here, you might interject that neither soil nor a volcano is a living system like a forest. So how is a forest an example of a dissipative structure? As a young Douglas fir forest grows old, it converts energy from the sun into living tissue, which ultimately dies and accumulates as organic debris on the floor of the forest. There, through decomposition, the organic debris releases the energy stored in its dead tissue. A forest is, therefore, a dissipative system in that energy acquired from the sun is dissipated gradually through decomposition or rapidly through fire.

Of course, rates of decomposition vary. A leaf rots quickly and releases its stored energy rapidly. Woody material, on the other hand, rots much more slowly, often over centuries. As the woody material accumulates, so does the energy stored in its fibers. Before the suppression of fire by such agencies as the U.S. Forest Service, fires burned frequently enough to generally control the amount of energy stored in the accumulating woody debris by burning it up, thus releasing the stored energy, which in turn protected the forest for decades, even centuries, from a catastrophic fire that would kill it.

Over time, however, a forest eventually builds up enough woody debris to fuel a catastrophic fire, such as those experienced over much of the western U.S. in recent years. Once available, the fuel requires only one or two very dry, hot years with lightning storms to ignite such a fire, which kills the forest and sets it back in succession to the earliest stage of grasses and herbs. From this early stage, a new forest again evolves toward the old-growth stage, again accumulating stored energy in dead wood, again organizing itself toward the next critical state, a catastrophic fire, which starts the cycle over.

After a fire, earthquake, volcanic eruption, flood, or landslide, a biological system may eventually be able to approximate what it once was through resilience — the ability of the system to retain the integrity of its basic relationships. But regardless of how closely an ecosystem might approximate its former state following a disturbance, the existence of every ecosystem is a tenuous balancing act because every ecosystem is in a constant state of disequilibrium from the pressure of forces outside it.

Thus, a 700-year-old forest that burned could be replaced by another, albeit different, 700-year-old forest on the same acreage. In this way, despite a series of catastrophic fires, a forest ecosystem can remain a forest ecosystem. In this sense, the old-growth forests of western North America have been evolving from one catastrophic fire to the next, from one critical state to the next.

Because of the dynamic nature of evolving ecosystems and because each system is constantly organizing itself from one critical state to another, we can only manipulate an ecosystem during part of an evolutionary cycle (through the decisions and actions derived from land-use planning) and hope that we are wise enough to care for the system in a way that may be favorable for us in the long term.

Thus, whether we like it or not, the balance of Nature is in fact being constantly achieved, although imperfectly and often in ways that cause us humans dismay and horror. Thus, while many forces are simultaneously at work, the old notion of an unequivocal, static balance of Nature will never be achieved because Nature always evokes the second law of thermodynamics, which states that the amount of energy in forms available to do useful work can only diminish over time. The loss of available energy thus represents a diminishing capacity to maintain "order," which increases disorder or entropy. When considering the notion of social-environmental sustainability, it is vital to understand that an "expenditure" of energy means the conversion of a useful or available form of energy (that with which work can be done) to a less useful or less available form.

Some forms of energy conversion, however, have problems of pollution associated with them, such as the conversion of nonrenewable fossil fuels to electricity. In the process of converting coal to electricity, pollutants, such as sulfur dioxide, are spewed into the air and carried hundreds or thousands of miles from the coal-fired power plants that produced them in a phenomenon known as acid deposition, commonly called acid rain.

Although healthy functioning ecosystems produce the vital necessities for life, an ecosystem that is compromised in such a way as to diminish its productive capacity has a diminished capacity to maintain life with unpleasant and sometimes devastating results for humans, which brings us to the human factor in the disruption of ecosystems.

Consider that the catalyst in many of the armed conflicts that took place during this century were disputes over land, which usually implied the resources contained therein, such as oil, water, or the land itself as space for growth. Even the recent conflict in Yugoslavia, where the Serbs attempted to remove the ethnic Albanians from Kosovo, their homeland, occurred because the Yugoslavian government wanted control of the rich deposits of oil, chromium, gold, nickel, platinum, coal, lead, zinc, and lignite in the province.[77]

Not only do people die as a result of such wars but damage, often severe damage, to the environment is also inevitable. If one could view such circumstances impartially, one might ask, despite the immediate injury to the environment, will the loss, which is both obvious and painful, result in less pressure on natural resources in the long term due to the loss of human life and thus future progeny? One might also ask with respect to humanity whether poverty, disease, war, carnage on the highways, murder, and the other horrific parts of life result in less demand for Nature's resources by reducing human numbers. Might it also be postulated that the loss of cultural diversity through the oppression or elimination of an entire people diminishes a form of natural capital for the rest of the world? Can we really answer these questions? Do we have the capacity — mental and otherwise — for understanding all the items that need to be added to the balance sheet when such questions are posed? Do we fully understand the ongoing process of self-organization, including evolution, and the interaction of the multitude of variables that comprise it?

We raise these questions as a way of suggesting that both the gains and losses of natural capital, including human/social capital, inevitably arise from land-use decisions and need to be incorporated into land-use planning. Accounting for natural capital in determining whether an action results in a gain or a loss requires that: (1) we determine in each instance what the natural capital is, and (2) we determine what, in our perception, constitutes a gain or loss.

Today, the evaluative process is usually tied to a form of currency Must we measure loss and profit only in terms of dollars? This measure does seem to be, by far, the easiest way to communicate to others why it is vital for our survival to stop compromising the ecological health of the planet. Because most understand wealth to be in the form of dollars rather than cultural capacity, as discussed earlier, measuring gains and losses in dollar terms, while challenging, may be the most communicative way to demonstrate losses, gains, and the "bottom line."

But is there a less transitory means to measure profit and loss than dollars, especially when many of the items on our new "balance sheet" may be elements transcending the material world — elements that would be diminished in value if measured linearly, that is, by measuring them in terms of dollars? Is there a nonlinear tool to evaluate profit and loss? If the process of evaluation is conducted as it typically is, to determine how well we are doing or whether a decision is right or wrong, is our dependence on a linear measure consistent with modeling our actions after the world of Nature?

We think that it is not. One reason why we feel this way is the fact that measuring loss or gain is becoming more complex due to the abundance of evidence that can be amassed either in support of or in opposition to a particular position or action. We are living in an Age of Information that is growing exponentially. "Evidence" or "fact," which one must remember is merely how one interprets a given set of data, can be brought to bear far more easily than in the past to either support or oppose a particular proposal, plan, or action.

Having said this, we find that when a stalemate is reached, when each side has exhausted its resources of what it considers to be valid hard data and facts, ethics begins out of necessity to play a role. The role of a judge in a legal dispute, for example, is frequently to bring ethics into the evaluation of the "loss" incurred as a result of some crime. Penalties for crimes are then tied not to any particular tangible, measurable loss, but rather to the intangible, immeasurable loss to a family, a community, or society as a whole.

Let's look at the multidimensionality of a particular decision and attempt to tie it to a net-gain model. A father decides to leave his wife and child because he discovers he has an incurable disease, does not wish to tell his family, and does not want his spouse or child to suffer the pain or financial costs of his disease. His wife is employed and has shared equally all the expenses for operating the household with her husband.

Now, if the parent proposing to leave his family were to assess the potential impact of his decision on his family, it might look like this. On the "benefit" side of this particular balance sheet, he might put the additional funds available due to decreased medical costs and lower household operating costs, the potential for closer bonding between mother and child, additional free time for the mother, and less emotional impact due to the lack of proximity of the mother and child to a dying family member. On the "cost" side of this balance sheet is the loss of a father, of a spouse, reduced income to support the child and cover household expenses, perhaps additional medical costs to cover treatment of emotional problems arising as a result of the departing father and husband, and so on. Finding the "bottom line" in this instance — ascertaining whether this was a good move on the part of the ailing parent — is really impossible to say. How can we evaluate the child's loss in terms of dollars? Wouldn't any attempt to do so diminish the meaning of this impact?

What we are suggesting in this discussion of land-use planning is that, before taking any action that affects the natural world on which we depend for survival, we must ask a multitude of questions that address both measurable and non-measurable elements. Then we must trust our judgment, intuition, and the collective wisdom to make the wisest decision.

Many checklists of sustainability and some environmental impact analyses ask such questions. They contribute to a nonlinear process to produce answers that will no doubt be challenged legally, but with no greater frequency than decisions produced by more traditional, linear, or "fact-driven" methods. We believe, however, that such nonlinear processes will better serve a community and/or the world in the long term, as opposed to a purely material measure used to evaluate the merits of a decision or action. By using a nonlinear process of evaluation, we will bring our minds and our hearts into the process. Nonlinear methods of evaluation are not only more creative but also more self-reliant because they incorporate intrinsic values and qualities, are far more elegant and multifunctional, and produce longer lasting results than do traditional linear methods. Such methods respond to an admonition of Albert Einstein, who once said, "The significant problems we face cannot be solved at the same level of thinking we used when we created them."

We posit that a solution created by a nonlinear process will be something more closely modeled after Nature. It must be further understood that a solution so derived is one that works here and now. It may require revision over time and as circumstances change, but if the solution is evaluated on a continual basis using the same multidimensional, heart-mind approach, the "problem" is less likely to appear and frighten us into using worn-out, brittle, linear, technical solutions. We cannot solve linear technological problems with linear technological solutions, just as we cannot "fix" our own dysfunctional thinking through our own dysfunctional thoughts.

Another way of viewing this concept of self-organization and balance is by examining the notion of a steady-state system. A steady-state system develops in quality as opposed to continually growing or expanding in size. A library, for example, that discards obsolete or worn volumes and replaces them with new books can be considered a steady-state system because it grows in quality by staying the same size.[78]

Self-organization occurs many times following natural disasters. In 1989, Santa Cruz, CA, experienced a significant earthquake. One of the authors was a planner for the city at that time. What followed this event was similar to the community response to several other natural disasters occurring in Santa Cruz over a 12-year period. The coming together of a community when some event affects all citizens, especially in cases where the impact creates the need for mutual assistance, demonstrates, in our opinion, the phenomenon known as self-organization. A primary characteristic of the resulting social system is its diversity.

In 1989, Santa Cruz experienced the effects of an earthquake that measured 7.1 on the Richter Scale. The similarity of experience, the shock and horror resulting from the lift and surge of an enormous force, brought the community together. It is during events like these when age, race, income, social status, and religion lose their power as divisive forces. The humanity of each person coming forward to help was all that mattered. Everyone seemed to be giving what they could. And the level of acceptance for anything anyone had to offer was high.

The story of the earthquake in Santa Cruz brings to mind a tune called "Hell and High Water," which was written by Warren Nelson for a historical musical about the town of Bayfield, WI, a small fishing village on the south shore of Lake Superior. The musical tells of a huge rainstorm and resulting flood. This poignant song illustrates that, "It seems it takes disaster and emergency, to show a town it's just one big family."[79]

Recreating the type of self-organization that occurs in a community after a natural disaster without the catalyst of a natural disaster is one goal of the planning process we are attempting to describe in this book. How can this be accomplished? A place to start is to characterize the catalyst in ways that we might translate into the planning process.

First, let us note that events other than natural disasters have drawn communities together in ways that would not occur otherwise — for example, the recent tragedy in Littleton, CO, at Columbine High School, where 12 students died as a result of two students opening fire in the high school building. What characterizes these events that create a sense of belonging, equality, mutual suffering, usefulness, cooperation, and place?

First, the event touches everyone in the community in some way, such as a sense of mutual suffering. Second, the event is easily translated into the experience of another with the resulting effect of empathy — one for another. Third, the event affects some individuals more dramatically than others and therefore some need more assistance than others. Fourth, there is a recognition that everyone has something to offer in the recovery process, if only a smile. Fifth, it is clear that the event could recur. In the case of an earthquake, aftershocks and the possibility that the major tremor was a precursor to something greater make a huge contribution to the sense of "community." Sixth, there is a sense of urgency. The time to act is now, which blurs the sense of tomorrow in the immediacy of the moment.

How can the planning process in a community recreate this type of community cohesion? First, the certainty of dramatic, impending change is the "event" that initiates the planning process, whereas the uncertainty of impending change that hangs over a community, if it chooses not to plan, is the reality that will affect everyone and may affect some in ways that are more dramatic than others.

For example, in many small towns in the region of northern Wisconsin where one of the authors lives, real estate sales are beginning to grow at a rapid pace. The heightened sales are, of course, accompanied by increasing costs. This trend in turn raises property taxes. Income in the area may not keep pace with the growth of property taxes, which stimulates the fear that people will not only be taxed out of their homes but also be forced to move, even though they may own their homes and want to stay. This is particularly true for the elderly who have resided in an area for a long time, are more likely to actually own their homes, and are less likely to have the resources to keep up with increasing property taxes. In this case, the needs of one segment of the community may be greater than the needs of a more affluent segment of the community.

The certainty of change, the uncertainty of its outcome, and the fact that change is constantly occurring may be one way of engaging the community. The invitation to become involved can be done in a way that emphasizes the importance of the contribution of all. How? By inviting all to share their vision for the future of their place. Most people in a community care about how the future of their place of residence or business unfolds. But what, one might ask, is the urgency? Why do we need to plan now? And, most importantly, how does the agency or body initiating a planning process do so in a way that draws people into the spirit of community without relying on fear as the catalyst or the "hook?"

One might, for example, point out to a community in an open invitation through news stories or in open pre-planning meetings that changes are occurring, that the impending changes will affect some citizens more than others, and that, without careful planning, the results of such changes could be a heightened sense of uncertainty, especially if there is no strong, organizing context of a shared vision to guide the collective future of the community.[49] Because people generally care about their places, the invitation is based on love for the community — not on the fear of change.

A celebration could be planned to launch the planning process, one that highlights the reasons people have chosen to live where they do. The fragility of everything that a community holds dear could help to bring poignancy to this kick-off event — a town's history, its natural wealth and beautiful features, its downtown, its favorite gathering places.

At one post-earthquake charette in Santa Cruz ("charette" is a condensed community design process led by design professionals), for example, the first activity of attendees as they entered the high school gymnasium was to show where they lived by sticking a pin in the city map. Second, after breaking into smaller groups to discuss the possibilities for the recovery of Santa Cruz's downtown, where about 60 buildings were seriously damaged or destroyed, each participant was asked to draw a heart where they felt the "heart of downtown" was. The same kind of thing can be done to engage people without having first suffered a disaster.

It is important to emphasize in the invitation that everyone's perspectives, ideas, feelings, and willingness to share their time and energy are both needed and appreciated. Questions not only need to be asked but also are an excellent place to begin the planning process: Why is our community experiencing these changes? Why did we not notice them before they reached this stage? How has growth changed our community? What are our options for addressing the issues, such as growth? In light of such questions, it must be repeatedly stressed that we, as citizens, need to help one another in order to protect that which we value in this, our tiny place on Earth, which brings up the concept of "waste."

Eliminating the concept of "waste"

"Waste" can be eliminated in two ways: by not producing it in the first place and by re-casting the perception of "waste" once it has occurred. The former method is considered in the book *Ecological Diversity in Sustainable Development*.[2] The latter is discussed in the following paragraphs.

In Nature, all so-called waste is fuel for other parts of the living systems. The word "waste," in our society, has many negative connotations, such as "a damaged, defective, or superfluous material produced by a manufacturing process; an unwanted by-product of a manufacturing process; refuse from places of human or animal habitat as in a garbage, rubbish, excrement, sewage."[3] The connotation of waste is something unwanted and thus unneeded, usually in the economic sense. Today, however, the perception of waste as a valuable and usable commodity is vital.

"Waste" is generally viewed in an affluent society as something to get rid of, to remove from sight, because it is deemed to pose problems. Waste is thus seen as valueless, something that has a cost associated with its disposal, however disposal is done. These costs are dollar costs. The costs in terms of loss of or damage to ecosystem services as a result of ostensibly "getting rid of" wastes are not counted on the balance sheet.

For example, there are the costs associated with damage to a watershed by improper operation of a land fill (a euphemism for a "garbage dump") or other forms of waste disposal; damage to a commons — the shared air of the world — from emissions caused by trucking waste from one place to another; damage to the soil from the release of various toxins that occurs during the breakdown of certain human-made substances and makes the soil unfit for agriculture and the water unsafe for human consumption. These "costs," when added to the dollar costs of disposal, form a significant sum when taken in the collective.

One would think, therefore, that the total collective costs of doing business in the current manner would send a clear message that there must be a better way, a wiser way to view "waste." By this we mean that the reuse and reintegration of "waste" into Nature's cycles would be far more prudent and safer ecologically and far more conservative of vital energy, which is, after all, what every economy is about — the allocation and cost of energy.

The Natural Step, a system developed in Sweden, offers a partial framework, based on science, for guiding "businesses, communities, academia, government entities, and individuals working to redesign their activities to become more sustainable."[80] The Natural Step addresses the need for waste conversion in two of its four "system conditions." System conditions are used in a shared mental model for problem solving. System Condition One, for example, states that "substances from the Earth's crust must not system- atically increase in nature," which means that fossil fuels, metals, and other minerals must not be extracted at a rate faster than their slow redeposit into the Earth's crust. System Condition Two states that "substances produced by society must not systematically increase in the biosphere," which means that substances must not be produced faster than they can be broken down and reintegrated into the cycles of Nature.

John Jackson, former Chair of Great Lakes United, a U.S.-Canadian environmental coalition, refrains from using the term "waste" and instead uses the phrase "valuable used materials." His report to the government of Ontario, called "Resources Not Garbage," admonishes the provincial gov- ernment to re-conceptualize waste in order to protect valuable resources, decrease the use of energy, and decrease contamination at the stage of pro- duction as well as disposal, including the release into the air, surfacewaters, and groundwaters of toxic contaminants from waste disposal facilities.[81]

Thus, to the extent that we view waste as a problem, rather than as a food or fuel for other parts of the Earth's living systems, we will continue to foul our own nest and diminish the Earth's capacity to support life upon it, including — or perhaps especially — us.

Municipal planning can be guided by the notion that waste will be minimized or noticed only when it occurs and is viewed as something potentially useful, something that will turn a profit either by its conservation in the sense of slow and wise use or in its economic conversion potential into a different, usable products. What sorts of things can possibly be viewed as wasted in a public process? Time, money, human resources, natural resources, and perhaps more if one engages one's imagination.

Time will be wasted if a particular experience is viewed as a waste of time. If, on the other hand, all experiences in the course of the planning process are considered valuable and thus attended to as valuable sources of information, time will be gained. There is, however, an all too common complaint about the waste of time and money related to planning efforts, for which there is ample evidence in the form of plans sitting idly on the shelves of planning departments, where their greatest utility is to gather dust. A complaint of this nature is a call for education, not defense, and must be viewed as an opportunity instead of an obstacle.

If all experiences are seen as useful, it is impossible for them to be viewed as a waste of time. Even if a city undertakes a very expensive planning process that leaves the community without a vision or a plan, some learning will have taken place if negativity does not override the collective ability to move forward in spite of what might be viewed as a setback. Learning experiences can sometimes be exeedingly costly in terms of both time and money, but if used as stepping stones, neither time nor money can truly be lost.

Creating a place in the planning process for all voices and the safety necessary for free expression is another way of avoiding waste. After all, what is frequently said in parking lots after public meetings or in hallways or restrooms — that which Peter Senge calls "left-column thoughts"[82] — can be lost or wasted information if not spoken to the larger group. Such thoughts may be critical to a fully informed, realistic, and meaningful vision and plan for a community.

Language plays an enormous role in our perception of the world, including our perception of something being wasted. If we use a negative word to describe something, the "thing" described becomes a negative and we feel negatively.

For example, if we say a person is wasting his or her life, the person becomes a negative, and we feel badly. This relates to the notion that we suffer to the extent that we choose to identify with our negative thoughts. In this illustration, we might suffer less or feel less badly in response to our perception of a wasted life if we were to view this person as afraid and perhaps in need of help.

If we were to lose our health or a loved one or experience a financial calamity, the challenge would become one of seeing these experiences as only part of the whole of our life and not letting them occupy a greater space than they deserve. If we cannot achieve this distance from the experience, we essentially choose to become the disease itself or, in the process, to lose our boundaries and become the departed person or become the poverty. To the extent that we choose to do this, we will suffer. The challenge is to use language internally that is positive in order for positive actions to emerge. This notion, is consistent with the words of Peter Outlaw, who said: "Watch your thoughts, they become words. Watch your words, they become actions. Watch your actions, they become habits. Watch your habits, they become character. Watch your character, it becomes your destiny."

In light of the above, it is wise to engage people with divergent ideas and politics in the planning process, people of varying ages and incomes, race and ethnicity, education and religion. In this way, we conserve rather than waste human experiences. With such a diverse group, conflict is more likely to surface, and some may view this as a negative and even as a waste of time. Conflict with civility is at times necessary, however, to arrive at a consensus of truth and must be viewed as both a catalyst and fuel for change.

In order to convert the notion of waste into usable resources as part of the planning process, we should design the process to include such things as carpooling to meetings or the use of alternative modes of transportation. People can also be asked to bring recyclable paper for note-taking to conserve trees and thus forests. Ask participants for their ideas and add these to the publicity surrounding the planning process because everything is, after all, interdependent.

Interdependency

We have already alluded to the fact that all forms of life are interrelated and thus interdependent as a co-evolving part of a dynamic system, that we cannot tamper with one part of the system without affecting the entire system itself. Eliminating the frogs from a wetland, for example, will have many effects — some understood, some not understood, and some of which we are unaware that we are unaware.

But the result of such a removal is the compromised or diminished integrity of the wetland system. The system's response will be to change in order to accommodate change itself (self-organization), but how, in what subtle ways, will the changed wetland affect related forms of life, including humans? Perhaps with this dynamic in mind, Gary Silberstein, a biologist at the University of California, Santa Cruz, noted, in a letter to a congressman in the 1970s regarding the need for measures to protect the northern California sea otter, that the destruction of any species is tantamount to burning a collection of library books, given the abundance of genetic and biological information encoded in any one species.[83]

Some will argue that our intervention in the non-human portions of the living world is part of evolution, that the disappearance of species is natural. Peter Raven, in a recent interview on National Public Radio, stated that the rate of species extinction is 10,000 times greater than ever before in the history of the planet.[84]

Interdependency describes the relationships among all components of all living systems, including human communities and societies. Recognizing this fact in the planning process will result in a greater diversity of citizen involvement. Applying this principle to the plan itself will produce a broader range of areas discussed and analyzed within the plan.

For example, a comprehensive plan typically contains the following elements: transportation, land use, economy, historic preservation, parks and recreation, housing, natural resources, open space, community facilities, and population. Are there other related dimensions of community that might be added to the list in recognition of the interdependency of all parts of the whole? What are the components of community that planning might serve for the overall well-being of the community?

Might, for example, the trusteeship of land as a biological living trust be worth examining? That is, to what extent are there privately initiated land conservation initiatives? What about an element that inventories and explores the possibilities of incentives that aid in the implementation of the plan? Community design, including architecture, is sometimes, but not always, included in comprehensive plans. Health care, including facilities for the poor and elderly, and government-sponsored community celebrations and activities that might come under the general umbrella of recreation are other possibilities. A community's cultural opportunities might also be considered.

The point here is to look carefully at both the whole and its components when planning for a community's future. New components or elements frequently surface during the visioning segment of the planning process. Someone in a town that depends heavily on tourism for his or her economic stability may, for instance, express a concern that the effects of unbridled growth in tourism itself will ultimately diminish the qualities of the town that attract the tourists in the first place. Diversification of the economy might therefore be an answer and could be covered in the economic element of the comprehensive plan, but other parts of this concern might be accounted for in an element called "Sense of Place." Be that as it may, this part of the plan could inventory what parts of the community combine to give its residents a sense of place and, more importantly, what can be done to protect, or even enhance, the qualities that visitors come from afar to experience.

chapter five

An alternative approach to comprehensive land-use planning

Thus far, we have been talking about land-use planning with a greater emphasis on the process than the end product — the plan itself. Henceforth, we will focus on a systems approach to land-use planning that applies to the process as well as to the product.

This systems approach is proposed as an alternative, possibly an interim alternative, to guide municipalities in issuing and implementing policy and regulations to control the use of land. A systems approach is ultimately intended to move government away from an authoritarian role in the use and development of land toward a more dynamic role as a service agency, where decisions are made by consensus and are guided by the community's vision. In this chapter, we will propose an alternative structure for a comprehensive plan and an array of nonregulatory approaches to implementing comprehensive plans.

Land-use planning and the notion of supply and demand

Supply-and-demand economics, in the guise of benevolent capitalism, dominates the global economy. After all, the world (especially Western industrialized society, which sets the example) has become, with the encouragement of industry and the media, a culture of never having enough, within which is fostered the modern mythology of economic growth as the panacea for poverty and provider of the utopian well-being of humanity.

Industry, business, and even government frequently resort to this model to justify an action or as an entire *modus operandi*. Supply-and-demand thinking has serious limitations, sometimes due to the misconception of both "supply" and "demand." This misconception is in turn linked to the failure to account for the multidimensional necessities of human beings and the natural world of which they are an inseparable part.

An example of the hazards that strict supply-and-demand thinking can cause, with respect to land use and development, is represented by a current power line proposal in northwestern Wisconsin. The justification for the proposed 345-kilowatt, 250-mile long power line is, predictably, consumer demand. This massive and controversial project would traverse the northwest corner of the state of Wisconsin *en route* to Wausau, WI, from Duluth, MN. From Wausau, it would distribute electricity to points south, including Illinois. Part of the controversy relates to the effects on the land of the 150-foot-wide swath that would of necessity be cut across the landscape to accommodate the extension of the power line and the potential impact of the electromagnetic field generated by the power line. A greater part of the controversy is linked to the source of the power itself, created by the flooding of 3 million acres of Pimicikamak Cree Indian traditional lands (Cross Lake region) in northern Manitoba, Canada, by Manitoba Hydro.

Unlike the dams and reservoirs in the American Southwest, water impoundments in Manitoba flood and/or make inaccessible thousands of square miles of northern forests, rivers, lakes, and muskegs. Forty-five percent of the power created by the diversion of two rivers coupled with the mechanical regulation of water levels of Lake Winnipeg goes to the U.S. Drowned trees and other accumulated vegetation prevent wildlife from reaching the shoreline of Lake Winnipeg; the local moose population has dropped, and permanent, noticeable changes have occurred to other species of animals that formerly flourished in the biotic richness of undisturbed boreal forests.[85a]

During a recent visit to the Cross Lake Manitoba Hydro project by representatives from Minnesotans for an Energy-Efficient Economy, visitors reported seeing "an ecological disaster [for which they] were unprepared."[85a] Spokesperson Michael Noble stated that the affected area is an "ecological wasteland for as far as the eye can see ... more than 50,000 square miles flooded, millions of trees ripped up and destroyed, silt-choked waters, formerly navigable waters ... rendered impassable to man, animals, and fish." On December 8, 1999, the *Winnepeg Free Press* reported on the conditions at Cross Lake in a front-page story as being "the worst situation anywhere in Canada. ...Seven residents in the community of 4000 have killed themselves in the past five months, and more than 100 others have tried as a result of the severe unemployment and despair."[85b]

The Wisconsin Public Services Commission is the public body responsible for determining the fate of the transmission line proposal. When queried about this 100-plus-year-old method for supplying power, which may become obsolete within a decade or two, the staff engineer to the Wisconsin

Public Services Commission stated that, when consumers create the demand, it is the duty of the Wisconsin Public Services Commission is to find ways to fulfill it.[86] This is an age-old hackneyed refrain.

"Supply" in this proposal is interpreted by the Wisconsin Public Services Commission to mean electricity and, following suit, "demand" is interpreted to be *for* electricity. Our view is that supply and demand in this instance are too narrowly defined, which serves to perpetuate a public utility model that will ultimately create more problems — in both time and space — in the long term than are solved in the short term.

In the case of electricity, "supply" is comprised of the finite natural resources that make the production of electrical power possible — coal, wood, or, in the case of Manitoba Hydro, the lands and the life they support that are necessary for hydropower, which amounts to 30,000,000 acres or 50,000 square miles over a period of 22 years.[85a] In addition, the "demand" may be seen as a demand for warm homes, cold food, television programming, or other services.

A large European manufacturer of home appliances, Electrolux, is an example of an industrial company that has shifted from being product oriented to being service oriented. Instead of focusing on refrigerator design, Electrolux focuses on the best means for providing their customers with cold food. Electrolux is therefore committed to the principle that environmental protection is imperative to the long-term survival of the individual, the corporation, and society in general. To honor the principle of environmental protection, Electrolux takes a holistic view of both product and production and does a complete life-cycle analysis of each product, from the handling of raw materials and manufacturing to distribution and recycling.[87] Electrolux's holism views both supply and demand as being inseparable parts of a dynamic system — Nature — of which we also are an inalienable part.

The simplified principle of supply-and-demand that is driving the global economy is inherent in the economic model described earlier, in which people or households supply certain services in the form of labor, entrepreneurship, and revenue to business and industry, which in turn provide products and services to the "households" part of this two-part model. And, as we discussed earlier, the missing part of the model can be collectively thought of as the free or inherent services contributed by each and every ecosystem.

If we thus add the free (or, more precisely, inherent) ecosystem services to the traditional two-part economic model of supply-and-demand, as well as the requirements of all three components, we will have a more useful model that clearly represents what in fact is happening in time and space as we humans interact with the rest of Nature. The general lack of recognition of this multidimensionality, however, continues to have humans operating under a dangerous illusion of somehow being in control of Nature and thus having a limitless supply.

So, how do we add necessities to this three-part environmental-economic model, which is composed of humans, business/industry/institutions, and

Nature — each with requirements, production of "wastes," and a scope of services that are inextricably interrelated with one another? By the same token, one might ask how the characteristics of inputs and outputs associated with each component are to be accounted for.

In the case of humans, we might address values as the basis for perceived necessities. In the case of Nature, we can only assume, through the results of scientific study, what might be required by other life forms and natural systems to maintain their health and integrity. This being the case, we can only address environmental constraints, or upper thresholds that we agree must be held inviolate.

How does the three-part environmental-economic model guide the way we alter landscapes to meet our perceived necessities?

In conventional land-use planning, the land is the commodity, or "supply," and "demand" is, at least on the surface, that for which the land is used: housing, offices, manufacturing plants, open space, public utilities, streets and sidewalks, agricultural fields, and so on. The challenge alluded to earlier is to see beneath the ostensible "supply" and "demand" in order to assess environmental constraints, human values (and perceived necessities), and, therefore, desired services. In so doing, we can thus more easily access alternative ways of supplying demand. To determine underlying demand, we need to ask, "What service is actually desired?" Demand is then restated in terms of perceived necessities and/or values that are required to achieve a given standard of living.

For example, we might see the demand for housing as the need for shelter, privacy, cohabitation, a place to cook and eat, and so on. Shelter can be provided in numerous ways, from the "beginner mansions" that can be seen springing up in suburban Denver, CO, to co-housing, which enables families to have not only their privacy but also the benefits of being with others in a shared space for dining, cooking, and/or recreational activities. Co-housing, according to Stella Tarnay, editor of the journal *CoHousing*, is "a progressive New Age movement, and in other ways as old as apple pie."[88] To view consumer demand in terms of perceived human necessities and the various services that could meet those necessities opens up a greater range of possibilities in terms of land use and development.

Another example is the demand for office buildings. Viewing this demand as the need for places to conduct business opens up many more possibilities than simply viewing the demand as a generic need for a new or expanded office building. Telecommuting (working out of one's own home) is rapidly surfacing as an alternative to the necessity of employees having to commute to and from work by automobile or mass transit and, of course, requiring an office at the end of the commute with the necessary office equipment and other infrastructure, as well as the pollution resulting in a certain contribution to air pollution in transit. Now consider that telecommuting could someday drastically alter the demand for land on which to construct and maintain office buildings. Also, consider the effects of electronic commerce, or e-commerce, on the potential future demand for land, not to mention the potential effect on energy consumption.

The demand for open space, if viewed as the need for places to experience a refuge of quiet, solitude, and peace in an open landscape uninterrupted by human developmental artifacts, could likewise be supplied by innovations in the design of a residential development or a commercial-industrial complex. Experiences of "open space" might, for example, be afforded in places other than, say, a greenbelt or an open transition area between a city and its suburbs. All of which is to say that we must begin to understand a more complex array of perceived human necessities and plan with this in mind.

What do we mean by human necessities?

The things humans consider basic necessities of life cannot easily be characterized once they are teased out of, and thus seen as independent of, the cultural context in which they were formulated.[89] Perceived necessities are modified in myriad ways by the values, customs, and traditions of their parent culture. And it is these very modifications, imposed as they are by time, place, and tradition, that make it difficult to speak with assuredness of "basic human necessities." One could speak confidently about such basic necessities only if the essence of humanity could be detached from the very characteristics that are unique to humanity itself, characteristics that are, according to author Jeremy Seabrook, "both the gift and the curse of any given culture."[89]

Because societies grow organically, our human emotions, sentiments, and faith germinate in and grow out of the perceived material realities of our daily lives. Human societies have always made sacred that which is useful to them, whether it be animists worshipping the trees and forest that sustain them or agrarian societies praying to their gods of seeds and harvest. Certainly one difference between us in Western industrialized society and the animists or agrarians is that money is seen as the root of our survival, the supreme guarantor of our well-being.

The answer to the prayers of meeting our rich Western industrialized needs has become enormously convoluted as a function of the capitalistic market, which, of course, does not respond to real human necessities but rather the flow of monetary transactions. And the market responds only to the power of purchase, which means those who have money can fulfill their whims, while those without cannot even acquire that which is vital to their physical survival.

Some necessities, such as those intrinsic to the spiritual fulfillment of the human soul, can neither be satisfied by the market nor twisted in such a way as to appear in concert with goods and services deemed by the market as vital to human well-being. Such necessities not only become invisible in society but also lie just beneath the skin of the very society that denies them; therefore, people turn in vain to consumerism, all the while wondering why a sense of fulfillment, a sense of "enoughness" eludes them.

What, you might ask, are the human necessities that a rich market economy, such as ours in the U.S., suppresses? There are two primary ones: creativity and meaning. Creativity is the response to our own needs of helping ourselves personally and helping others through our own efforts, to give of our own substance, to invest the personal gift of our ideas, our toil, our sweat in the collective effort of communal life. Unfortunately, such a collective endeavor as community has been largely disgraced and defiled in the U.S. by our legacy of and national pride in our extreme individualism.

Indeed, business people assure us (through a continual, intrusive blitz of advertising and media hype) that being able to find meaning in life is something that the market not only provides but is also the very source of the meaning that we as humans seek. If we listen to the advertising, we are to find in buying the sense of personal significance, community, and spiritual meaning that are as much the essence of being human as are the physical necessities of food and shelter. But to substitute consumerism for spiritual transcendence is to become the quintessential George F. Babbitt of Sinclair Lewis' novel.

To acknowledge some of these suppressed human necessities when planning for sustainable community development is to accept that it is not only the poor but also the rich who require liberation from their yoke of chronic insufficiency and want. With the latter, however, it is liberation from the hidden, inner poverties tied to an outer existence in material wealth. While many would smile at such a statement, thinking the rich "have it made," one might consider the addictions of all kinds, including drugs and alcohol; the suicides, murders, and mutilations; the fragility of relationships; the breakdown of families and associations; and the isolation and fear of one another. They affect the rich as well as the poor because they are the complex of symptoms characteristic of the pathogens that arise when the market is elevated above the humanity of society, when humanity itself is pressed into service of the economy through institutions that put the creation of monetary wealth — the money chase — over the well-being of people and their environment.

Once we have learned to fulfill our own basic necessities, which has much to do with wise planning for sustainable human communities, to enjoy the inner security of a modest and safe sufficiency ("enoughness") we will no longer succumb to the kind of competition that destroys both human cultures and the environments upon which they depend (including our own) to feed the perceived need for perpetual economic growth at the expense of our very survival. With this in mind, we turn now to a discussion of "demand" in terms of a more complex array of perceived human necessities.

Understanding demand in terms of a more complex array of perceived human necessities will help us find alternative ways to deliver the desired services

To analyze supply, relative to a particular demand, we need to ask what built-in, nonnegotiable constraints impose limits on the perceived supply? In the three-part model above, services performed by all parts of the model can be both intrinsic and extrinsic and thus quantifiable or nonquantifiable. For instance, the beauty and inspiration provided by a national forest cannot be measured linearly or perhaps measured at all; therefore, the descriptive model proposed is not, for this very reason, value free or predictive. It is, however, precisely because of the model's dynamic and transitory nature that it maximizes our potential to discover heretofore unseen relationships within and among its three components.

In the case of land for human use, we need to respect the diverse array of structures and functions of a healthy ecosystem which provide both goods and services to humanity. Ecosystem *structures* include the structure of food chains, the characteristics of soil, the composition of species within plant and animal communities, and the complex structure of such nonliving matter as large woody debris, which, ironically, is more alive in many ways than was the live tree.[57,60] Ecosystem *functions*, on the other hand, include biological productivity, decomposition, hydrologic flux and storage, and biogeochemical cycling and storage. Ecosystem *goods* include food, construction materials, and fiber for fabric in addition to medicinal plants, tourism, recreation, and wild genes with which to maintain the hybrid vigor of domestic plants and animals. Although we discussed ecosystem *services* earlier,[90] additional services include the biophysical regulation of climate, maintenance of the gaseous composition of the atmosphere, and storage and cycling of essential nutrients.

By asking to what extent any of these structures, functions, goods, and services would be compromised in the process of developing a piece of land, we could set constraints to development that would protect the land for both present and future generations. This approach is intended to be more consistent with systems thinking and thus more consistent with sustainable community development, which in turn is based on the interrelatedness and interdependency of the parts to the whole. After all, a system, any system, is defined by the total functioning of its parts — not by its structural components in isolation of one another.

Structural components of the comprehensive plan

Some states, such as California, mandate not only comprehensive planning but also the specific elements of the comprehensive plan. Mandated elements frequently include such subjects as transportation, land use, housing, preservation of historic sites, open space, economy, and natural resources, all of which must fit together in an overall structure.

Overall structure

The elements of a comprehensive plan represent an understandable and rational division of community requirements for which a vision, goals, objectives, and strategies are developed to implement the plan. An alternative framework for such a plan is one in which the elements are more closely tied to community values and a wider array of perceived necessities for both the human and non-human communities. Such a structure is intended to be dynamic and organic, or "a complex structure of interdependent and subordinate elements whose relations and properties are largely determined by their function in the whole."[3]

To achieve such a structure, it is necessary to apply systems thinking, which involves focusing on the unity of the functional whole rather than on individual parts in isolation of one another. It has been said and oftentimes proven that failing to understand the connection among things produces solutions today that become problems tomorrow.[91]

Thus, when creating a comprehensive plan that is intended to guide a community toward the realization of its vision, the "whole" is the community in reciprocal relationship with its surrounding landscape, and the "parts" of the community are the interactive, interdependent elements.

The "state of the system" or "state of the community" is described by whatever material and non-material "standing stock" is of importance in the community.[75] For example, the amount of open space with public access, the absence of visible air pollution, trust in public officials, and the number of households above the poverty line may all be matters of community concern ranking high on the list of values. These could also be seen as indicators of community well-being. Useful indicators are clearly related to some value, measurable, sensitive to change, and generally comprehensible.

Later, in the implementation segment of the comprehensive plan, indicators can be used to determine the extent to which a value is being retained or compromised. We will discuss indicators further on in this chapter, but first we must address the role of values.

The role of values

In developing a comprehensive plan, identification of community values is an essential first step. Value is defined as "something (a principle or quality) intrinsically valuable or desirable."[3] Finding out what citizens care about is vital to a community's future. These concerns frequently fall into categories; a suggested three-part categorization of values is social, ecological, and economic. These values can serve as the present, nonnegotiable parameters or criteria for organizing the elements of the comprehensive plan and also serve to guide the spirit and content of the plan.

Community values can also be understood as those things that connect a person to "place" and, when retained, continue to feed and nurture that sense of place in a community. Identification and recognition of community values also set the stage for community involvement in the creation of policies, laws, and regulations that are both meaningful and functional. The following model describes a cyclical process of community involvement and self-regulation tied to community values.

In a Progressive Community Planning model, community values are linked to a sense of place, which is linked to community cohesiveness, which creates community involvement and collaboration, which produce meaningful policy and laws to guide land use that are tied back into community values. It is the explicit intent of this Progressive Community Planning model to demonstrate that trust is fostered through the formation of responsive policies and laws.

Lack of trust in public officials, and government in general, is a common feature of society today. The lack of trust in public officials and government may occur because trust is something that can only be generated through actions that genuinely respond to the community values expressed by the citizenry. Although trust depends to some extent on shared symbols, language, and desires, trust is earned when there is evidence that one's attitudes, thoughts, and actions are consistent with the promises or commitments that one makes. In short, one is a votary for the truth — one's word is one's bond, and one's actions are evidence of the authenticity of that bond. Trust is also built upon reciprocal self-disclosure,[92] which is discussed later under "Mining for meaning — obtaining community values."

Diversity is at the hub of the Progressive Community Planning model, as it relates to all parts of the cycle. Collaboration, tied to diversity, will theoretically produce the greatest number of possible solutions. Adversarial means of problem-solving produce a limited range of solutions as opposed to those achievable through collaboration, according to former U.S. Secretary of Labor Robert Reich, who went on to say that there is a space between actual and potential solutions that can only be occupied when adversaries venture into it together.[93] Either party alone cannot occupy this space because it is a place where cooperation, not rugged individualism, is the quality that both characterizes it and makes it functional.[93] In this sense, the Progressive Community Planning model, with diversity at the hub and collaboration as an essential step toward raising the level of consciousness in land-use planning, could help to counter a feature of our culture that defeats community well-being — the American love affair with "rugged individualism."

Noted author and philosopher Barry Lopez commented on this feature of our society in an interview with Kenneth Margolis.[94] Lopez stated that he attempts, in his writing, to assist readers in their understanding of the landscape "as not only something that is living but [also] something that includes us and upon which we are subtly dependent. In a profound, dynamic, and spiritual way, we have created, particularly in North America in the last 200 years, a culture of independent people... ." Although, continued Lopez, the price of such independence is unknown, we find the accounting to rapidly become obvious through such things as social violence and indifference toward one another, as well as the myriad environmental problems that each generation seems quite willing to compound for personal gain before passing the baton of consequences to the next generation — and in many cases to all in the future.

That said, conflict is a welcome part of the process in our model of Progressive Community Planning, and collaboration is essential. Further, we believe this model leads to less regulation because, in our experience, citizen involvement and the need for regulation may be inversely and linearly related: the greater the involvement, the less need there is for regulation, which is one of the goals of planning that we are proposing in this chapter. To fulfill this goal, however, we must consider the elements of a comprehensive plan.

Elements of the comprehensive plan

If we model the comprehensive plan after an ecological system, what are its component parts? To begin, we need to describe the system. One way of describing a system is to deal with the elements of that particular system, which would include identifying its composition, structures, functions, and services.

In a community, such as a town or city, there are actual physical structures (such as buildings and bridges), social structures (such as a school system, economy, and government), and ecological structures (such as soil characteristics, floodplains, wildlife corridors), and so on. Not only are parts of each structure interactive within the structure itself but also the structures as whole entities interact with one another. In addition, each structure provides specific functions in goods, products, and services. The type and degree of interaction and the actual number of variables involved are probably beyond human understanding. But recognition and acceptance of interdependency and the complexity of the whole are possible and important if we want our planning process, implementation, and its outcome to reflect Nature.

This essentially represents an ecosystem approach to land-use planning. According to Henry Diamond and Patrick Noonan, authors of *Land Use in America*, the ecosystem concept could, in an ideal world, provide a framework for defining domains of land-use planning and management.[90] Although the ecosystem approach is criticized because of its fluidity and the lack of rigid operational definition, this fluidity is precisely its greatest virtue, according to Diamond and Noonan, who stress that an ecosystem concept recognizes that the goods and services depend on processes and that the artificial boundaries of jurisdiction and/or ownership we inscribe on the land often have little relationship to these processes. Diamond and Noonan go on to say that the ecosystem concept helps identify not only which patterns of land use are likely to entail conflicts but also which citizens must be involved in the resolution of those conflicts.

We propose that, in developing a comprehensive plan, each element contain the following: (1) a statement of perceived necessities and values stated broadly enough to encompass the requirements for integration of human and non-human living systems, (2) a description of the current state of the particular component of the community system (composition, structures, functions, and services), (3) an analysis of what is working and what is not and why, (4) what external conditions offer opportunity or pose threats, and (5) a statement of goals, objectives, policies, and outcomes. In addition, the results of this planning process should include subplans for implementation, monitoring, and periodically revisiting the vision statement and parts 1 through 4. Thus, the planning we are recommending, as an ongoing process, is really a way of thinking. The plan is never either perfect or complete.

What distinguishes the format we are recommending from the conventional format of most comprehensive plans is the accounting for the structure, function, goods/products, and services of both the human and non-human components of the system when designing a desired outcome for the human future. Typically, a comprehensive plan has an element called "environmental quality" that primarily defines constraints to development. In the proposed comprehensive planning format, ecological considerations, including constraints, are built into each element of the plan. Further, this approach places a strong emphasis on community values, both broadly speaking and in association with each element of the comprehensive plan.

Developing a comprehensive plan

Throughout, it is important to provide clear and understandable explanations for each part of the process and to emphasize creativity, innovation, and imagination rather than blindly following prescribed planning steps. It is also important to make sure that all participants agree on certain ground rules to create a meaningful process and to build resilience into decision-making. Some suggested ground rules would be to: (1) focus on issues and not personalities; (2) share all relevant information; (3) use the consensus process; (4) agree on the definition of significant terms or words; (5) when stating a problem, offer a solution; and (6) disagree openly in the meeting rather than leaving discussion of such matters for the parking lot after the meeting.

In a recent presentation, Darrell Morrison, landscape architect from the University of Georgia at Atlanta, used four words to characterize the landscape plans that he believes his clients are seeking: mystery, complexity, coherence, and legibility.[95] Might these words also apply to the world in which many humans would choose to live — a world with contrasting features that, when in balance, provided the necessary sustenance for the human body, mind, and spirit?

A community's comprehensive plan should capture the essence of what people living in a place would like to sustain. A community's plan for its future should therefore be characterized by community values. When developing a comprehensive plan tied to community values, creativity, imagination, and innovation are useful tools to access. How do we help communities to think outside of their self-imposed box? How can we help communities access their creative, imaginative, and innovative selves in order to maximize the usefulness, meaning, and community-wide importance of the plans they create?

We believe, as alluded to above, that we should start by considering where people are in their personal growth and development and the things they care about — the intrinsic qualities they hold dear about their communities. After all, shared personal values become community values. Values are personal standards by which we judge behavior or events to be right or wrong, good or bad, fair or unfair, just or unjust. Values are generally taught to us at an early age, but they can also come from later experiences and from introspection at different stages in one's life. Openly expressed values frequently sound noble and good, but really understanding other people's values is critical to understanding why they feel the way they do as well as to knowing how to effectively use public comment.[69]

Values and needs are closely related, in that the former underlie the latter. Examples of values are control, freedom, rationality, private enterprise, freedom of speech, privacy, and so on. Some values are more fundamental in that other values are derived from them. The rights to privacy, to bear arms, and to enjoy freedom of speech, for example, derive from the general concept of individual freedom.

Values are thoughts and play a critical role in creating our realities. And, it has been said that for every thought there is an effect; that thoughts precede our visceral response to the outside world and therefore our perception of the world. Values give meaning to our experience of the world. Based on our values, we judge something as good or bad, right or wrong, etc., then, based on the meaning we attach to an event or the behavior of another person, we feel such things as being afraid, happy, annoyed, or sad.

Because most data from the public are value-laden, it is important to assess one's own values if one is to be open to what others have to say and to listen more objectively. James Creighton, in his *Citizen Participation/Public Involvement Skills Workbook*,[69] warns that the bulk of public comment will be general and emotional. It will be an important source of information about values people want applied in the situation, but it may lack specificity. Organized interest groups, on the other hand, have the commitment and resources to translate their values into specific, concrete proposals. As a result, there is a tendency on the part of agencies to view the data from interest groups as "valuable" while regarding the data from the general public as "over-emotional and illogical."[69]

Further, our interpretation of public comment as over-emotional and illogical may be tied to a conflict of the expressed views with our own system or of the agency we represent, or both. Creighton advises that, "Any system of public involvement must value emotional data from the general public as a valuable source of information about values or it will build a bias into the public involvement for the kind of specific, documented contribution that can only come from the organized interests."[69]

Without permission to express one's feelings, emotions, and sense of values and the safety to do so, how is the planning process going to have any social validity, let alone sustainability, in a democratic society? Kill the processes that make and keep a society free, and that society will wither like a flower's blossom in a hot wind. Values, and the feelings and emotions they represent, are critical to wise planning because they build nonlinearity into the process of determining the future of one's sense of place.

Asking people what they value about their community, what is important to them, is a way of truly determining their perceived needs — those that go beyond the basic necessities of survival. Needs determined in this manner are more likely to reach the needs often secreted in the privacy of one's heart and thus frequently overlooked in standard practices of governing or managing people. For example, many communities have permitted vast numbers of fast-food, drive-through restaurants to line their commercial thoroughfares. Many people, especially families, value this quick and reasonably inexpensive source of meals; some say they need to have fast-food restaurants so they can "grab a bite to eat" on the way to work or run errands on their lunch hour and have a "meal on the run."

What are the potentially deeper needs being met by the conveniences of fast-food restaurants? Affordability leaves funds for other things and leaves a person feeling "wealthier." Assistance in doing more than one thing at a time (eating while driving in order to run errands) could help one's self-esteem through the resulting sense of accomplishment, winning the praise of others, being seen as a better mother or spouse, and so on.

Perhaps marketing in general attempts to link these two related human needs — material or external wealth and internal wealth in the form of self-esteem — and capitalize on the human inclination to look to the outside, material world to fulfill needs not met from within. If we simply and gently venture forth with this understanding during the planning process, to see what people are really looking for in life, we may be able to open up and call upon creative, out-of-the-box solutions that meet needs in healthy, humanitarian, environmentally sound, and truly economical ways. By encouraging thinking systematically, honoring differences, and looking for common ground, we may also further this process of getting at real needs.

This approach to comprehensive planning — dealing as deliberately as possible with people's deepest values and needs — is intended to open up a wider array of options for realizing a community's vision, ways and means that are imaginative — creative solutions that are elegant and tend toward the ever-elusive win-win situation and perhaps are even cost-free. Be that as it may, setting the stage for planning is critically important.

Setting the stage for planning

Properly setting the stage for planning is critical to the overall planning process. It represents an important part of leadership: knowing your audience, knowing their sense of place, and knowing their history.

Setting the stage for planning involves gathering all available information about a community that is reasonable within time and cost constraints. Materials to gather include recent census data, any longitudinal studies on community demographics, previous comprehensive plans or planning studies, economic studies, maps, city budgets for the past 5 years, any technical or scientific studies relative to the community's health and well-being, and any information that describes existing conditions. A view of a community's history is usually available in concise form, through the local historical society, in public documents, or even in previous comprehensive plans.

During this phase of planning, with the help of the community's elected and hired officials, identify people in the community who are important to interview; these people need to represent a cross-section of the community. Interviewing key people in the community is a multipurpose activity that helps the planner-facilitator obtain what we call an issues-actors map of the community. Through one-on-one interviews, we can gather information about both surface and subsurface issues, concerns, ideas for change, and the existence of others in the community who might be helpful in providing a perspective and deeper knowledge of the community.

Simultaneously, maps not already available should be prepared. The geographic information system (GIS) makes possible the mapping of any type of data that are available. Maps to gather include a community's zoning map, land-use map, soils map, wetlands-floodplains map, maps of other environmental constraints (fault lines, for example), demographics map, functional classification map (streets), a map of street conditions, and so on. All the gathered information can be used as reference materials during the planning process, as well as for development of and inclusion in the plan document itself.

All of the activities associated with the planning process should be made public through press releases, community website announcements, etc. Informing as well as educating the citizenry throughout the planning period will help to ensure and/or encourage the citizens' continued involvement beyond the development and adoption of the plan.

In addition to announcing meetings and issuing interim progress reports, keeping an interactive website up to date and/or creating a newsletter can be very effective in keeping the community engaged in the planning process. By visiting with the editor or manager of the local newspaper, it might be possible to initiate an ongoing column or display piece that, in addition to keeping the community abreast of the planning process, defines planning jargon, or contains pithy or provocative quotes that affirm the need for planning for one's community.

In these early phases of the planning process, a community survey, designed with the help of the citizen planning advisory team, would help create the information base necessary for creating a useful and meaningful plan. There are many models for these types of surveys, and software for manipulating the data is available. During the early stages of the planning process, open meetings with the community, where citizens feel safe to express their ideas and feelings, are essential to creating the plan for the community's future. When have we attracted enough people? Should there be a specified percentage-of-the-community threshold required for moving forward? Or should representativeness be the determining factor? These are questions to ask early in the process. Earlier in the book, we discussed the importance and process of attracting a diverse group to such meetings.

Step 1: mining for meaning — obtaining community values

A nonlinear planning process is assured where individual and community values play a vital role. To achieve competency at the level of a group is to act in meaningful and purposeful ways, and recognition of individual values is an early and important first step.

Failing to bridge the knowledge gap between planner and citizen is a common flaw in community planning. Transactive planning, as purported by John Friedman, in *Retracking America: A Theory of Transactive Planning*, emphasizes mutual learning and dialog where the "scientific knowledge of the planning expert is joined with the deeply personal, experiential knowledge of the client."[96] In Friedman's model, the joining of two distinct modes of knowing will guide community action. This interaction requires mutual self-disclosure of values, and, absent this kind of disclosure, "messages may be exchanged, but the relevant meanings are not effectively communicated."[96]

The language of planners is conceptual and intended to present the results of research — findings that can be reproduced. It is a kind of knowing quite unlike the community members' kind of knowing, which is tied to personal experience and is less systematic and orderly than the processed knowledge of the planner.

Viewing both kinds of knowledge nonhierarchically and as equally essential in the planning process is key to bridging the knowledge-action gap. All of this requires each individual participating in the process to remain open to others, to accept differences and conflict as necessary and probable, to stay on the lookout for common ground, to stay in the present, and to retain our various and competing individual dimensions of intellect, morals, emotions, and empathies in mutual tension. A tall order, but truly the active ingredients in maintaining relationships and therefore the possibility of productive action.

This role of values in the planning process is further amplified by Ralph Keeny's *Value-Focused Thinking: A Path to Creative Decision Making.*[97] Values are described through the individual and group process of discovering the thinking or reasoning behind desired areas, where the need for change is perceived. Values surface through questions addressing desired outcomes and why a specific outcome is important: "For most public problems, values, rather than facts, are the aspect of the problem about which many members of society will have knowledgeable viewpoints. Discussion of the details of the consequences of various alternatives often depends on technical and complex concepts from various professional fields. Hence, without discussion of values, many people are excluded from participation and others are limited to minor contributions."[97]

While values can range wildly within any given group of people, finding the common ones — the common ground — is key to bridging the gap between knowledge and action. Discovery will only occur through face-to-face communication and by "staying in the conversation," so to speak, following the principles set forth above, thus uniting the processed knowledge of the planner with the experience-based knowledge of the community member.

Tapping into individual values can be accomplished in a number of ways at the very beginning of the process. One way is to ask people to list five or six reasons why their community is important to them. Citizens participating in the process of city planning in Fort Collins, CO, in 1997 were asked to voice their most deeply held values. These core values then became the basis for the vision, goals, and actions.

Stated values cannot be prioritized or separated from one another. They are mutually *inclusive*. In Fort Collins, for example, they form the foundation for how the citizens want to work, live, learn, and plan for the city for the next 20 years. The four core values of the plan for Fort Collins are "sustainability, fulfillment, fairness, and choices."[40]

By "sustainability," the citizens mean the long-term social, environmental, and economic health of the community. For Fort Collins, this translates into "quality human-scale urban design, energy-efficient building practices, economic health, diversity of housing, public safety, environmental protection, and mobility...."[40]

"Fulfillment" is defined as the availability of opportunities for experiences that are culturally, recreationally, socially, and learning oriented, the existence of a distinctive urban environment with avenues established to connect the citizens to the natural environment through a system of open spaces. "Fulfillment" also includes an emphasis on providing alternatives to the automobile as a means of transportation.[40]

"Fairness" implies open government, the opportunity for participation in planning and decision-making, safe and affordable housing, economic and employment opportunity, equal access, and a wide range of community services. Finally, to the people of Fort Collins, "choices" means the opportunity for people to shape their own environment tempered by a recognition of the needs of the broader community. "Choices allow us to buy goods and services where we want, have places of quiet repose next to places of bustling activity, have quiet streets and homes, and have offices with access to the global market," and so on.[40]

The most important statement made in the city plan, with respect to the description of core values, is probably: "In Fort Collins, we enjoy life, rather than merely exist."[40] Values thus set the stage for what a community wants and its perceived needs. It is critical to understand these values when moving to the next step of creating a vision.

Step 2: creating a community vision

Creating a community vision can take many forms. When working with the City of Ashland, WI, in the creation of a their comprehensive plan, one of the authors, Jane, adapted a technique suggested by Geoffrey Ball and Associates,[98] a California-based consulting firm. The author had recently moved from the Monterey Bay on the coast of California to Ashland, a city of 8000 on the shore of Lake Superior. The cultural, climatic, and demographic shift was significant, and she welcomed the challenge of being a planner in a place so unlike the place from whence she had come. The 30-member citizen planning group, appointed by the mayor to develop a comprehensive plan, was extremely diverse, ranging from retired ore dock and railroad workers to hospital and college administrators, small and large business owners, political activists, and housewives.

Prior to doing this work, the author had visited with as many of the "main actors" in the community as possible — those acknowledged leaders, as well as long-time community activists, and then some folks that had just been around for a long time and were well known in Ashland. The purpose was not only to get her bearings and learn as much about the community as possible before venturing forth in guiding development of a comprehensive plan but also to disarm any fears someone in the community might have about her. After all, she was indeed an "outsider" in a part of a world where one remains somewhat suspect until they have lived in the community for at least 20 years.

Thus, she found herself, fresh from California, bearing a Jewish surname, driving a Japanese car (which stood out in a City Hall parking lot dominated by General Motors), a female in a mostly male-led town and recently hired to guide them in community planning. She felt that there was significant potential for community members to be skeptical, as it seemed that many older people in Ashland had either not traveled or traveled very little and therefore had rather limited views of the potential for change in their town. In addition, many seemed unaware of the forces from outside of their community that might cause rapid and unwanted change in Ashland. And, finally, many remembered the industrial past and the boom town that Ashland once was, with an abundance of jobs and activity, prosperity, and national prominence. This was a past that for some merited resurrection.

With the above in mind, the author's job, as she saw it, was to establish trust and to reassure those with whom she visited that she was not bringing any particular template to the planning process, that she could not help but be influenced by her many years as a planner in a very different place, but that she would guarantee them an open process, where all points of view were welcome.

After an initial orientation of the planning task force to the job at hand, the group undertook a visioning process, which, by the way, was not preceded by a process of soliciting values (the author's understanding of the process did not include that step at the time). As an introduction to the visioning process, an exercise was used in which the group was asked to imagine that they had been to a beautiful exotic place (Tahiti, perhaps), where they had lived very comfortably. They had been in touch with a number of friends and relatives in the community, who reported that some wonderful and significant changes had taken place in Ashland but provided no details. The group was left with only their imaginations to determine what those changes actually were. At this point, each member of the task force completed the story by jotting down their ideas about what they would have liked those changes to have been and to elaborate further on how they would like their community to change.

Next, individuals formed smaller groups to share their personal "visions" and form a collective "vision" to bring back to the larger group. Ball suggests that each group present a symbol to accompany their vision because symbols often reach beyond words.[98] A list of at least five to seven suggestions for inclusion in a shared vision were requested as part of each group report to the whole gathering. This sharing of ideas is an important function in that it helps participants become more aware of the amount of commonality that exists with the group as a whole — a magic moment in which perspectives change about what is possible.

Following the magic moment, one member of each group is chosen to be part of a subcommittee to summarize all the data and develop a symbol for the vision. With data summarized and a symbol in hand, a meeting is called at which the summary is reviewed by the full group that adds, modifies, or revises elements or parts of the vision. Once consensus is reached, the group signs the vision statement as a record of its acceptance.

At this point it is useful to explain the value of modeling our activities after Nature and how the comprehensive plan itself could be guided by certain ecological principles.

Modeling the plan after Nature

These principles should be offered for discussion and evaluation by the group, as they are intended to set the stage for systems thinking and/or simply encourage participants to think of the community in terms of the whole when focusing on its individual parts. In a well-designed comprehensive plan, linkages between various components are made clear. Consider the notion of waste.

No waste. The plan should demonstrate that the community can, in its future, make use of all waste to fuel other systems and that, to the extent humanly possible, feedback loops mimicking Nature will be created and/or restored. This can, for example, translate into what the Rocky Mountain Institute calls "plugging the leak;" that is, developing a local economy where purchasing power cycles within the community as much as possible, thus continually recycling the energy represented by the money spent.[99] The plan can feature strategies for greening existing industry, attracting new green industry, and incentives for retrofitting existing business, industry, and institutions to operate more sustainably, all in that portion of the plan designated for economic development. Recycling, repair, and recovery can also be emphasized under economic development.

Planning for alternative modes of transportation — such as bicycle, pedestrian, and mass transit — will illustrate the attempt to diminish the amount of waste in the community, as air pollution created by automobile exhaust represents a waste product of fuel combustion. "No waste" or "resources, not garbage" could in fact be a major theme of a city's comprehensive plan, which naturally leads to interdependency.

Interdependency. The scope and range of the elements that comprise a comprehensive plan are as important as how they relate to one another. When we begin with consensus on the understanding that everything is interrelated, the task becomes one of discovering connections that may not be readily apparent.

One must consider, for example, how in the comprehensive plan does transportation relate to population? The necessities of transportation are of course directly tied to the demographics of the population. By way of illustration, if a large number of school-age children live in the community, the plan should accommodate bike routes, both on- and off-street. On the other hand, should a major portion of the community be elderly, then adequate means of transit for the elderly must be included in the transportation element of the plan.

A service that was offered in the city of Washburn, WI, is an excellent model of the latter case. At one time, the local historical museum owned a vintage Packard, which had a lovely taxi logo painted on its front doors. Anyone in the community could call the museum and request a ride, at no cost, any time during operating hours of the museum. Although the large elderly population in Washburn particularly enjoyed this service, a variety of people used it, which brings us to diversity.

As stated above, diversity of voice must and will be apparent in a comprehensive plan created through an all-inclusive planning process. Diverse elements, such as those described earlier, are the hallmark of a thorough and complete plan. These elements, in the collective, should reflect the richness of the community and be seen as dynamic, co-evolving, and interdependent because interdependence is nonlinear.

Nonlinearity. This characteristic may be best revealed in the nonhierarchical structure of the comprehensive plan. Composition, structure, function, and services of the community system are all interrelated. This translates into a model that does not place one structure above another or make one more important than another, as the healthy functioning of one is related, if not directly dependent on, the healthy functioning of the others.

The resulting plan is a series of highly interactive components, where none overshadows another. The extent to which a comprehensive plan is balanced might also be gauged according to the values articulated by participants in the planning process. These values must be linked and interwoven into all elements of the plan. The community's vision, likewise, must be reflected in all elements of the plan. Following this explanation of modeling the plan as product after Nature, work begins on the core elements.

Step 3: developing elements of the comprehensive plan

A community is a system comprised of many interactive parts. Each part has composition that creates a certain structure that allows particular functions to occur that in turn produce services used by humans. A complex pattern of interactions between the human world (with its social and economic composition, structures, functions, and services) and Nature (also with its composition, structures, functions, and services) describes the "arena," so to speak, within which a comprehensive plan is developed.

A primary question addressed by a comprehensive plan is "How do we, as humans, continue to receive the goods and services we want and need without compromising the ability of the ecosystem — of which we are an inseparable part — to deliver those goods and services over time?" If we go back to the three-part model discussed earlier, which describes the complex set of interactions and intra-actions between humans and the rest of Nature, we begin to understand what sorts of considerations are integral to the planning process.

In a healthy system, there is a free flow of goods and services — energy — between all parts of the whole. In a healthy system, households provide labor, capital, and entrepreneurship to industry, commerce, government, and other institutions; in return, revenue, goods, and services are produced by these entities for household consumption. Also in a healthy system, households and the commerce-industry component deposit, into the environment, waste that can be used by other living systems and provide services, in the form of stewardship, to the environment. In return, Nature, or the environment, supplies humans with the entire list of ecosystem services described earlier in this book. Thus, all three parts provide energy (goods and services) to the other parts, and, in a healthy system, it is only energy that is exchanged. This is an economic model based on the flow of usable energy.

A well-designed, comprehensive plan can help to sustain this flow of usable energy. The focus of the plan is thus on any and all parts of a community where one can possibly exert some control: transportation (or circulation and parking), land use, community appearance and design, community facilities and services, parks and recreation, cultural resources, safety, economic development, housing, natural areas and open space, and environmental quality, which translates into the quality of air and water, fertility of soils, sustainability of biotic resources, usability of energy, and level of noise.

Our suggested approach attempts to bring together the necessary considerations of environmental quality into all other elements, demonstrating the inseparability of Nature from the human community as well as the composition, structures, functions, and services of each. Some states, such as California, require environmental impact reports (EIRs) for all municipal comprehensive plans; in California, such reports are called General Plans, and EIRs are required under California Environmental Quality law, but these reports are usually written after the planning process is complete. We believe planning that considers both dimensions simultaneously will produce more creative, dynamic, sustainable, and conscious plans.

Thus, for each "part" of the community, an element of the comprehensive plan must be fully developed. Within each element, adherence to the community vision and to identified core values must be kept in mind. What is valued and therefore what needs to be retained as an identified value is ultimately what each element accomplishes. In addition, the overall composition, structures, functions (both material and non-material), and services must be identified. Parallel structures, functions, and services in Nature are noted, where identifiable, as a means of connecting our thinking throughout the planning process to the rest of Nature, the health of which is essential to community well-being and longevity. Determining where there are parallels in Nature is itself a productive exercise for those participating in the planning process. It assists participants not only in understanding similarities, interrelatedness, and connectedness but also in understanding the possibilities for restoring broken connections.

Each element of a comprehensive plan should contain the following information.

Composition and structures
The plan should include a description of the nature of the particular "part" of the community system and its current status, as well as the structures that make up the whole. Structures are both physical and programmatic.

Functions and services
Also included should be a description of what is enabled by the structures within each "part" and an evaluation of how well the functions serve. To "take stock" of each part of the system, an assessment is done to determine internal and external conditions affecting the integrity of a given part of the system (in this case, a community) and what parts of the system require improvement or replacement. Internal conditions are discovered by asking what works, how well, and why and what does not work and why.

External conditions are determined by asking what outside forces pose a threat or perhaps offer an opportunity. For the economic development element, for example, a strength might be that tourism provides many jobs and much income to local businesses; a weakness might be that, due to a tourism-dominated economy, many residents must travel elsewhere for basic goods and services. A threat to the integrity of the local economy might be the inability of local government to keep up with the impacts of tourism on the infrastructure and, consequently, the possibility that deterioration of the infrastructure could diminish the attractiveness of the town to tourists. An opportunity might be the availability of funds from the State Department of Tourism to study ways to lessen the impacts of growth in tourism on the community's infrastructure.

Parallel structures, functions, and services in nature, where identifiable

Structures in Nature parallel to the structures defined in the land-use element as "corridor" and "edge," for example, are structures in Nature with the same name. "Edges" in Nature are transition areas between such things as a forest and meadow or streamside vegetation and a stream's floodplain. They function as suitable habitat for particular species of plants and animals. Their services to humans might include providing places to more clearly view birds and other wildlife, as do other natural areas. Parallels in Nature to the element of community design and appearance could be simulated by structures in Nature's land forms (hills, ridges, plateaus, ravines, etc.), which function as a stormwater system and serve humans in this regard, as well as creating hills for hiking and a variety of habitats for enjoying the sights and sounds of wildlife and the seasonal display of wildflowers.

Parallels to the community facilities and services element in Nature include wetlands, which, like sewage treatment plants and water treatment plant facilities, function to filter and store sediments, heavy metals, or organic compounds that would otherwise drain into larger bodies of waters. A massive parallel to the economic development element in Nature would be ecosystem services, which provide energy, solar income, and other forms of natural capital to humans. An obvious parallel to the housing element in Nature is a healthy habitat that provides shelter and nesting grounds and, for humans, serves to provide places for recreation and reflection.

Critical issues emerging from the earlier analysis

These are simple statements expressing conflicts or problems that must be addressed during the planning horizon of, say, 10 to 20 years. In the economic development element, for example, a critical issue might be growth of tourism in the city and its potential negative effects on the infrastructure, both in terms of capital and services.

It is here that values begin to play a key role. Each critical issue represents a "decision situation," as described by Keeny.[97] The question to ask, in order to get at individual values, is "What would you like to achieve in this situation?" This will produce a list — non-ranked and non-prioritized — of potential objectives and the basis for further probing. The process should include participants creating their own personal lists. These then become part of a group discussion. Redundancy should not be a concern during the group discussion.

Various devices for helping to elicit objectives or statements that describe a way of reaching a specific goal include wish lists. For example, the facilitator could ask: "If you had no limitations at all, what would your objectives be?" with regard to the identified "decision situation."[97] As these objectives are refined, they become specific in terms of desired outcomes or results and are quantifiable and action oriented.[49] A clear objective will explain what you plan to do and how. A well-written objective is measurable in that its achievement is easily determined. After objectives are identified, participants should be asked what they want to achieve by overcoming a particular problem and why doing so is important. These statements will, in our opinion, lead back to goal statements.

Formulation of goals
A goal is an end toward which effort is directed, a desired outcome. It is qualitative in nature. A goal emerging from an analysis of critical issues relative to economic development could be "The city's economy will be diverse and balanced, preserving a sense of place while providing for the economic well-being of residents."

Policy definition
Define policies that address time frames for implementation and the parties responsible, in addition to any costs.

Checklists
Next, prepare a checklist to evaluate the goals, objectives, and policies. The purpose of this final part of each element is to assess the potential impact of the plan on the integrity and well-being of the surrounding landscape that supports the human community. If goals, objectives, and policies are designed to perpetuate or sustain the human community, they will also best serve the natural systems supporting human life. Sometimes, fundamental directions will emerge as part of the planning process that may appear in each checklist at the end of each element.

One such checklist is an adaptation of a checklist from Sustainable Seattle, an organization formed to stimulate sustainability in Seattle, WA. The *Checklist for Evaluating the Sustainability of Community Ideas and Project Proposals*, adapted from Seattle's list by Philipp Muessig of the Minnesota Office of Environmental Assistance, is prefaced with the following words:[100]

"Like wisdom, sustainability (also known as sustainable development) is an ambitious goal. Rather than an endpoint or static condition, sustainability is a process whereby a community increasingly takes actions and develops attitudes which simultaneously strengthen its natural environment, its economy, and its social well-being. This checklist is meant not so much to be used literally, but as a guide to thinking about the interrelated issues sustainability calls upon us to consider."

The list is divided into five areas: community development, ecological health, social equity, and connections, trade-offs, and the long term. The community development section asks questions pertaining to inclusiveness, use of local resources, mobility, quality of life, public safety, education, community history, community identity, and neighborliness. The checklist asks that the user rate a statement after each category from "strongly agree" to "strongly disagree." Under community identity, for example, a statement reads: "Helps citizens feel a sense of belonging to the community and a sense of ownership in it."

The ecological health list covers ecosystems, land use, waste reduction, reuse and recycling, energy, clean water, clean air, healthy buildings, and peace and quiet. The economic health list covers meaningful work, business variety, economic vitality, economic self-reliance, and economic feasibility. The social equity list inquires into who gets the benefits, who pays the costs, fairness to other communities, fairness to other generations, and affordability and access (housing, services, and other opportunities). And, finally, the connections, trade-offs, and long-term list addresses the seven generations test, the big picture, trade-offs in the community, trade-offs outside the community, and improvement over time.

Such a checklist can be used to guide each community in creating a plan that engenders sustainable development, as it takes into account the links among social, economic, environmental, and community issues. Below is an example of a comprehensive plan element that demonstrates this approach.

Follow-up

Monitoring the implementation of the plan is covered in Chapter 7. And, finally, annually revisiting to the plan — particularly the vision and goals — is critical to keeping the process alive, rather than making the plan itself sacred and static.

Sample comprehensive plan elements: transportation

We have chosen the transportation element to use as an example because transportation is a problem (and becoming more so) not just from a spatial point of view but also from an environmental point of view. In fact, the future of communities, towns, and cities is at the root of contemporary debates about travel and transportation because the form and population density of the community, town, or city are prime influences on both the volume and pattern of its mobility. Form and population density are also factors in the accessibility transportation is designed to deliver.

For most of the 20th century, traffic has been seen as an inevitable and necessary part of modern progress. "The calm and quaintness of life before the automobile," says Jay Walljasper, editor-at-large of the *Utne Reader*, "might be nostalgically mourned, but most Americans seem thrilled at the possibility of going to more and more places in less and less time."[101] Our cities, suburbs, and countryside have all been carved up and blanketed with motorways and parking lots. "Million of trees have been chopped down," laments Walljasper, "tens of thousands of houses torn down, and thousands of communities ripped apart, all to meet the needs of the ever-escalating volume of traffic."[101] In Los Angeles, for example, it is said that 60% of the land area is dedicated to transportation.

Building new, bigger, and faster roads has become the major preoccupation of government at all levels in the U.S. during much of the past half century. Billions of dollars have been and continue to be spent widening and straightening streets and highways in almost every urban and rural setting throughout the U.S. An entirely new profession — traffic engineers — has materialized to accomplish this feat, and they now wield far more influence over the planning and layout of communities than do elected officials, business people, or citizens groups combined. Traffic engineers have a single goal — enable cars and trucks to move easier and more quickly through both town and countryside.

When their motives are brought into question, they invariably invoke the issue of public safety in their proposals for newer, wider, and smoother streets and roads. The American Road and Transportation Builders Association, for example, attributes unsafe roads to a scarcity of road construction, saying that opponents have been tying up needed new lanes. "Adding capacity has not been an aggressive strategy in most urban areas," says association president Peter Ruane, who spends two hours a day driving back and forth between his Maryland home and Washington, D.C., office.

On the flipside of the coin, however, studies have shown that narrow streets are actually safer. The city of Longmont, CO, which is a booming suburb of Denver, examined 20,000 accidents on local streets over an 8-year period and found that "as street width widens, accidents per mile per year increase exponentially."[101] This finding flies in the face of traffic engineers, who have long held that narrow streets and traffic congestion are safety hazards that must be remedied.

The Surface Transportation Policy Project, which advocates alternatives to driving, argues that more roads attract more vehicles and add to urban sprawl, much as a larger house induces people to fill it to capacity, just as they had done their smaller house. "If we want to curb ... congestion, we need to curb ... [the] spread [of roads], so people can get around without driving everywhere," says group spokeswoman and Washington, D.C., resident Barbara McCann, who needs no car to commute.[101]

Randy Tucker, a spokesman for the land-use watchdog group, 1000 Friends of Oregon, says, "No one has ever been able to build their way out of congestion. That belief ignores the negative impacts of building roads, which often ... facilitate[s] more sprawl, which creates more congestion in the future."[101] In essence, the level of consciousness that created the problem of traffic congestion in the first place is not the level of consciousness that can fix it, which simply means that building more roads and widening others is *not* the solution.

Peter Headicar, a Reader in Transport Planning at Oxford Brookes University in England, states the problem eloquently. He says that basic questions about the urban future in the context of transportation are not often posed because "they are both politically uncomfortable and tractable only over the longer term — hence conveniently forever deferrable in the present."[101]

Most comprehensive plans project only 10 to 20 years ahead, which is a barely perceptible interval of time in the evolutionary scale of the settlements themselves. Public attention is captured instead by more immediate problems and with attempts to "solve" those problems independently of any coherent longer term transportation strategy for the community, town, or city. The urbanized areas of most communities have long been slowly restructured into places that can only function on the basis of extensive use by automobiles. Had the long-term trajectory implied by such restructuring been investigated, it would have been clear that it was never socially or economically sustainable in large measure because it is not environmentally sustainable, especially when large trucks are included.

According to John Whitelegg, a professor at the School of the Built Environment, John Moores University in Liverpool, England, trucks emit 77% of all particulate emission in road transportation, 19% of the nitrogen oxides, and 47% of the sulfur dioxide.[101] All these have serious effects on health, such as respiratory and heart diseases. Research in the U.S. has shown rates of death from both lung and heart diseases to be 37% higher in the most polluted cities compared to in the least polluted cities. The International Agency for Research on Cancer classifies benzene and particulates, which are both present in the exhaust emissions from trucks, as cancer-causing chemicals. Diesel exhaust itself is classified as a category of pollution that is "probably carcinogenic."

Now consider congestion, as measured by the average number of hours per year that Americans spend behind the steering wheel in snarled traffic. The most congested urban areas, where drivers are "motionless, bedeviled, and hung up," according to the Texas Transportation Institute, which is part of Texas A&M University at College Station,[101] are, in descending order:

- Los Angeles, CA: 82 hours (= 10.25 working days)
- Washington, D.C., and suburban Virginia and Maryland: 76 hours (= 9.5 working days)
- Seattle-Everett, WA: 69 hours (= 8.6 working days)
- Atlanta, GA: 68 hours (= 8.5 working days)
- Boston, MA: 66 hours (= 8.25 working days)
- Dallas and Houston, TX: 58 hours (= 7.25 working days)
- San Francisco-Oakland, CA: 58 hours (= 7.25 working days)
- Portland, OR-Vancouver, WA: 52 hours (= 6.5 working days)

The average in 68 areas nationwide was 34 hours, or 4.25 working days.

The nationwide study by the Texas Transportation Institute found congestion just about everywhere in urban centers, even in places that just 15 years ago were freewheeling. Despite the fact that some cities are getting a handle on traffic, the spidery network of clogged traffic arterials continues to grow across the landscape, especially in urban areas, with the worst growth in bumper-to-bumper driving in Indianapolis, where the average time a motorist spends stuck in traffic grew by 225%, to 52 hours (6.5 working days) per year, between 1992 and 1997. Moreover, those cities that placed a higher emphasis on replacing and/or increasing roads did not decrease congestion and delays.

In addition to the physical congestion are the tensions that arise among drivers which today are known as "road rage." Road rage is turning increasingly deadly, as exemplified by a woman who was charged in November 1999 with the shooting death of another woman in a fit of rush-hour rage outside Birmingham, AL, on a stretch of road where it can now take an entire hour to travel 20 miles.

These kinds of circumstance are causing communities across North America to rethink their issues with traffic. Eugene, OR, for example, once required all streets to be at least 28 feet wide, but now allows some to be as narrow as 20 feet. Wellesley, MA, chose to narrow their congested main street and widen the sidewalks to encourage walking as a mode of transportation. Even the cities of San Bernardino, Riverside, and Beverly Hills in auto-happy southern California have chosen to narrow their major commercial streets.

With the above sketch of transportation in mind, we will give the human component of the transportation system and Nature's counterpart in each of the following examples, as a means of connecting our thinking to the rest of Nature throughout the planning process.

Composition and structures

Composition

The overall composition of a community's transportation system should be described, which means generally describing the individual components. For example, a community may only have provisions and facilities for private motor vehicles and pedestrians but no provisions or facilities for public transit or for bicycles, such as safe riding paths and racks for parking bikes.

Structures

Next we inventory structure. The community's transportation system has two types of structure: (1) the physical structure, which consists of streets and highways, sidewalks, bikeways, and sometimes tracks or other guidance hardware for mass transit; and (2) the programs, such as designated times that parking is prohibited on certain streets to provide safe travel for bicyclists commuting to work, or such incentives as express routes for cars having two or more passengers during commuting hours to simulate carpooling, or transit passes for city employees.

Parallel structures in Nature

Transportation systems in Nature have structure as well — habitat corridors used by wildlife to move from one area to another, migratory paths, waterways for spawning fish, and so on.

Functions

Functions reflecting community values

Ultimately, system functions should represent community values. Values associated with a community's transportation plan may include safety, convenience, and efficiency; however, the plan must offer a variety of choices for moving into, out of, and about the community and contain built-in incentives for non-automobile travel.

Because the automobile usually far surpasses other modes of transportation and has a major influence on land use, analysis of its role in the community is critical. The following are some questions one might ask in this regard: (1) How do community members use their automobiles? (2) What value do they place on automobile use? (3) What are the environmental, social, and economic impacts of automobile use?

Relative to this issue is a recent report from the Centers for Disease Control in Atlanta, GA.[102] William Dietz, Director of Nutrition and Physical Activity at the Centers for Disease Control, reports that obesity, the cause of 300,000 deaths annually in the U.S. (second only to tobacco-caused deaths), is now being studied from an environmental perspective. Community design, says Deitz, is contributing to the problem of obesity. Urban sprawl is stimulating a continual rise in the use of automobiles. Neighborhood design that includes cul-de-sacs, no sidewalks or bike trails, and distant schools and shopping centers requiring travel by automobile diminishes the possibilities for physical activity. Twenty-five percent of trips made in the U.S. are less than one mile, and 75% of all trips are made by car. Reversing this trend might be aided by rethinking how we plan for transportation in our communities.

"Two centuries ago," writes Jungian psychologist James Hillman, "there was a good deal of walking in Europe, especially in and around gardens."[103] Those gardeners, says Hillman, not only were the great developers of the time but also were moved by aesthetic considerations, whereas the developers of today are moved almost solely by economics.

Hillman discusses the importance of walking: "I have found in my psychological work with people that, during periods of acute psychological turmoil, walking is an activity to which one naturally turns."[103] This observation was made in Zürich, Switzerland, where he practiced as a Jungian analyst for a quarter of a century before moving to Dallas, TX.

Walking in Dallas does not come easily, according to Hillman, because a person walking along a street "stands out more oddly, more suspiciously, than does a winded jogger in [a] red warm-up suit, yellow-striped shoes, and earmuffs."[103] Although walking around the city for hours in the early morning or late at night can be meditative therapy, Hillman wonders if people who take such walks are regarded either as prowlers or victims in the eyes of their fellow human beings. Hillman's point? We must plan our communities to give freedom to our legs and thereby give freedom and health to our minds. If we all walked more, would "road rage" be a problem?

In addition to or in lieu of walking, one can ride a bicycle.[104] Cycling, like walking, is good for one's health, fitness, convenience, and independence, especially if one is too young to own a car, as well as for the local environment, where a bicycle makes only slight demands on resources and space. A number of countries have been successful in fostering use of the bicycle — Sweden, despite its winters, and Switzerland, despite its mountains.

Cycling involves leaving behind the social insulation of the automobile and getting out among the people, which repopulates the streets with human faces and individual personalities. In this way, the streets become friendlier and thus safer and more sociable, which helps to reclaim our communities from automobiles and trucks and make them more personable, like they once were. To accomplish this, however, one must positively favor those modes of transport that one wishes to make flourish, such as walking and cycling, which means creating an overall vision for the kind of transportation system that is required for a healthy, sustainable community. Such a vision must be one in which automobiles and trucks are replaced by walking and cycling as the nonnegotiable heart of the vision.

One thing must be kept in mind, however, when such a vision is crafted. It must build toward what people want (a positive) through kindness, tolerance, and education — not by trying to move away from a perceived negative. Any measure perceived as discriminating against motorists will likely cause staunch opposition to the end desired.

Parallel functions and values in Nature

Recognizing the functions and values of Nature's transportation corridors may alter how a community plans for its own transportation needs. Nature's transportation corridors enable wildlife to reach food and water, provide habitat, and serve as routes for certain migratory species. In addition, animals, like humans when they walk or ride a bicycle, do not pollute the environment in their passing. To recognize these values to the non-human biotic community is to also recognize needs. These "needs," if we choose, could be translated into desired future conditions and so stated in the development review process, or, at the very least, designed as constraints to development. These corridors and habitats further serve human needs, which could also be discussed in an Open Space element.

Services

Services based on functions and values
Transportation services should be tied to identified functions and values. Transportation services typically fall into two areas or categories: utilitarian and recreational. Utilitarian services include ways of getting about safely and efficiently to obtain the basic necessities of life — get to work, obtain goods and services, and so on. Recreational services might include the need for safe and convenient places to bike, roller blade, stroll, run, cross-country ski, snowmobile, and so on.

Parallel services in Nature
By parallel services, we mean the services of Nature's transportation systems to the non-human natural world. But, because it is difficult for humans to separate function from services in the natural world — that is, to understand what services are available to the non-human natural world that are not also available to humans — we will focus instead on the services to humans offered by Nature's transportation systems.

Nature's corridors provide services tied to human values and the healthy functioning of community. These uninterrupted areas of the landscape connect people to the natural world, provide quiet and restful places for renewal, and enable us to view wildlife and birds, as well as allowing them to offer their free services of ecosystem maintenance. Some may describe these services as utilitarian; others may view them as recreational.

Current status and analysis of structures, functions, and services

Next, look at the whole of the existing transportation system — structures, functions, and services — and assess what works and what does not work, which includes reviewing and considering such things as a survey of street conditions, accident data, transit ridership data, any reasonably current transportation studies, and so on. This examination can produce a list of assets and liabilities, strengths and weaknesses, opportunities and threats — characteristics to take advantage of and characteristics to overcome, whatever language seems right. Areas covered should include such things as condition of streets and roads, parking, traffic, and public transportation.

Critical issues yield goals, objectives, and policies

Following this inventory, participants brainstorm ways to overcome weaknesses and take advantage of strengths. Helpful in this process might be to remember the words of Sir Lawrence Olivier: "Exploit your weaknesses, aspire to your strengths." Or, those of Pogo: "We are surrounded by insurmountable opportunities."

The information produced during this brainstorming activity is then used in the development of a list of critical issues, which typically reveal community values. Goals are then formulated to reflect functions and values of the human system and Nature's system for delivering goods and services — the local economy and the ecosystem. A goal, as stated earlier, is an end toward which effort is directed, such as: "Our community's transportation system improves air quality, manages traffic congestion, encourages walking, and supports effective land use." Because some people are not comfortable with goals that are stated as a present-tense endpoint, this statement could read: "Our community's transportation system will improve air quality, manage traffic congestion, encourage walking, and support effective land use [while enhancing mobility]."

Objectives are then formulated to achieve goals, and policies are defined to carry out programs. An example of a goal and related objectives follows. The example is adapted from the principles and policies contained in the transportation element of the plan for the city of Fort Collins, CO.[40]

Goal: The physical organization of [name of place] will be supported by a system of integrated alternative means of transportation that together optimize access and mobility while reducing dependence on the private automobile.

Objective 1, Land-Use Patterns: Land-use patterns, as created by zoning and the approval of individual developments, will support effective transit, an effective and efficient roadway system, and alternative modes of transportation. High-density residential and specified nonresidential land uses must be within walking distance of transit stops.

Objective 2, Multi-modal Streets: Main travel corridors will provide for safe and convenient use of all modes of transportation, including motor vehicles, transit, bicycles, and pedestrians.

Objective 3, Street Design Criteria: The community [give the name of the place] will establish criteria for designing streets that will support transit, ride-sharing, and non-motorized modes of transportation; will minimize conflicts between the modes of transportation; and will be compatible with surrounding land uses.

Checklist to evaluate goals, objectives, and policies

The purpose of this final part of each element of the comprehensive plan is to check the potential effect of the plan on the integrity and well-being of the ecosystem supporting the human community. If goals, objectives, and policies are designed to perpetuate or sustain the human community, they will also best serve the natural systems supporting human life. Fundamental directions will sometimes emerge in each checklist at the end of each element as part of the planning process.

Possible questions to ask in association with the transportation element include:[100] Will these goals, principles, and policies result in a reduction of vehicle trips and vehicle miles traveled? A wider range of alternatives to the drive-alone automobile, including walking, bicycling, and public transit? Local street designs that encourage use by pedestrians and bicyclists and discourage high-speed traffic? Greater opportunity for effective, efficient, and affordable transportation for low-income households, elderly people, and others who comprise the portion of the population that does not own automobiles?

Specific proposals for improvements in transportation, such as narrowing an existing road to encourage forms of transportation other than the automobile, adding a new road, expanding an existing one, or expanding the transit system should conform with the goals, principles, and policies articulated in this element of the comprehensive plan — as well as be subject to an environmental review checklist discussed later.

Following are other elements found in most comprehensive plans. Our descriptions discuss some of the nuances that you may want to consider in developing these elements. Not all have a complete discussion of structures, functions, and services as above in the transportation element.

Sample comprehensive plan elements: land-use

A land-use plan — in map form — is part of a land-use element (formulated according to the sample element above). Creating one should start with an analysis of environmental constraints, which can be represented on GIS-created maps, as well as with a land-use map and a zoning map. Citizen participation in the creation of this plan can take the following form, starting with an explanation of structures.

Community structures

Community structures, or types of places, can be described in a number of ways. As mentioned above, the City of Fort Collins, CO, used corridors, districts, neighborhoods, and edges.[40] In the well-known book *Pattern Language*,[105] the authors describe patterns that are useful in building and planning. All the patterns are related. Some of the town patterns or community structures named are neighborhoods, neighborhood boundaries, web of public transportation, main gateways, activity nodes, promenades, sacred sites, access to water, and so on.

A good place to start identifying structures would be for citizens to review the existing map of land use and environmental constraints with the planning team. Citizens should be encouraged to note any special features that are not conveyed by the land-use map.

Recently, one of the author's undertook this process as a citizen appointed to a town land-use planning committee for the small rural township where she lives. When examining the town map, committee members, who had lived in the area far longer than the author, noted special places that they viewed as sacrosanct. One was a point of land along the shoreline of Lake Superior called "Houghton Point," which, although privately owned, had for decades been used by the public, with the owner's consent, for hiking, picnicking, and simply viewing the Great Lake.

Another feature many of the participants viewed as extraordinary and worth preserving in its present form was simply an open field along the lake side of a two-lane highway which also contained an historic plaque and a place for motorists to pull over, stop, and read the plaque. The entire area represented what planners would call a viewshed. At this point in the discussion, members of the planning committee simply wanted to say these areas deserved special attention in terms of recommended land-use policy. Both Houghton Point and the field were consequently designated as conservation areas.

Members of a planning group may come up with their own designations for structural elements for their community. It is important to keep the number of units to a manageable size and to make sure these structural units are carefully defined. A list of possible structural elements — with definitions — could be offered, but creativity by the participants should be encouraged.

Structural components should provide an organizational structure for the plan as well as form the bridge to the development of regulations that implement the plan. Thus, structural components, or types of places, should remain simple and few. Later, when goals, objectives, and policies are developed, these types of places can be further defined. For example, if a structural component is "neighborhood," a further step would be to break the neighborhood component down into (1) multi-family residential neighborhood; (2) single-family residential neighborhood; (3) low-density, mixed-use neighborhood; (4) high-density, mixed-use neighborhood; and so on.

For the purposes of this discussion, we will use the following structural components to describe types of places: neighborhoods, districts, corridors, gateways, nodes, and edges. Neighborhoods are areas dominated by residential uses. The New Urbanist approach to planning would say that, ideally, all neighborhoods should contain destinations that are within walking distance, such as schools, parks, and convenience shopping. The human scale, spatial relationships, and availability of facilities for non-automobile travel create neighborhoods that are compact, pedestrian friendly areas. Neighborhoods are linked by travel routes. Neighborhoods can be further defined as already mentioned.

Districts are larger areas of activity. Several neighborhoods may make up a district. Such neighborhoods would be linked and may share schools, shopping areas, or public areas such as parks or playgrounds. District composition and definition can easily be translated into the language of zoning ordinances. Districts are destinations and may include the following types: commercial, downtown, industrial, residential, conservancy, and agricultural.

Corridors connect districts and can be corridors for human travel or natural corridors, such as ravines or greenbelts. Collectively, these natural or "green" corridors create a network that links such open spaces as natural areas and parks to areas of the city where residents live and work.[40]

Gateways are the primary places of entry into a community from the outside. These areas frequently are where a community makes its first impression. For this reason, they are an important place to make a statement about a community's identity even as they say "Welcome."

Nodes are strategic focal points. They can include viewsheds, or places that offer a particularly beautiful view of the natural or built environment, or simple places that form focal points, such as a vestpocket park or a central park.

Finally, edges are boundaries between areas of contrasting character. They can be used to protect sensitive habitat or plant communities, as open space, or as a boundary between the developed community and a rural landscape. Edges are designated in planning more frequently than in the past in order to counter sprawl.

Functions and services

Examining these structural components should be done critically. Are these components where they are wanted and to the degree they are wanted as they currently exist? For example, if a particular area of a community has long been devoted to shipping and warehousing, would this still be the most desirable use of the area or should it be changed? Would the structural element "industrial district" remain on the map or would it be replaced with something like "public recreation district?"

Most planning efforts address the future in terms of guidelines for alterations to existing development or for new development. In Ashland, WI, for instance, much of the waterfront was for decades devoted to industry, specifically such things as shipping and sawmills. Following the departure of much of the industry, however, the decision was made to convert the abandoned industrial sites to public use, including trails, a marina, and other recreational opportunities. Further, nearly the entire shoreline was rezoned to reflect the desired future development of waterfront recreation.

Next to be considered are the identify structure, function, and services in Nature or areas of environmental protection. Some areas, such as wetlands and shorelands, are typically already protected by state law. These areas should be designated on the map along with other constraints — soils, sensitive plant communities, areas with identified endangered or threatened species, fault lines, and so on. The structures identified above should be shown on the map, and all of this should be overlaid on the current land uses. GIS mapping will help with this process.

Once this process is completed, a series of questions should be addressed regarding how the land is used and could be used: How large does the current pattern of land use allow us as a community to grow, both geographically and in terms of population? (The latter question will require some mathematical calculation.) What sort of character or sense of place is afforded by the current pattern of land use? How far does the average adult travel to work or children to school? To what extent does the existing pattern of land use allow for convenient access to goods and services? How much open space is there, and how much land is allocated for housing, industry, commercial uses, parks, and recreation? What protection is afforded places of spiritual, cultural, or historic value by the current pattern of land use? Is there enough housing? Is there enough medium- and high-density housing? What sorts of uses do we want on our waterfronts?

Checklist

Although the above exercise will lead to a map that shows the location and amount of each desirable land use, an impact analysis should follow. It is important for the analysis to address the following questions: How much potential growth in population is represented by this plan? Given the amount of land allocated for commercial and industrial uses, how does potential housing balance with job potential? How does the amount of parkland and public open space per capita compare with accepted standards? (This last question begs another: Are the accepted standards acceptable?) How do the designated uses of the edges relate to extraterritorial uses adjacent to the edges? How will this pattern affect opportunities for recreation and economic development as defined by the goals of the respective elements of the comprehensive plan?

Sample comprehensive plan elements: community facilities and services

The community facilities and services element, like the others, can be patterned as suggested above — composition, structures, functions, and services. Major parts of this element include such facilities as sewage treatment plants, water treatment plants, and solid-waste disposal facilities. What is most difficult with this particular element, however, is to depart significantly in the goals, objectives, and policies from simply expanding or otherwise improving the conventional infrastructure in which communities have typically invested thousands, if not millions, of dollars. Federal clean water laws regulate the operation of such facilities, which, in turn, frequently dictate the type of equipment and other hardware necessary to maintain "safe" standards. And, typically, the hardware dictated is that which is currently available — experimental methods or equipment are not usually permitted.

Although this reality may result in meeting immediate needs for waste-water treatment by conventional means, in looking to the future a community's goals could suggest that research be directed toward alternatives, and there are examples of such forward thinking. Along the Hay River in Dunn County, WI, an alternative to the standard high-tech, plastic-and-steel solution to sewage has been created.

The village of Dunn has made a wetland, filled with gravel and cattails, as part of its new wastewater treatment system. The Wisconsin Department of Natural Resources noted that the method would be a cost-effective alternative to standard treatment plants. The idea for the constructed or artificial wetland came out of a contentious public hearing that addressed upgrading the village's sewage treatment plant. Residents were very angry about the possibility of more treated water being dumped into the Hay River. The frustrated citizens noted that the downstream lakes receiving this water are polluted, as indicated by an algae bloom each summer. As a result, a new system is in place. It is a dual system, funded in part with state dollars because of the innovation it represents.[106] Another similar system exists in Drummond, WI, where a natural bog is used in the city's waste treatment system.[106] These projects represent communities that not only recognized the service an ecosystem can perform but also took advantage of it while protecting other natural resources.

Certain innovations in the standard technology of stormwater management actually represent huge cost savings. In Grayslake, IL, a development named Prairie Crossing has drawn national attention for an entire range of nuances, one of which is the way stormwater is handled. Rainwater typically flows down a road in a gutter, then through a pipe, and finally into a retention pond. Along with the water come road salts and other petrochemical pollutants. At Prairie Crossing, however, pollutants are washed out of the water with the aid of a natural filtration system, so that by the time the water reaches the lake, it is clean enough to swim in, and the Illinois Department of Natural Resources is using a portion of the lake for a hatchery in which to breed endangered species of fish. This plan saved the developer around $1.8 million over the cost of the entire development by not having to put in traditional curb and gutter storm sewers.[107]

Water resources and water treatment also fall under the category of community facilities and services. The need for facilities can be greatly affected by social change. For example, if a community is educated in the conservation of water and the potential effect of their lifestyle on water quality (and acts on what it has learned), the need for public infrastructure in this area could be lessened. Put differently, the need for the physical structures could ultimately be lessened by the creation of social structures or systems in the form of educational programs, community campaigns to conserve water, or community "cleansweep" programs, where specific toxic materials can be taken to a site for safe handling and storage in order to prevent these substances from going to landfills, where they leach out and ultimately end up in the soils and, through the soils, in groundwater.

Community programs to achieve the elimination of waste of all kinds can take many forms. In 1973, for example, the mayor of Curitiba, Brazil, Jaime Lerner, devised a creative solution to the collection of garbage in the streets of the *favelas* (slums), where either collection of garbage did not exist or the streets were too narrow for conventional means of garbage collection. His solution was to pay people for their garbage by offering them tokens for public transit in return for separated and therefore recyclable trash. To the farmers who took the organic waste to use as fertilizer for their fields, the city gave tokens that could be exchanged for food. "Kids scour the *favelas* for trash, and can spot the difference between polyethylene terephthalate and high-density polyethylene bottles. The tokens give the poorer citizens the means to get out of the *favelas* to where the jobs are, while promoting cleanliness, frugality, and the reclaiming and recycling of waste."[108]

Solid-waste disposal is the subject of much innovation in the U.S. Yet the amount of materials recycled or recovered is a small percentage of the potential.[10] The message here is that, even though the technology and, in the case of recyclables, the markets may exist, social attitudes or entrenched behaviors still keep us overloading the natural "sink" with indigestible, unusable, and in some cases toxic waste. Added to this is the reluctance of industry to raise itself to the higher standards of trusteeship of the Earth being advocated — not yet legislated — by multinational programs and other efforts in this country.

For example, the Council of Great Lakes Industries recently called upon the environment directors of Michigan, Minnesota, Wisconsin, and Ontario to withdraw support of each government entity from the efforts of the Lake Superior Binational Program To Restore and Protect Lake Superior (a program of the International Joint Commission) by producing a Lake Superior Lakewide Management Plan. The reason for the Council's vehement plea to governments to withdraw their support from the Lake Superior Lakewide Management Plan was that implementation of the plan, which would reduce the load of nine persistent, bioaccumulative toxic substances found in the lake, "would occasion severe economic disruptions and extreme lifestyle changes within the Lake Superior basin."[109]

This response (and others like it) to potential limitations placed on the ways in which society has for so long conducted business reveals a fear of a major shift if the limitations are mandated. Responses such as this may also reflect an element missing from many of the recommendations and mandates emanating from interest groups, environmental organizations, and government — the suggested alternatives. In some cases, business and industry are taking responsibility for developing alternatives by diversifying, making investments in infrastructure or operations that help them comply with higher standards, or even offering alternatives to the recommendations themselves. In other cases, however, they are simply digging in their heals and threatening or undertaking lawsuits.

In the community planning process, we advocate imaginative solutions rather than unreasonable demands. Long-term goals can be fairly radical, but the objectives and policies must make sense to a broad audience, be reasonable, and be both politically and financially possible. This is not to say that a comprehensive plan cannot call for major change. It can, and the changes called for, if tied to community values, will most likely resonate with the larger community. An important framework to keep in mind with the development of each element of the plan, however, is the existence of the social, economic, and environmental dimensions of each part of the community system, all of which must be addressed as part of the planning process. This is done not only to discover where there is a potential problem but also to formulate innovative, multi-purpose, long-term solutions.

Community services also include all government services, which, in many communities, are frequently the focus of much complaint as a result, no doubt, of the police powers of cities and such things as property taxes, fines, and various forms of regulation. It is precisely this kind of division that motivates the type of planning process we are advocating — a process that lessens the division and may actually lead toward less regulation, more meaningful taxation, and more personal responsibility for one's behavior.

When formulating goals, objectives, and policies for community services, becoming aware of what misconceptions may exist between the citizenry and the government would assist in this creative process. Such awareness may also reveal needed services as well as creative ways of providing them.

The City of Santa Cruz, CA, for example, has drafted a General Plan for 1990–2005 that includes the following goal and objective, which we believe represent an innovation in city government:[110]

> "Goal 1.1.7. Work with community groups to create a center for community organizations in order to build constructive inter-relationships between individuals, groups, organizations, and City government by providing opportunities to come together in cooperative and synergistic ways, to facilitate networking, and, lastly, to gather and disseminate information about local and global issues.

> "Objective 1.1.7.1. Examine the feasibility of developing a community 'earth room' displaying the City's community vision and relationship to the global community and issues including our Sister Cities."

Community services not currently provided might also be suggested by goals. The need for new or expanded services could come from the kind of exploration undertaken in each element of the plan and then be brought back to the community services element. For example, discussion and work on the economic development element might reveal that, due to the generally low wages offered by area jobs and low median income when compared with the region or the state, many parents must each hold a job. This recognition might lead to the development of objectives and policies addressing daycare.

The City of Santa Cruz General Plan is illustrative of this point in that one such policy directs the City to work with the county and daycare providers to "expedite and facilitate the development of accessible, affordable and quality childcare spaces to meet the demand for services." In related programs, the City is directed "to develop a mechanism to obtain and preserve planned childcare sites" and "investigate employer-provided childcare programs and explore the feasibility of developing such programs within the City."[110]

Curitiba, Brazil, has established a municipal poetry center, where people can come to write poetry and have it bound into book form. Such a service must surely contribute to the "livability" of a place. In the process of making improvements in Curitiba, the focus was not on the environment, but rather on simply making the city be as livable as possible.[111] Such a process, we suggest, would be strongly tied to community values, be understandable, and be one to which a greater number of people could more easily contribute.

Sample comprehensive plan elements: cultural resources

Many times the character and appeal of a community stems from its cultural milieu. A community's historic resources provide a cultural link to the past. Historic buildings, sites, and landmarks, for example, serve as reminders of the past and help to educate a community about its history. These remnants of the past in some communities are a prominent part of their appearance. Other cultural resources include the visual and performing arts, museums, and archeological resources.

The review of the past, both what has disappeared and what remains, is a critical step in the planning process. Below the surfaces of today's built and social environments is a former pattern of community — physical, social, economic. Traces of the past can be experienced at historic and cultural sites such as Civil War battlefields, or restored or preserved places such as Williamsburg, PA, or in the glacial scars on the rock faces of mountains. Some patterns exist today that have existed for hundreds, if not thousands, of years — wildlife migrations paths, undisturbed plant communities, old growth forests, mountains, vernal pools, public ritual, religious ceremonies and rites, language, and so on.

Lerner, the mayor of Curitiba, refers to the physical past that underlies today's world as "ghost maps."[111] Introducing the idea of "ghost maps" to the planning process helps to form a bridge to the past. The notion of ghost maps, like the other efforts to create connections and an understanding of interrelatedness of the parts to the whole, contributes to the organic nature and multidimensionality of the planning process as well as the final plan. The organic nature and multidimensionality of the planning process are accomplished, in part, through the cultural resources element of the comprehensive plan, which looks at and plans for the cultural history of a place, including architectural and archeological resources and visual and performing arts.

The underlying questions in the examination of the past as well as existing cultural resources include: What does the community value that merits restoration or preservation? What can we understand from the past that will aid us in our attempts to create a positive and meaningful future? What mistakes from the past do we want to correct, rather than repeat? Finally, there is the underlying question of what natural patterns exist that are nonnegotiable. Learning about these patterns, their importance, and the heritage they represent will contribute significantly to the meaning and resiliency of the community's plan.

Sample comprehensive plan elements: economic development

Similar to the community services and facilities element in terms of a challenge to think "outside of the box," so to speak, is the economic development element. An analysis of economic development in most communities simply means determining whether existing commerce makes a substantial contribution to the community's tax base as well as providing enough jobs and meaningful work. Once determined, a follow-up question would be, generally speaking, "How can we improve on the situation?" But the most important and usually unasked question is "How much is enough?"

We suggest, that when considering the local economy and its relationship to the regional economy, all of a community's assets should be included on the balance sheet, including those for which a dollar value may not be easily calculated or even understood. For example, in Jane's community of Ashland, WI, a huge store of natural capital is represented by Lake Superior, a natural feature that daily provides most local citizens with a great deal of pleasure — recreational, spiritual, and aesthetic. Putting a dollar value on these pleasures does not make sense. Yet, when people complain about low wages and high property taxes due to the absence of large amounts of industry and commerce, Jane finds herself reminding them of the other forms of wealth to which they have access — the inestimable value of the lake and the surrounding forestlands inhabited by huge populations of wildlife, the many lakes and trails to explore, the opportunities for silence and beautiful vistas, and so on.

These values are like fringe benefits to everyone employed in the region. Now, admittedly, this line of reasoning does not go far with some people. But everything comes at some cost, and residents of this region are paying daily to protect a relatively pristine area by not being more densely populated and by not being a greater generator of jobs. Add to this that people are being attracted to the area, like many rural places in America these days, for the very qualities that accompany low wages and little employment. Thus, the area is looking at imminent growth and now has the time and space to plan what economic development could look like so that it does not compromise the beauty, splendor, and charm for which there is a growing demand and a diminishing supply in the U.S.

Economic development will, according to Paul Hawken, start to wear a different face in the coming decades.[108] In "A Road Map for Natural Capitalism," authors Lovins et al. claim that "business strategies built around the radically more productive use of natural resources can solve many environmental problems at a profit."[112] The businesses following this road map will raise their resource productivity, close their production loops, and shift to a solutions-based business model. They will also "reinvest in restoring, sustaining, and expanding the most important form of capital — their own natural habitat and biological resource base."[112]

Companies pioneering the way include independent power producer AES. This company has long pursued a policy of planting trees to offset the carbon emissions of its power plants, which has turned out to be a smart investment because a dozen brokers are now creating markets for carbon reduction.[112] Perhaps other innovations in industry and commerce will have a ripple effect and filter down to the local level in terms of efforts directed toward economic development.

Advances in industrial ecology are one such area. Industrial ecology is the "multidisciplinary study of industrial systems and economic activities and their links to fundamental natural systems."[113] As a field of study, industrial ecology, however, cannot by itself support the achievement of a sustainable society or global system of human societies. "Significant cultural, ethical, and religious evolution are difficult but also necessary."[113] For example, in societies where women do not have professional opportunities or equal rights, equity — a foundational tenant of sustainability — will make achieving a sustainable society impossible to the extent that features of inequity remain fixed.

Developing community goals tied to economic development, as opposed to economic growth, will be a good first step. (See *Setting the Stage for Sustainability* for an indepth discussion of the "growth/no growth" dilemma.[63]) If we continue to believe as a society that economic growth is necessary to maintain full employment, which implies continued increases in resource consumption, we will all soon realize that this is impossible, as resources are finite. On the other hand, economic development — where quality of life is improved or at least maintained, where the wealth of a community is the sum of all its assets, and where new and/or expanded parts of the economy focus on resource productivity, closed-loop technology for production, and a solutions-based business model — enhances the possibilities for sustainable community development.

Paradigm warning

Although we have been discussing a number of models or paradigms in this book, we would like to offer a caveat, or maybe even a disclaimer. We believe that paradigms, like mindsets, can be dangerous and that continual wonder, exploration, and critical thinking fuel the creative process and are part of extended learning. We believe, as does Donella Meadows, noted systems analyst, that the highest "leverage point, or "place within a complex system ... where a small shift in one thing can produce big changes in everything" is to remain unattached to paradigms, "to realize that NO paradigm is 'true,' that even the one that sweetly shapes one's comfortable worldview is a tremendously limited understanding of an immense and amazing universe. It is to 'get' at a gut level the paradigm that there are paradigms, and to see that itself is a paradigm, and to regard that realization as devastatingly funny. It is to let go into Not Knowing."[75] And, as co-author Chris says, "honor your ignorance," as that is the place from which brilliance is often born.[114]

chapter six

Implementing the comprehensive plan

In this chapter on implementing the comprehensive plan, we will travel further into the realm of change necessitated by the problems we are facing with our current methods of land-use control. We will look at some of the major issues with zoning ordinances, which are considered a primary tool for the implementation of plans, and then into proposed alternatives for land-use regulation. All of this is premised by our belief that community planning, done in a way that mirrors Nature's biophysical systems, will result in less — not more — need for regulation. This is not to say that regulations will cease to exist, only that communities can provide incentives or simply the opportunity or education that will help achieve the same goals as those that justify the existence of land-use laws and regulations.

Zoning ordinances

Zoning law, discussed earlier in the book, and the policing powers represented by zoning ordinances are a result of state statutes that authorize municipalities to regulate the use of land. Zoning law must also be designed to protect the health, safety, and welfare of all citizens.

Zoning ordinances and greed

The most frequent complaint about development standards, as set forth in zoning ordinances, is tied, we believe, to individuals not understanding the purpose of setbacks, limitations to building height and size, driveway placement, and so on. While zoning ordinances usually contain glossaries, rarely do they contain the kind of annotation that explains the way in which such requirements as setbacks protect the health, safety, and welfare of the community. Also high on the list of complaints about zoning laws, under the general rubric of "arbitrary and capricious," are any control on architectural design as well as regulations concerning signs.

It is certainly true that simply explaining the broader purpose for development standards will not necessarily overcome the desire of many in a free society to get what they want when they want it. Some call this greed. Some call it arrogance and greed. Others call it ignorance.

We suggest that all of the above are tied to fear — fear of losing one's rights, however they are perceived; fear of being less than the government or being overwhelmed by the government; fear of having less than someone else has; and so on. Further, we suggest that fear drives the social dysfunctions that lead us to destroy, disrupt, and otherwise interrupt social and community progress and well-being. (For a more in-depth discussion of these fears, see *Resolving Environmental Conflicts: Toward Sustainable Community Development*[115] and *Setting the Stage for Sustainability.*[63])

Much of what we hope to engender by the process we are describing herein is a reduction in the fear of individuals, to cultivate a connection to place and to one another, to assist in the discovery of common ground and values, and to forge lasting solutions and relationships. When we look carefully at the choices communities have made that have produced permanent or significant damage to natural systems, such as the construction of massive shopping centers or huge casinos in the middle of the desert, some basic fears might be discovered. The authors know people who love to visit the glitzy lounges and performance venues of Las Vegas or Reno. It provides an escape from the hum-drum or other parts of life that people feel they need to flee. The fear of too much hum-drum (the inability to be comfortable with oneself) or too much of whatever is often the seed of change in our communities. Fear produces vast markets for products and services. Fear allows developers to come unchallenged into communities where economic problems are prominent. Once in such communities, developers believe they have greater access to development approval than in communities where economic well-being gives decision-makers greater confidence in saying "no" to such a developer.

Content of the zoning ordinance preface

At the very least, we suggest it is necessary to include a preface to zoning laws that contains specific explanations (an expanded glossary, if you will) of the common elements of each requirement set forth in the development standards found in the zoning ordinance. Such explanations will help the reader and/or user of zoning laws to understand their connection to the requirements of the Earth in terms of its health, the community in terms of its livability, and the citizens in terms of their health and well-being.

Percent impervious surfaces

There is a direct relationship between the amount of impervious surface (such as a paved road) on any one site and its affect on the runoff and infiltration of water. The greater the area covered by an impervious surface, the greater the amount and level of contamination of the water flowing over it from such things as automotive oil. In addition, the gutters and storm drains that line paved streets redirect runoff which results in less water infiltrating into the soil, where it can be purified and stored and can ultimately replenish the supply of usable groundwater.

Long-term costs, both social and economic, are associated with the pollution of water and an insufficient supply of water. Minimizing the amount of land we cover with impervious surfaces will contribute greatly toward maintaining both the quality and sufficiency of the water supply.

Building setbacks

A building setback is the distance from a property line required for a building or structure. The requirement of keeping property lines free from the encumbrances of buildings is related to maintaining access between buildings for the control of potential fires, to protect personal privacy, and to protect the spatial scale of development with respect to such public infrastructure as streets and sidewalks.

Required setbacks from lakes, rivers, streams, and wetlands reflect recognition of the impacts that human-caused disturbances to the natural landscape have on the quality and availability of water. Setbacks from wetlands, in particular, are in recognition of the social, economic, and environmental values of wetlands with respect to the health of a community. These values include: (1) filtering pollutants, sediments, and nutrients from the water passing through them, thereby protecting the quality of water in streams, rivers, lakes, and wells; (2) storing runoff from rain and snowmelt, thus helping to prevent flooding and the damage it causes; (3) providing habitat for waterfowl, fish, and other creatures; (4) acting as a shoreline buffer, thus preventing erosion from waves and currents; and (5) providing beautiful open spaces, thus enhancing the quality of life, the economic value of private property, and the economics of tourism.[116]

Plans for erosion control and contouring the land

One reason for requiring plans for contouring and controlling erosion is to minimize sediment transport by water during and immediately after construction. Sediment transport is a major source of damage to water quality and to the general health and ecological integrity of a community's water catchment. In windy Las Vegas, airborne soil erosion from disturbed undeveloped land and land under development contributes to a notable decrease in the city's air quality.[117]

Grading plans are also based on an understanding that the less disturbance there is to the natural landscape, the lower the impact of the development process and finished product on water quality and the health of other natural resources. To the extent possible, conformance with the existing topography is desirable.

Similar to the effects associated with impervious surfaces, long-term costs, both social and economic, are associated with sediment transport, which diminishes the quality of a community's available potable water.

Open space requirements

While setback requirements are sometimes spacious enough to qualify as an open space requirement, an open space requirement frequently stands alone in larger developments. This stand-alone open space requirement is based on the general understanding, alluded to earlier, that the more contiguous and well designed an open space system is, the better it can be protected in a relatively natural state and the lower will be the impact of a given project on the surrounding ecosystem.

The need for such protection of the landscape is exemplified by the effect on indigenous species of the degree of habitat connectivity or habitat fragmentation. Fragmentation of the landscape has resulted in a loss of plant and animal communities, the creation of abundant edge habitat at the expense of interior habitat, the alteration of natural disturbance regimes, and the loss of variability of ecological processes over broad spatial and temporal scales.[118]

The retention of open space can also be justified by understanding the human need for contrast in one's environment, such as passive spaces to serve as a welcome relief from the built environment. Each type of environment has a sensory impact on humans in that we might presume the more intense the development, the more stress on our senses. Additionally, provision of open spaces in a development typically enhances property value.

Although not in the context of a zoning ordinance, we could add to the above that the demand for open space by home buyers is on the rise. In November 1997, for example, *The Wall Street Journal* published a survey revealing that natural open space topped the list of desires for people wanting to purchase new homes. Paths for walking and riding bicycles came in second, gardens with native plants placed third, and areas of wilderness in close proximity came in fifth.[119]

Requirements for landscaping

The requirements for landscaping are tied to a general understanding that for ecosystem health to be maintained or enhanced, the landscape surrounding a development must be left as much intact as possible to protect the ecological processes that not only catch but also allow the infiltration, storage, and purification of stormwater. Further, the larger the percentage of healthy, indigenous vegetation that remains on a project site, the greater the benefits to ecosystem integrity and health. Thus, landscaping requirements can be seen as a way of maintaining and/or replacing something that may be lost in the development process. It can also be seen as a way of beautifying a site, tying it into the surrounding landscape, creating sound buffers, creating a natural cooling system, and so on. Finally, enhancement of a landscape typically heightens property values.

Design controls: site design, architecture, signs, and graphics

Before offering suggested language for a zoning ordinance preface, we will discuss design controls in general — their basis, difficulties encountered with their establishment and/or implementation, and potential guidelines.

What is design? The dictionary definition that we believe is most relevant to government controls over project design is an underlying scheme that governs how something develops or unfolds and how it functions. We believe a project design should be compatible with the overall design for a community and support the meaning and implementation of its vision, goals, objectives, and policies.

We believe further that a design dictates function, much like species composition in a plant community yields the community's structure, which in turn yields its function. How well a new project or development functions in a community will be tied directly to its design (read: composition and structure). To maintain community integrity, each new development must demonstrate its consistency with the overall design of the community as revealed in its comprehensive plan. Whereas a good design in this context will be clearly relevant to the overall character of a community by contributing to its social, economic, and environmental well-being and sense of place, a poor design will seem irrelevant and out-of-touch with the desires of the citizens.

Design is something that, like planning, is always occurring. To plan for a town or our own lives, we analyze tradeoffs, consider alternatives, and then choose a course of action. Design differs from planning in that it addresses the way things look and the way they work. A community that has clearly defined its vision and has consensus on community values will more easily find the path to good design and a proposed development design. It will either feel right or it won't.

Design emphasizes our physical relationship to the rest of the world. It can affect how we feel while walking down a street or sitting in a park. How a town looks reveals a community's self perception. It tells the visitor a lot about who the community is. As Mark Twain once said, "We take stock of a city like we take stock of a man. The clothes or appearance are the externals by which we judge."[120] This is but saying that definition is important for the development of a community, both from within and without. Such definition can be accomplished through published design guidelines that illustrate what requirements are necessary in order for a project to obtain approval.

Design guidelines can be used by municipalities to assist in the development review process or by peer review committees. Many cities, including Santa Rosa, CA, have adopted design guidelines. Santa Rosa first published design policies in 1980.[121] While the policies are broad, the city felt that overly restrictive or overly definitive standards would hamper the designer and might result in citywide monotony. Generally, Santa Rosa's site planning policies cover the appropriateness of setbacks, the height of buildings, circulation patterns for traffic, site coverage (percent of land covered by an impervious surface), parking, and landscaping, including outdoor lighting. The policies also cover the relationship of a proposed development to adjacent areas (including developments), the amenities of natural open space, and considerations of shared solar energy. Its architectural design policies cover scale, mass, bulk, and proportions of acceptable developments; suitability of design to the surrounding neighborhood and/or the streetscape; consistency of building materials and quality of workmanship; utility and mechanical facilities and their relationship to other structures; and accessory elements on the site. Sign and graphics design policies address size, scale, location, and materials of such things as signs and billboards with respect to the placement of lighting, proximity to buildings and roads, and so on.

These types of considerations are common in many municipal design standards. A consistent feature in *all* of the municipal design guidelines we have reviewed is protection of the unique character and heritage.[121,122] There is a human parallel here that cannot be overlooked. Perhaps communities that have discovered the value of preserving and protecting the unique character and heritage of a place have decided, like people who have ventured within to heal or grow, that finding one's True Self — we could call this the soul — is the key to sustaining a quality life. Travel writer Arthur Frommer has said that, "Among cities with no particular recreational appeal, those that have preserved their past continue to enjoy tourism. Those that haven't, receive almost no tourism at all. Tourism simply doesn't go to a city that has lost its soul."[120]

Many cities, like people cut off from themselves, have gotten used to mediocrity, hum-drum, or even ugliness; it has become who they are, an identity, so to speak. Many accept this state of being as an inevitable part of progress. For the city, it might be shopping malls and chain restaurants and motels; for the individual, it might be a job that provides an income and nothing else. Although the tools to make a city or one's life memorable and beautiful are neither new nor rare, access to them requires deliberate action.[120] Deliberate action sometimes does not occur, however, until there is some major threat. For a city, this could be the unintended consequences of a major new industry — losses not anticipated; for a person, it might be a sudden recognition of one's mortality or some awareness of permanent change in, let's say, physical strength or flexibility. In any case, a moving force in the direction of self-realization may simply be the full recognition that we do not really miss something until it is gone.

But how can we bring a community to an understanding of the images that communicate their values and their vision? One technique, used by the City of Fort Collins in its comprehensive planning process, is called a Visual

Preference Survey. Such a survey was conducted on cable television, by videotape, and in public meetings, resulting in more than 1500 participants.[123] While a Visual Preference Survey is considered a useful planning tool for soliciting community attitudes on a range of issues, it does not allege to address all of the relevant issues facing a community during the comprehensive planning process, such as management of growth, transportation, economic development, and so on. But a Visual Preference Survey is an effective tool for getting people initially involved in the community planning process on a general and interesting level.

The use of visual images to solicit comments allows people to respond to such questions as, "Do you like this image? Do you think it is appropriate for Fort Collins?" These questions put the issues in terms that can be readily understood, thereby making it easier than asking the public to spontaneously suggest an acceptable development pattern or density.

Results of this survey may be useful to other communities, even though the sample of respondents was not scientifically drawn, because those surveyed were simply those that chose to be surveyed. The findings, however, may be starting points for discussion in a community wishing to create its own design manual. Participants of this survey clearly favored a coherent system of open space — including sidewalks, paths, and parks — that connected all parts of the city. Every image that related to a body of water or edges of waterways rated high. What citizens preferred in the built environment were historic buildings — with historic colors, building materials, sizes, and shapes. This, of course, would translate directly to design guidelines for new development in the vicinity of existing historic structures. Participant preferences for downtown development included mixed-use development with commercial enterprises on the ground floor and professional or residential space above, interesting shop windows, outdoor cafes to stimulate pedestrian traffic, street trees, and street furniture. Preferences for the residential streetscape included narrow streets with on-street parking to slow the speed of traffic, neighborhoods completely connected by sidewalks, and connector streets with planted boulevards to minimize their width and facilitate pedestrian crossing.

The images receiving the lowest ratings included those showing an automobile-dominated environment. Streets, parking lots, and shopping areas designed only for the convenience of the automobile received poor ratings from a community that values the outdoors. Participants may fear that if such development is allowed Fort Collins will lose its individual character.

Such an exercise can provide credible substantiation for design standards. Even in the absence of such specific data, it is, in our opinion, still incumbent on a city to offer a rationale for design standards as well as to set forth legal findings necessary for the issuance of a design permit. This language should be found in the preface to the zoning ordinance, which most likely contains provisions for design review, such as design permit, design approval, development review, and so on.

Suggested language for use in a preface might be

> The purpose of these standards is to protect and en-
> hance those characteristics that make our community
> interesting, memorable, and attractive, and, in order
> to protect our unique character and heritage, the city
> of XYZ has established design guidelines for develop-
> ment. They are intended to protect all those places,
> both natural and human-made, that give our commu-
> nity its special character and identity. These include
> historic buildings, sites, and neighborhoods and other
> features of our community that have either cultural or
> spiritual significance. There are social, economic, and
> environmental reasons for design standards, as well.
> If the resulting design enhances people's connection to
> this place, we anticipate that there will be a stronger
> will toward creating a stable economy and stronger
> forces at work safeguarding our environment. With
> these things in place, we see a community of strength,
> resiliency, home, and heart.

Additional language could be added to explain site design, architectural design, and signs and graphics.[122]

Site design

Good site design has a plethora of rationale to support it. For example, buildings designed and sited to have a strong functional relationship to one another will make it easier to collect waste, promote economy of scale in operations in general, and help to form a legible site — one that simply makes sense.

To the extent that a development can minimize its disturbance to the natural amenities of the site, it is contributing to the well-being of the com-munity. A site's topography and natural amenities should therefore be rec-ognized and used to assist in the design and situation of proposed structures (for reasons explained under the discussion of a plan to control soil erosion) by fitting a development within the context of a landscape. Another reason is that a community's true economy is realized only when all of its assets are put on the balance sheet. It thus behooves a community to maintain its natural land forms, habitats, edges, waterways, and so on in a healthy condition.

Site plans should be compatible with the immediate environment, including development on adjacent parcels of land and streetscapes. This sense of spatial and temporal compatibility is part of creating continuity and weaving a new development, however one defines it, into the existing land-scape.

While an existing landscape might include a strip mall, that does not dictate that new development must necessarily be a continuation of the strip mall design if it is below current design standards. Insertion of new and progressive building design into a dated area is a challenge to the developer and the development-authorizing agency. Here, the opportunity exists for creative solutions that can stimulate rehabilitation and renovation in adjacent developments.

Many derelict neighborhoods in some of the nation's largest cities are being rescued in this manner, usually due to someone recognizing the value, either architectural or social, of reviving a building or a place. Such activity causes a ripple effect that can be seen in the gentrification of old, run-down neighborhoods in many of the country's large cities. With the improvement of one property, people in adjacent areas see the possibility of creating a critical mass that will give rise to heightened property values overall.

Architectural standards

Architectural standards, like other design standards, have social, economic, and environmental relevance. If a community has decided, as Santa Rosa, CA, did, that natural building materials such as wood, stone, or brick contribute to the character of place, then such a value can be reflected in the community's architectural design standards.[121] Like Fort Collins, CO, the Santa Rosa community saw both social and economic value in having the ground floors of commercial buildings be engaging to pedestrians, through interesting display windows, courtyard entrances, provisions for a sidewalk cafes or sitting areas, and so on. Both cities also recognized the importance of including measures of energy conservation as part of architectural design — a standard that clearly has both economic and environmental implications.

An architectural design standard growing in popularity is that all buildings should achieve a sense of human scale. This design standard is particularly relevant in places where people recognize the importance of creating nodes of activity or neighborhoods within larger cities, consistent with the approach of New Urbanism.

Sign standards

Sign standards have given rise to some of the most contentious debates in the realm of land-use regulation. In some cases, freedom of speech and expression have been added to the sign industry's arsenal in their fight against sign standards, particularly when it comes to billboards. While states such as Vermont and Hawaii have banned freestanding billboards, most communities have given up, have embraced sign proliferation, or continue to try to find ways of controlling signs. More and more, communities are passing sign ordinances with sunset clauses for the most offensive types of signs, such as billboards or freestanding, portable signs.

In an undated publication of the U.S. Small Business Administration in cooperation with the National Electric Sign Association, a strong case for signs is set forth. What can signs do for the community and neighborhood?[124] According to this publication, signs enhance the environment by making certain zones of the city more attractive and dynamic and giving the area a particular atmosphere. They also perform two major community safety functions — reduction of traffic accidents and crime. Government studies found that vehicle accidents actually decrease at highway intersections that sport commercial signage, and ambient lighting from signs is a major crime deterrent in urban areas.

The most difficult claim to fight, for a community that wants to control the proliferation of signs, is that they are the most efficient, effective, and consistent revenue-generating device for small business. Against such a backdrop of fearing the loss of one's freedom of expression and claims of public safety and economic necessity, the sign wars persist. But signs, like other design features of the community, should measure up in terms of their contribution to the overall well-being of a community — socially, economically, and environmentally. Sign placement, number, size, materials, and illumination have a collective effect on the overall tapestry of a community. Just how prominent a role they should play is up to each community.

Redesigning zoning ordinances

Next, we offer some ideas for modifying the standard zoning ordinance. Our ideas are based on the belief that a zoning ordinance can serve as a tool for social change and thus educate as well as provide the rules for land use. In so doing, we will again allude to the work of Donella Meadows regarding systems and their healthy functioning.[75] When describing places in which to intervene in a system to change its dynamics, she lists points of leverage in an ascending order of their effectiveness.

Now, if a zoning ordinance seeks not only to guide development in a way that achieves a healthy balance between human necessities and the environment but also to continually educate, it must seek an effective leverage point in the socioeconomic system of a community. The weakest place to intervene in a system to effect change, according to Meadows, is numbers or something tied to numbers, such as parameters or standards. Yet, development standards dominate zoning ordinances and, as we alluded to above, represent a source of conflict and frustration to many developers, which stimulates resistance in the form of noncompliance and/or lawsuits.

The system, in this case, is the community with its values, beliefs, and traditions. If it is a typical community, there is a significant segment of the population that does not want its perceived rights of private property infringed on by any form of land-use regulations. If Meadows is right, the parameters contained within land-use regulations will have the least effect on potential change in that social reality because of people's resistance to any perceived loss of personal choice. Meadows notes that if a system is chronically stagnant, changing parameters will rarely kick-start it. By the same token, if a system is wildly variable, changing parameters is unlikely to stabilize it, and if it is growing out of control, changing parameters will not act as a brake to slow it.

Slightly more effective than intervening at the numbers level is to intervene at the level of material stocks and flows, which means rebuilding the
system. Rebuilding or revamping the socioeconomic system of a community
in order to achieve a more lasting relationship with the Earth is, of course,
a long-term goal implied by all herein. It is, however, a place that a zoning
ordinance does not intervene. Instead, it is a part of the socioeconomic system
of a place and does not contain built-in mechanisms for changing the system
of which it is a part.

Moving up the list of leverage points, we reach built-in mechanisms that
are supposed to retain a steady state by providing a goal and a signaling
device to detect deviations from the goal as well as a response device to
correct each departure. Do zoning ordinances contain the kind of mechanisms that keep the socioeconomic system (the community) in a steady and
safe state? Although penalties and fines are built into zoning ordinances for
this purpose, we do not think they promote a steady-state system.

If current development standards in zoning ordinances serve only to
frustrate developers, why not use incentive-based development standards,
as we believe people respond best when they feel they have a choice whereby
they can retain their dignity? In some places, for example, developers are
provided incentives to produce something to improve the quality of life in
a community — affordable housing, parks, improvements in infrastructure,
childcare facilities, public art, and so on. We discussed some of these mechanisms earlier, such as incentive zoning, planned unit developments, and
more. Such devices should have a prominent place in zoning ordinances.

In addition, a new development can contribute to quality of life in a
community by its ripple effect, particularly if the community is made aware
of the fact that every development simultaneously has positive and negative
effects on both the community and its surrounding landscape. With this in
mind, a community can encourage developers to seek ways in which they
can mitigate the negative effects of their projects while enhancing the positive
effects. Municipal governments could also make significant contributions to
an improved quality of life by reaching out and asking developers for their
ideas of how to maximize the positive effects while minimizing the negative
effects of their development and by seeking to understand what the trade-
offs might be.

Affecting the flow of information is the next highest level of intervention.
This means creating a new loop for delivering feedback to a place where it
was not previously going. As an example of this, Meadows uses the U.S.
government's 1986 action requiring that every industrial operation emitting
hazardous air pollutants report those emissions to the public. No fines or
penalties would result — the pollutants would simply be reported. By 1990,
emissions had dropped by 40%, which can be attributed, it is believed, to
industries simply not wanting to be listed in the Top Ten Polluters or even
being known as contributors to poor air quality.

So how can a zoning ordinance provide a new form of feedback, one that
might be currently missing, as, according to Meadows, a missing feedback

loop is a common cause of system malfunction. An example of such a feedback loop, which should be restored to the right place and in a compelling form, would be pricing that reflects the true cost of a product. If, for example, gasoline at the pump were priced according to the costs of protecting the shipping channels in the Middle East, the costs of shipping, the costs to clean up air pollution tied to the burning of fossil fuels, and so on, we would see a much higher cost per gallon at the pump. In turn, a higher cost at the pump would serve as a compelling reminder of just how expensive it is to continue to rely on gasoline combustion engines to maintain our standard of living. Most people, particularly in the U.S., do not want to know about the real cost of gasoline or to pay more to operate their automobiles, which might infringe on their freedom of choice.

If, on the other hand, a zoning ordinance were aimed at this leverage point, it could legislate that for every acre of shoreland lost to development in a community, a fee is charged to the developer which goes into a fund for public purchase of such lands when available.

Simply changing the rules is the next level of intervention. This can include incentives, punishments, and constraints. As Meadows points out, "Rules change behavior. Power over rules is real power."[75]

Although we have been suggesting throughout this book that we will ultimately change the rules by modifying the process for arriving at land-use regulation, leaping to such change without the inclusive process described in these pages would, in our opinion, be tantamount to folly, which leads us to the next level — self-organization, or the ability of a system to change in response to change.

A zoning ordinance can provide the spark plug for taking advantage of this inherent quality of the human community by encouraging such experimentation as the wetlands-as-sewage treatment mechanism. Compost toilets, living machines, and other alternative ways of meeting our needs while minimizing our ecological footprint could appear in zoning ordinances in a number of ways. For example, a zoning district could be created for eco-industrial parks, where a full range of innovation in technology would not only be allowed but also be required.

The development of such a provision may require the cooperation of state and, perhaps, federal regulatory agencies, but if such a provision resulted in eco-industrial parks that were then monitored and studied, further innovation in land-use regulations might result. Encouraging such diversity may not be popular because it suggests losing some measure of control, but we feel it is necessary to lose some control by reaching into the areas of unknowns — and even institutionalizing such a process — if society as we know it is to survive on this planet.

Intervening at the next level — goals — means, in the context of the zoning ordinance, ensuring that the goals of the community are reflected in the zoning ordinance regulations.

Intervening at the level of the mindset or the paradigm out of which the system arises means having the development code, which includes zoning ordinances, reflect an understanding of the community's deepest set of beliefs about the nature of life. We believe that land-use regulations can serve to influence and redirect community-held beliefs or assumtions of our culture. Examples offered by Meadows include: (1) that one can own land, (2) that growth is good, (3) that Nature is a stock of resources to be converted to human purposes, and so on. Therefore, while the development code must reflect an understanding that the assumptions exist, it must not reflect the assumptions *per se*. That is, the development code could leverage social change if an awareness of these assumptions underlies the creation of the regulations. Other paradigmatic assumptions that a zoning ordinance could possibly influence are that (1) government is separate from the citizenry, (2) land-use law is arbitrary and capricious, and (3) laws seek only to control but not to educate, inform, or serve as a catalyst for creative solutions.

Finally, the highest level of intervention is the power to transcend paradigms (we mentioned this earlier in Chapter 5). A zoning ordinance can intervene in a socioeconomic system (a community) at this level by containing built-in mechanisms for flexibility and nuance which, in spite of the extra time or costs associated with administration of the ordinance due to its lack of traditional structure, remain part of the development code. The additional time and/or costs associated with implementation of such flexibility and nuance will be seen as a long-term investment in the building of a sustainable community.

Thus, systematically moving a community toward environmental trusteeship and sustainable development can be engendered by a body of land-use law — a zoning ordinance. To be effective, however, the zoning ordinance must continue to evolve in a way that reflects an understanding of the leverage points in a community that will not only produce the necessary changes but also promote a sense of community well-being, both human and non-human alike.

Other regulatory approaches to land-use control

While there is a strong legal basis for restricting the use of private property, our effort in this book is to arrive at a place where regulations will be obviated by citizen initiative or where the regulations are so consistent with community values, vision, and goals that compliance is generally not an issue. Be that as it may, there is still a very strong case to be made for the protection of legitimate public interests. Like the recommended zoning ordinance preface, any legislated land-use control must be explained in terms of social, economic, and environmental benefits.

Preservation of farmlands

The amount of farmland, forests, and other open space that has been lost to development doubled during the 1990s, according to a government report.[125]

Between 1982 and 1992, the amount of land converted to development was 1.4 million acres per year, but that amount rose to nearly 16 million acres between 1992 and 1997. According to the National Resources Inventory, a study by the U.S. Department of Agriculture, this increase translates into 3.2 million acres annually. It is difficult, however, to blame farmers because development has greatly increased the value of land, which provides a windfall profit to many farmers who live near cities and choose to sell their farms. On the other hand, it is precisely the selling of the farms that is hurting not only the environment but also the very quality of life around the nation's cities.

The rate of development jumped more than fivefold in Pennsylvania, from 43,110 acres per year between 1982 and 1992 to 224,640 acres per year between 1992 and 1997. Altogether, 1.1 million acres of land were converted to development during the 5-year period, second only to Texas, where 1.2 million acres were converted to development during that same time — 139,000 acres annually between 1982 and 1992 and 243,900 acres annually between 1992 and 1997.

Pennsylvania and Texas were followed by Georgia, Florida, North Carolina, California, Tennessee, and Michigan, although some cities and states attempted to curb the conversion of farmlands to development by paying farmers to stay in the business of farming. By voluntarily selling easements, farmers continue to own the land until they die or choose to move, but they are barred from pursuing activities other than farming. Such programs help to control urban sprawl while simultaneously maintaining clusters of farms necessary to ensure a viable supply of local agricultural products and the required network of support.

A survey of existing government policy, laws, and legal decisions gives credence to the creation of devices for the protection of food-producing lands.[126] The U.S. Farmland Protection Act, for example, states that a "continued decrease in the Nation's farmland base will threaten the ability of the United States to produce food and fiber in sufficient quantities to meet domestic needs and the demands for our export materials." The concern represented by this statement — namely, that existing and/or potential agricultural lands may be undervalued — is real because most people living in the U.S. are so far removed from food production that they have little appreciation of the social value of farmland, and the outlook for small, private farms seems bleak due to the continued growth of corporate farms.

This being the case, the concern represented by the above statement could affect how a community planning committee views its agricultural lands and their future. In addition, local farmers and/or farming interests, should they exist, could also raise the awareness of community planners.

Boone County, IL, for example, protects farmland with a mechanism that kicks in when an application is submitted for rezoning from exclusive agricultural district to rural residential district. In this instance, no tract of land with a 25% or greater percentage of its soils classified as Class I or II soil or with a 50% or greater percentage of its soils classified as Classes I, II, and

III will be rezoned unless it meets the requirements of: (1) the slope of the tract is 6% or greater, (2) manmade or physical features act as barriers to farm operations, and (3) it contains at least 20% wooded area as judged by the U.S. Forest Service criterion for the evaluation of tree cover.

A law like this has merit in terms of influencing social change because it so clearly relates to a human need for survival — in this case, food and the business of farming. Such a law also has merit because a community might not see the need to protect some of its farmlands, believing that this necessity can be taken care of elsewhere, say central California, often seen as the breadbasket of the nation.

Other regulatory tools include zoning for a large minimum lot size, fixed area-based zoning, and sliding-scale zoning.[127] Large minimum lot zoning, for example, is intended to encourage the protection of agricultural land. The incentive to the property owner for creating a larger lot out of a collection of smaller lots, perhaps 80-plus acres, could be the tax advantage of owning land with agricultural value instead of the value assigned to land for speculative development. The resources protected through such zoning include agricultural land, rural landscape, and viewsheds, but would not preclude residential development, only the establishment of residential subdivisions.

Fixed area-based zoning allows the creation of a smaller parcel within a larger one (e.g., one dwelling lot of up to 2 acres within a parcel of 25 acres). Like minimum lot zoning, the resources protected include agricultural land, rural landscape, and viewsheds. With sliding scale zoning, on the other hand, the number of dwellings per area decreases as the size of the parcel increases. Also, smaller parcels not suitable for farming may be developed at a higher overall density than larger farm parcels.

Another example of this is found in a Lincoln County, OR, law (Ordinance 1.00075), which addresses rural residential development in agricultural areas. It states that rural residential development can be accommodated on land within agricultural areas not suited for agriculture or commercial timber production, and such residences will be allowed if they pose no threat of conflict with prevailing farm and forest practices.

If a community decides that agriculture will not be a part of their community, the value must be respected and portrayed in the plan. As we try to find alternative and more effective means for creating sustainable development, the question that arises over and over again is whether a community really knows what is best for itself over the long term. If the process through which the community arrives at decisions that affect how the land is developed is inclusive and value-laden and produces multidimensional solutions that serve human needs while protecting ecological health, the answer most likely is "yes." The decision-making process is intended to continue beyond the actual plan-creation phase and includes mechanisms for monitoring the success or failure of resulting goals, objectives, policies, and laws. Thus, if subsequent monitoring reveals that a recommendation is not yielding the desired result, modifications can be made.

Population growth rate and new construction

Nationally, growth in the number of new houses built was estimated to have increased by 10% between 1990 and 1998, going from 102.3 million houses constructed annually in 1990 to 112.5 million in 1998.[117] Although a few states have experienced growth of more than 20% (such as Utah and Idaho at 22% and Arizona and Georgia at 21%), Nevada topped the list with a leap in the housing market of 48% between 1990 and 1998 — from 519,000 to 767,000 houses built annually.

According to Damon Eilek, a site superintendent for American West Homes, Inc., "The houses here [in Las Vegas] are sold out beyond what we can build. There's really no end in sight. I hope it continues." Houses are selling so quickly that the land is not even prepared for construction before a "sold" sign appears, which is not surprising to Marc Perry, a demographer who helped to prepare the housing report, because Nevada has been the fastest growing state every year during the decade of the 1990s. "As Nevada grows," said Perry, "and its base population gets bigger, it's going to be increasingly difficult to sustain this rate of growth. You can't keep growing at 5% a year."

Houses are built so quickly in Nevada that prices remain low despite the thousands of new residents flooding into Las Vegas each month. When one of the authors (Chris) lived in Las Vegas from 1990 through 1992, he received a new, huge telephone directory every 6 months because of the tremendous increase in population. When he looked at one newly constructed house in 1990 and found the kitchen counters to be pulling away from the walls, he asked the contractor if they were going to be fixed. "Naaah," he replied, "someone will buy it." And someone did.

Las Vegas is not only rapidly destroying its surrounding landscape but also depleting its supply of water. While the author lived there, he saw more waste of water than anywhere he had ever been, even in the tropics. At some point, Las Vegas will run out of water unless, of course, the citizens can get someone else's water, as they have attempted to do. The upshot is that unlimited continual growth is not ecologically viable for any community, town, city, state, or nation — hence, the necessity of policy and laws.

A survey of existing government policy, laws, and legal decisions also points out examples of jurisdictions that regulate growth, one of the most controversial types of planning law.[128] In Oceanside, CA, the municipal code contains a system for controlling residential development. This system, or ordinance, limits the number of building permits allotted. Those permits are allotted on a point system that accounts for such factors as the effect of new construction on public facilities and services, the quality of the architecture and the site for its proposed use, and the desirability of housing for low-income persons or senior citizens. In the case of *Construction Industry Association, Sonoma County (California) v. City of Petaluma* (522 F 2d 897, 9th Circuit, 1975), for example, a decision was handed down by the court that builders would get points for good architectural design, for providing low- and moderate-income dwellings, and for providing various recreational facilities, all of which must conform to general municipal plans and municipal design plans.

Given our reasoning about the necessity of finding innovative ways of controlling and directing development, which includes growth, we believe it may be possible to arrive at a natural cap on development and growth. While pressures from the outside will undoubtedly continue to exist, the laws and policies in place may be so infused with a community's shared vision and the values it embodies that neither the limits to growth nor the availability of resources will be exceeded without further planning or adjustments to accommodate the community's vision and goals. Through such a process, innovative solutions might be sought to either stem growth or reconcile more growth with a community's immediate landscape and its environmental constraints, both of which depend on what a particular community wants.

The following examples of attempts to regulate growth are taken from Jane's experience in two cities, where growth management was a major focus of planning efforts. In Santa Barbara, CA, in the 1970s, growth became a major election issue and swept in a new majority to the City Council. It was an "anti-growth" majority, which, following a citizen referendum that called for a cap to the city's population of 75,000 people, directed the planning department to devise techniques for regulating growth. One technique proposed was to change the regulation of development density from units per acre to bedrooms per acre, with the assumption that bedroom occupancy was generally 1.3 persons per bedroom in the typical household. This would give developers more flexibility with number of units while simultaneously giving the city greater assurances of not exceeding the population cap.

In Santa Cruz, CA, where a county-imposed limit on the annual number of building permits issued forced most of the development into cities (primarily Santa Cruz), an attempt to regulate growth took the form of regulating the size of a household. The proposal required owners of rental dwellings to get a commercial-residential permit. The permit was issued if the property owner agreed to a number of conditions, including: (1) allowing only a specified number of residents to occupy a dwelling in relation to the number of defined bedrooms in the dwelling, and (2) allowing only a specified number of off-street parking spaces. Because more than 50% of the dwellings in Santa Cruz were rentals, this was essentially a form of population control.

In another attempt to have greater control over population growth while simultaneously attempting to increase housing affordability, a City of Santa Cruz housing task force proposed changing the multifamily residential density standard from units per acre to population per acre. The intent was to encourage the development of a greater number of smaller units but also clearly was another means for managing growth.

Such mechanisms are usually weak when it comes to actually preventing growth, as revealed in both Santa Barbara and Santa Cruz, both of which continue to experience tremendous pressure for further development because they are both beautiful towns with highly desirable climates. In Santa Barbara, for example, there currently is an effort underway to get some control over effects of growth that include: (1) a predominance of upper income households, (2) traffic congestion, and (3) a high number of people who commute outside the area for work.

Currently, work is underway in Santa Barbara to take a systems approach to finding solutions to the problems the city is experiencing. They are developing a systems model for the interaction of housing, business, and public infrastructure in order to rectify the current imbalance in these areas.[129]

Preventing traffic congestion

Controlling the effects of automobiles, including traffic congestion, is usually a point on which much consensus can be found. One of the authors (Jane), having lived in large to medium-sized communities for 43 years, has a great appreciation for the low traffic density of the community in which she now resides. They have what is locally known as a "rush minute" each morning between 7:30 and 8:00 a.m. and then again each evening between 4:30 and 5:00. She finds this is a splendid relief from the traffic of urbanized areas and it generally is not taken for granted.

Some cities are actively forging creative solutions to traffic-related impacts. In Minneapolis, MN, for example, on the west bank of the University of Minnesota campus, traffic-calming devices are employed. These include blocking off residential streets at one end to decrease traffic, a technique that is apparently borrowed from Sweden. In another example, the court found in *Hass and Co. v. City of San Francisco* (1979) that it was lawful to limit the height of future residential high-rises in order to reduce traffic congestion in neighborhoods, as well as protect the light and air that would be available to neighbors and protect aesthetic values, which brings us to nonregulatory methods of controlling land use.

Nonregulatory methods of controlling land use

There is an array of nonregulatory tools available for managing our use of the land, such as processes initiated by citizens groups and specific laws that enable and provide incentives for citizens to initiate actions aimed at protecting the land. We will begin our discussion with incentive-based tools.

Incentive-based tools

Incentive-based tools, which are described in great detail in a number of publications, such as *Common Groundwork: A Practical Guide to Protecting Rural and Urban Land: A Handbook for Making Land-Use Decisions*,[38] include outright purchase of land, donated conservation easements, purchase of development rights, and transfer of development rights.

The outright purchase of land from a willing landowner by a government agency or a not-for-profit conservation organization is generally for the purpose of protecting natural resources or providing public access. An example might be private land within a national forest or national park. On the other hand, a landowner may choose to donate some amount of land to a government agency or a not-for-profit conservation organization and reap tax advantages in return.

Donated conservation easements enable landowners to permanently limit future development on their property. Such an easement is a voluntary legal agreement between the landowner and a public agency or a not-for-profit land trust. Under such an arrangement, the landowner retains both the ownership of and the right to use the land, but within the terms of the conservation easement. There are, of course, tax advantages associated with such easements.

Purchase of development rights is a government-initiated or not-for-profit-initiated program that pays a landowner (who wants to protect his or her property from the potential of future development) for the development rights. Purchase of development rights takes the form of a legal agreement that places a permanent conservation easement on the properties.

Transfer of development rights, on the other hand, is a program that creates a private market for buying and selling the right to develop property. A transfer of development rights program begins by dividing a community into "sending" and "receiving" zones. Sending zones are areas that a community wants to protect from further development. Receiving zones are areas that are able to accommodate new growth, usually because they are already served by existing infrastructure such as sewers, roads, and water lines. In such a process, the right to develop the land is separated from other rights associated with property ownership, such as privacy and the right to lease or sell the land. Property owners in a sending area sell development rights to developers to use in receiving areas, where higher than normal densities are typically allowed.

Such programs are complicated to administer but provide advantages to the community at large as well as to program participants. Advantages include the guidance of development to areas that can most easily support it and the preservation of lands that cannot. "In addition, local governments do not have to spend funds to acquire land or development rights. In contrast to cluster zoning, which protects land parcel by parcel, transfer of development rights can help to preserve large tracts of open space in the community."[38]

The number of possible incentive-based tools is probably limited only by the resourcefulness and creativity of individuals and groups interested in furthering responsible land use. An understanding of community values and the multidimensional requirements of both humans and the ecosystems on which they depend for personal and social survival releases the creative forces of experimentation and discovery with respect to incentives for wise management of the land.

Incentives themselves

In describing new techniques for controlling land use, we have mentioned incentives, which are frequently money based, and the usefulness of such incentives in achieving better land-use practices. Examples of such incentives include tax advantages; actual payment to private landowners (in the case of purchase of development rights); allowing higher than usual building densities on certain pieces of land, thus making development more profitable; and so on.

Our society frequently rewards socially desirable behavior with some form of monetary gain. Children are rewarded in this manner, although gifts of dollars, while common, are seen by some as impersonal. Government rewards citizens in the form of tax benefits, such as tax write-offs, which are sought by most taxpayers. Such a reward system, in Pavlovian terms, serves to reinforce behavior and values associated with material wealth, which in the long term may be a deterrent to building sustainable communities and thus a sustainable society.

That money is used as an incentive is symptomatic of a society in which the full range of human requirements typically goes unrecognized. The recognition of the multidimensional and oftentimes nonhierarchical needs of humans may produce incentives not yet on the radar screen, so to speak, of government agencies attempting to evoke compliance with policy and laws.

The lack of recognition of the full range of human needs usually starts with the individual. It is generally understood that humans operate in a way that allows them to survive, and each human most likely defines his or her own survival daily. One person's survival depends on the retention of a particular job or a set amount of income and family relationships, while another's may be tied to gardening, reading, and a modest subsistence income. Although everyone is clearly different, the result is a survival-based way of life, regardless of how "survival" is defined, that usually leaves some built-in human needs both unrecognized and unnurtured.

For example, the workaholic who spends most of his or her time earning an income and commuting to and from work may overlook the need for physical activity or spiritual development. Overlooked or ignored parts of ourselves are sometimes awakened, and the experience can be like drinking a cool glass of water or plunging into a refreshing pool after a long, hot desert journey. Most of us are familiar with the kind of person who generally shows little feeling but can cry easily when the national anthem is played or upon seeing a public service announcement on television about child abuse. This experience can be an awakening, even if not recognized as such. These awakenings reveal parts of ourselves that perhaps have been long neglected. These undiscovered or unattended parts of ourselves keep us from fully understanding others and thus may be part of the reason why incentives not only are tied to material gain much of the time but are also seen as more valuable than simply giving recognition for something done well.

Rewards in the form of community recognition are, in our opinion, much too infrequently used by local government. For example, a city's Beautification Committee could, on a monthly basis, publicize and recognize contributions to the beauty of a community by local citizens, businesses, or institutions who have maintained a lovely flower garden, applied a new coat of paint to a building or house, put up a new business sign that sets an example for appropriate signage that blends into a community's character, and so on. This kind of recognition can encourage others to reach beyond their normal behavior for the benefit of their community as a whole. Such a "recognition committee" need not emerge from government; it can be citizen based.

A freely formed group in a town where one of the authors once lived gathers each Christmas season, walks together through this small community, usually during the evening, and selects homes with extraordinary holiday decorations. They stop, sing a carol outside the home, and, when and if an occupant appears, award the occupant with some small gift in recognition of the beauty they have contributed to the town. Elsewhere, during a community planning process, the leaders made certain that at each stage of the process a celebration of the group's progress took place. This not only contributed to team building but also was a reward of a non-monetary nature for the work of each participant. The concept of having fun must be recognized and encouraged in all of our work in community building because it can be seen as a reward in and of itself. Discovering what might be fun for others fits right in with discovering and appreciating the full range of human needs and is itself a fun process.

Incentives built into land-use laws, however, will most likely remain tax benefits or some other form of economic benefit because the value of property is typically viewed in terms of dollars and cents, even though some landowners think of their property as priceless and irreplaceable. A person who holds his or her land in such high esteem is a likely candidate for a conservation easement, which not only honors the intrinsic value of the land itself but also offers the reward of permanent protection for the land. An extrinsic reward designed to have an intrinsic reward imbedded within it could contribute greatly to our progress in building community. On the other hand, should a straight monetary reward be preferred, it might still help to raise one's level of consciousness if it is made clear how the act being rewarded is tied to other dimensions of community — social, economic, and environmental.

Ideally, incentives would not be needed to achieve responsible land-use practices. Land trusteeship could result from education, inclusive government process, and recognition or rewards for leadership in this area. Currently, the City of Ashland, WI, is planning a community event to celebrate years of citizen-driven work to revive the life of its waterfront and make it more accessible. This low-cost effort will no doubt have valuable long-term gains. The purpose of this celebration is threefold: (1) to recognize and acknowledge that the community has something to offer the city in developing the waterfront; (2) to recognize and acknowledge the current success in redeveloping the waterfront as a form of reward that, it is hoped, will instill friendship between the government and the citizens and stimulate further contributions to civic and community life; and (3) to draw, from the community, its memories, stories, and photographs relating to the waterfront, which has had a rich and colorful history.

This information will be used to design a series of interpretive "stations" to complement the recently completed waterfront trail, which travels from one boundary of the city to the other — a distance of about five miles. At these stations, signs will contain information about historic sites; existing industry along the waterfront, such as the power plant and an international paper-folding equipment plant; the types of fish caught in the lake; the history of the largest remaining ore dock on the Great Lakes; special seabird nesting areas; and so on. Inviting citizens to share their stories, memories, and photographs is a form of recognition and reward in and of itself for simply being long-time residents in a particular place, which is exactly the kind of activity that builds community.

Another example of this occurred several years ago in the town of Washburn, WI, when the town decided to apply to the Minnesota Design Team to conduct a three-day charrette to help the community discover ways to improve its town, which in this case drew around 200 citizens, or about one fourth of the community. The 17-member Minnesota Design Team — comprised of planners, architects and other design professionals, engineers, sociologists, and landscape architects — volunteers to go to communities in exchange for travel expenses. Team members are hosted by local families.

Before their arrival, the Minnesota Design Team sent a manual to help the community prepare for their visit. The manual described communities seeking the team's assistance as being commited to the future and wanting to make the most of the biophysical components of its environment as they define the community. These communities also realize that no one person or group of people are in and of themselves wise enough to know the best course of action for the community's future. The community therefore sets out to involve as many of its citizens as possible in the creation of a shared vision of the future that incorporates the ideas and core values of the community as a whole. To crystallize ideas, to clarify core values, and to energize the community effort, an outside group of eyes, ears, and minds is invited to help them — in this case, the Minnesota Design Team.[130]

The experience for most people involved with the Minnesota Design Team was very positive, as the team was well trained in active listening. The value they placed on the contributions of all participants was a form of reward that has had lasting value to the community of Washburn in the form of heightened citizen participation in the affairs of government and citizen-initiated projects, such as protection of and enhancements to the city's water-front trail, which brings us to the notion of a development review.

Development review

There are many opportunities for producing the type of development that does not compromise an ecosystem's ability to deliver services that sustain life. The most proactive level is during the community planning process, where the vision and goals are created, tied to a community's core values, and interwoven into an evaluation of the potential effects of proposed actions on the ecosystem. This process, of course, should yield zoning laws and land-use policy consistent with the community's vision and goals. And this process may indeed stimulate citizen initiative, both at the individual and organization levels, aimed at reaching these goals.

Citizen-initiated development review

Earlier in this book, we discussed the Land Development Guidance System of the City of Fort Collins, CO, and the reasons why it failed. One of the reasons was the administrative costs of handling the complexity and another was the absence of fixed rules. If we analyze this approach according to the systems theory described above, we see that such a point system is inter-vening at the weakest point — numbers. That is, if the system was designed to raise awareness and serve as a catalyst for social change with regard to development and appreciation of the nonnegotiable constraints of the eco-system, it was taking the least probable approach.

Another such point system for development is being proposed by the Conservation Fund. The system is in response to what is perceived as a mounting pressure on developers to produce more environmentally friendly developments.[116] The Conservation Development Evaluation System is a rating system created to evaluate the effects of the development on such things as long-term water quality and landscape integrity over the develop-ment's lifetime.

The primary purpose of the Conservation Development Evaluation System is to get developers to think about environmental concerns early in the planning process. The system is intended for use in rating new and existing developments and to encourage developers to strive to meet rig-orous standards and achieve multiple ratings for their developments. It therefore is not a piece of legislation nor does it purport to set the stage for recommended legislation. This is a strength of the Conservation Develop-ment Evaluation System, but its weakness lies in the same aspect as that of the Land Development Guidance System of Fort Collins, namely its empha-sis on points, which are awarded or deducted for satisfying a specified criterion.

Some of the ratings of the Conservation Development Evaluation System are much more stringent than the norm. The ratings of the Conservation Development Evaluation System lie more in the realm of positive feedback loops, however, and thus are more likely to change behavior of people than is the legislated but optional point system of Fort Collins.

This system presents a method of evaluating "conservation developments," recognizes the site-specific constraints and limitations on planning and design, assumes that the pre-development condition of the site is usually disturbed, is not intended for undisturbed land or high-quality natural areas, acknowledges that each category may not apply to every development, and emphasizes impact on water quality. The core criteria by which each development is rated are (1) site design and construction practices (percent impervious surfaces relative to conventional development, preservation of natural features and/or change in land form, sediment and erosion control); (2) stormwater management (rate and volume of runoff); (3) open space (management of open space, environmentally constrained open space); and (4) protection of natural resources (development of a protection plan for natural resources and existing vegetation, such as native plant and tree conservation and/or newly planted vegetation).[116]

The tactic of awards or incentives for encouraging more sustainable development is also used by the forestry products certification system. Certified forest products are wood products produced by a system that has been certified for sustainable practices, from logging and milling to manufacture and distribution. The market for certified wood products is growing as consumers become more familiar with the practice of sustainable forestry.[131] As these markets and their attendant demand grow, it is likely that more and more businesses associated with forest products will pursue these markets and thus change their behavior toward the environment. Be that as it may, for some consumers there is a certain status associated with owning what might be viewed as a designer wood product — SmartWood products do carry a label, much like many designer clothes.

Endorsements, like certification, represent a positive feedback loop in a system, and a process that will result from just such a project endorsement is gaining steam in Traverse City, MI.[132] The peer review committee of the Traverse City Area Chamber of Commerce New Designs for Growth program is comprised of architects, civil engineers, realty agents, surveyors, developers, homebuilders, and conservationists. All share an interest in seeing that principles of good growth management and progressive community development are applied to any project with potential significant impact.

In its two-and-a-half years of existence, the review committee has become so influential with community planners, government officials, and developers that its endorsement often assures friendly reception of project plans by governmental staff members. It has done 25 reviews to date and all but two have received final approval. The Chamber has also produced a design guidebook for use by developers. The mission represented by the guidebook is "to preserve and enhance the quality of our natural resources and environment as the basis for a healthy economy."

A statement by Keith Charters, coordinator of New Designs and administrator for the review committee, demonstrates an understanding of the use of leverage points in a system to achieve change: "Bad development is not the fault of developers, contractors, or realtors. It is the fault of bad rules, rules that affect the layout, look, site usage, and signage of projects and that specify where they can go."[132] In addition to the peer review committee, New Designs has undertaken a massive education program, holding workshops for officials and residents in 47 of the 93 jurisdictions of the region, which could ultimately affect goals and mindsets in the community. This committee is also seen as a stop-gap mechanism to help shape and control growth until local communities get their master plans and zoning ordinances updated.

We support the approach of the Traverse City Area Chamber of Commerce New Designs for Growth peer review committee on a number of counts: (1) it is citizen based, (2) it is nonregulatory, (3) it has a strong educational component, and (4) it attempts to intervene at nearly the highest level for success — to change goals in the community. We also believe that such an organized effort emerges from a process that is inclusive, vision-driven, tied to clearly defined goals, and high profile.

Such an organized effort brings the citizenry to government on a regular basis and, if carried out in an emotionally safe, civil, and dignified manner, can provide a very productive adjunct to government processes. This citizen-based independent review process should ostensibly be carried out by planning commissions, which can work quite well if the appointed members do not feel obligated to carry out the political agenda of the person — mayor or city council person — who appointed them. This is not to say that citizens on a peer review committee would not themselves have personal agendas, but rather it is to say that a citizens committee can choose to operate more freely — without the legal and political constructs of a government-appointed body. Such a multi-interest citizen's group has both advantages and disadvantages, as does everything, but on balance represents the essence of democracy and democratic processes and therefore represents an opportunity to be seized.[133]

Advantages of such a group include its diversity of interests — a characteristic of stable systems. Such a group also provides an arena in which participants can simultaneously address the interconnected aspects of a project. Finally, a process encompassing a multi-interested cross-section of citizens may succeed in resolving controversial matters unlike less diverse decision-making bodies because individual participants have most likely spent time in other settings identifying and justifying their positions.

Disadvantages of such a group include the fact that their work, due to the consensus process, often takes considerable time, more time than in processes where decisions are based on a vote of the majority. Although a multi-interest group process can lead to solutions based on the lowest common denominator because of the wide diversity of interests represented, an excellent facilitator, one who understands both systems and processes within systems, can often help such a group to choose solutions based on a much higher, it not the highest, common denominator. Such a facilitator also helps all participants to work together, in spite of the fact that solutions reached by such groups are not enforceable in a way in which a court order or law would be.

Obstacles to development review

Revised or new land-use policy could take the form of a new or revamped development review process. This process, if consistent with the type of planning we are advocating, would have a strong component of community involvement. Public participation is, after all, as important at the community planning level as it is at the stage where significant development is being proposed.

Some governments look at community involvement, like strict zoning regulations, as a threat to new development, as many developers do not want to invest the additional time needed for development approval. This frequently is a business decision, as time is money and time spent for adequate community review or government review that does not ultimately allow development is seen as a poor investment of time which equals a loss of money — a chronic problem in Corvallis, OR, and a growing problem throughout much of the state.

The Oregon legislature, through a 1995 land-use law, has essentially made it more difficult for the public to comment on residential development requests. House Bill 3065, pushed through just days before the end of the year's legislature, cuts the approval process in half and forces comments to focus on the legal merit of a subdivision.

"The idea is to get emotions out of land-use decisions," said Drake Butch, of the Home Builders Association of Metropolitan Portland.[155] The lobbying group, along with the Oregon State Home Builders Association, pushed for the bill's passage. "It's not fair to developers to keep delaying the process with appeals when their proposed developments meet all the legal requirements," Butch said. He went on to say that it is costing developers too much money to go through the approval process because of delays for public comment and appeals.[134]

The effect of this law is to: (1) steal choice and self-determining government from the people who live in the area of the proposed development; (2) give preference to residential developers, an increasing number of whom are absentee or even from out of state; (3) force local people to accept absentee interests; (4) limit — and perhaps even undermine — the scope of a local people's potential vision for sustainable community development within the context of their own landscape, especially for the desired future condition of their landscape; and (5) curtail or even eliminate the ability of local people to actively mourn for the continuing loss of their quality of life and their sense of place as outside choices are forced upon them, often by people who will not have to live with the consequences of their imposed actions.

The whole purpose of choice is for local people to guide the sustainable development of their own community within the mutually sustainable context of their landscape. After all, the local people and their children must reap the consequences of any decisions that are made. To limit their choices is to force someone else's consequences upon them, often at a great and increasingly negative long-term cost, first socially and then environmentally.

When preferential treatment is given to residential developers, including absentee developers, local people are at a serious disadvantage when it comes to planning for long-term community sustainability within the context of a finite landscape. While the focus of sustainable community development is long term, the interests of most residential developers are strictly short term, which usually counteracts long-term planning based on long-term environmental consequences. Further, it is exceedingly unlikely that absentee residential developers are going to have a vested interest in the long-term welfare of a community once they have made their money.

As noted in the above quote, it is the letter of the law that the residential developers want strictly enforced. But the letter of the law lacks moral consciousness, ignores the values of local residents, and discounts long-term planning for sustainable community development, all of which have consequences that are critical to the long-term social-environmental sustainability of a community. So, long after the residential developer is gone, the community is left to deal with the environmental errors caused by too much haste because the letter of the law was held to be inviolate and shielded from challenge while the people's core values and quality of life were discounted in favor of quick profit.

Finally, as noted above, the expressed purpose of the law to limit public debate is to "get *emotions* [feelings, human values] out of land-use decisions," which effectively slaughters the quality of human relationships while enforcing the law to the letter for the benefit of residential developers. But emotions, the force behind relationships, are based on personal and collective values, which are the heart and soul of a community.

Debates over the use of a given piece of land, be it in Oregon, anywhere in the U.S., or elsewhere, are indeed fueled by personal values that are expressed as emotions. These debates, and the emotions they evoke, not only help the participants to integrate the proposed changes into their consciousness but also are a necessary and vital form of grieving over the imminent loss of a safe and known past and the invasion of an unknown and uncertain future; after all, we live each day at the intersection of yesterday and tomorrow.

Curtail public debate, whether in an open meeting or by shortening the length of a public comment period (which steals people's legal right to express their feelings through both statements and questions in exercising self-determination), and trust and emotional well-being wither like a dying leaf in a hot wind. To be healthy, people must be allowed to grieve and given permission to grieve for their perceived losses, which is one of the functions of public debate. Only when people have moved through their grief is rational long-term planning for sustainable community possible.

Grief, although difficult at best, is vital to the emotional acceptance of a painful circumstance and to the reshaping of oneself in relationship to an outer world that reflects a new reality based on that painful circumstance. We, in our fast-growing American society, are daily faced with the death of beautiful things that we have long cherished, such as a small forested hill near our home where we have spent many a happy hour over the years enjoying seasonal flowers, fresh breezes, and the silence of open space.

Suddenly, we are confronted with the prospect of a housing development (255 single-family houses, 230 apartments, and 38 townhouses — an actual case) on 103 acres of that hill, and our sense of impending loss and grief is acute. Now we begin to go through the following stages of grieving that prepare the way for change over which, we the people, have less and less control because private interests are too often deemed more important than the public good of self-determination:

1. Denial of or resistance to change is how we isolate ourselves from one another because we see change as a condition to be avoided at almost any cost. We become defensive, fearful, and increasingly rigid in our thinking; we harden our attitudes and close our minds. If one becomes defensive about anything, starts to form a rebuttal before someone is finished speaking, and filters what is said to hear only what one wants to hear, one is in denial.
2. Anger, the violent outward projection of uncontrollable fear in the face of change, renders one temporarily "insane" ("I won't accept this!"). One's anger, however, is not aimed at the person on whom it is projected; it is aimed at one's own inability to control the circumstances that seem so threatening or emotionally devastating.
3. Bargaining is looking for a way to alter the circumstances based on more "acceptable" conditions (to cut a better deal, if you will), which is a function of public debate and the purpose of labor unions.
4. Depression is when one becomes resigned to one's inability to control or change the "system," whatever it might be, to suit one's desires. One feels helpless and deliberately gives up trying to alter circumstances. One becomes a "victim" of "outside forces," and one's defense is to become cynical — to project forward one's distrust of human nature and motives, even when nothing bad has happened. A cynic is a critic who stresses faults and raises objections but assumes no responsibility. A cynic sees the situation as hopeless and is therefore a prophet of doom who espouses self-fulfilling prophecies of failure regardless of the effort invested in success.
5. Acceptance of the ultimate outcome allows one to transcend the purely emotional state and reach a point where emotion and logic integrate. In so doing, one can define the problem and in turn transcend it. But acceptance of the problem must come before transcendence is possible.

Initially, we resist change because we are committed to protecting our existing values, representing as they do the safety of past knowledge in which there are no unwelcome surprises. We try to take our safe past and project it into an unknown future by skipping the present, which represents change and holds uncertainty, danger, and grief.

Those of us who have been trained to deal primarily through our intellect, which is but the first step in grasping the loss of someone or something we love, are too often cut off from our feelings and therefore try, as best we can, to minimize the pain. On the other hand, those who are in touch with their feelings and acutely aware of their pain are quickly accused by the moneyed interests, such as residential developers, of caring more for a wooded hill, wildflowers, or a butterfly than for people, which is implicit in the above-mentioned land-use law (House Bill 3065) pushed through the Oregon legislature in 1995.

The builders and developers in Oregon have found a way to directly intimidate people opposed to their commercial developments, effectively rendering silent any opposition at public meetings held to discuss their planned enterprise.[135] Such cases are known as "strategic lawsuits against public participation," or SLAPP suits. The Oregon House Judiciary Committee reviewed House Bill 2805 (aimed at stopping strategic lawsuits against public participation) in March 1999, after receiving statewide testimony concerning the abusive lawsuits. During the testimony, witnesses said they had ended up having to defend themselves in court after voicing their opposition to various proposals dealing with the use and development of land.

Although House Bill 2805 would protect citizens from lawsuits as a result of presenting facts, stating opinions, or expressing feelings at public meetings, it would not protect them from such statements made in letters to newspapers, such as letters to the editor. The bill also provides for courts to award attorneys' fees, other costs, and even punitive damages to defendants winning suits under the bill's provision and provides immunity for testimony given in public meetings.

Backers of the bill were pleased on May 12, 1999, when the Oregon House passed it by a wide margin, because, as Evan Manvel from 1000 Friends of Oregon, said "Public participation is critical to statewide planning and Oregon democracy."[135] Liz Frankel, from the Corvallis League of Women Voters, agreed, but cautioned that, while Joe Chandler (a lobbyist for the Oregon Building Industries Association, a statewide homebuilders organization) did not push very hard in the House, he will in the Oregon Senate. Although the Oregon House passed House Bill 2805 in May 1999, it was severely altered and then defeated in the Senate in July of the same year. Jeff Lamb, chairman of Oregon Citizens for a Voice in Annexations, said the defeat of the bill "will just add to the cynicism and the apathy" that already exist among voters. "It will be … a very chilling denial of what Oregon prides itself on … citizen involvement."[135]

Representative Kurt Schrader, a Democrat and the bill's sponsor, criticized the Senate action, which he contended put an end to the "opportunity for lawmakers to reaffirm the right of citizens to directly participate in the democratic process without fear of retaliation. …It's awful hard to go against money," which, according to Lamb, proved that, "He who has the campaign contributions will make the rules and the little guy will not have any immunity for participating in public debates."[135]

The Senate vote on the bill was along party lines to table the bill, with the Republicans engineering the defeat. Republican Senator Neil Bryant defended reducing protections for people testifying at public hearings on the grounds that speakers need to do the research necessary to make sure their testimony is accurate, which deftly removes social values and the feelings they engender from the democratic process.

It is no surprise, therefore, that in the material world, where money seems to reign supreme, special interest groups, such as developers, often make grieving for the loss of our environment and our attachments to it a most difficult and uncertain process in which the need to defend personal values and the feelings they engender against cold materialism is all but a foregone conclusion. We have almost no social support for expressing grief. Although our tears and honest discussion of our feelings may be signs of grief work well done when sitting beside the bed in which a loved one is dying, our tears and frank discussion are far more difficult and dangerous in a public meeting.

Nevertheless, people have long used rituals to help themselves and one another mourn and recover from grief. Most of our customs of contemporary mourning are directed at the acute loss of the people and pets that we love; these customs are important in the first weeks and months of the grieving process. But environmental and social losses are intermittent, chronic, cumulative, and without obvious beginnings and endings. It is therefore necessary to encourage, support, and develop (not curtail) socially acceptable customs of grieving (open public debate) and socially acceptable places of grieving (open public meetings) for environmental and social losses, those which alter the context of our lives just as surely as the loss of a person or a pet.

Because one's sense of loss is usually heightened by the sudden appearance of an unwanted circumstance over which one has no control, an alternative approach to development being considered in Corvallis, OR, could be for neighbors to hear what a developer has planned for a parcel of land before the houses are plotted and for developers to allow neighbors to have their say on a proposal before it is sent to public hearings.[136] For neighbors, such an alternative might help ease the fears of unbridled growth and for developers it might help to avoid costly battles in public hearings and in court.

Although all cities in Oregon must create citizen groups to involve people in land-use planning according to state land-use laws, in Corvallis the planning commission filled that role prior to the formation of the Corvallis Committee for Citizen Involvement, which is intended to act as a neutral clearinghouse for information. While a city can legally choose its own planning commission to fulfill the requirements of the state's land-use law, it is not recommended.

The Corvallis Committee for Citizen Involvement is seeking answers and inviting residents to help search for ways of getting citizens involved early in the development process — before ground is broken and houses go up. As noted above, one option might be to add an ordinance to the city's land-development code that would require developers to meet with neighbors *before* submitting development plans. Regardless of what option the committee recommends, says Kathy Seeburger, associate planner for the city and liaison to the committee, the goal is to remove barriers to citizen participation in the local land-use process: "You'd allow folks to understand what's happening early on and allow an exchange of ideas." In addition, the committee is working on a series of brochures that would illustrate how land-use decisions are made and how citizens can give effective testimony during public hearings. The committee is also thinking about rewriting public notices of land-use proposals to make them more reader friendly.

This said, it is our contention that development in and of itself may be neither good nor bad, aside from how we personally feel about it, but those who make their money from development need to make sure that socially responsible analyses of fiscal impacts of a given development have been conducted.

Fiscal impact analysis

Decision-makers who are concerned about having the development process thwarted and potential growth in the community discouraged because of a development review process that is open to community debate need to consider not only the collective intelligence of the citizens but also the right of citizens to participate in creating their own future. At the same time, however, a city would most likely benefit from conducting a fiscal impact analysis on all new proposals.

A fiscal impact analysis can provide a picture of the costs and benefits of a land-use project, and the following questions should be considered: Does the proposed business have a business plan? Are options for diversification built into the plan? How many employees will be needed, both short- and long-term? What are hiring practices of the business? How many jobs will this business mean to the local community? What sorts of adjustments will be needed in city infrastructure to accommodate this amount of growth? What will be the impacts, if any, on police, fire, and waste collection services, on the capacity of the sewage and water treatment plant, and so on? Will there be an impact on local schools and the available supply of housing? Will there be a short-term gain for the community with a long-term loss, or will it ultimately be a wash in terms of revenue added to the city?

A modified fiscal impact analysis would, of course, incorporate what is now called an environmental impact analysis, which analyzes the interconnectedness of three kinds of capital — social, economic, and natural.

Although a traditional fiscal impact analysis, as described in the series of questions above, does assess some social factors, such as schools, jobs, and housing, it only marginally touches on environmental effects by assessing the impact of a development on waste collection services.

If we assess the true cost of bringing a new development to a community, we would be looking at long-term social, environmental, and economic costs as well as gains — for example, potentially polluting emissions spewed into the air and/or water, which can be costly economically and socially for the company as well as the community but are always costly in the environment for the collective unborn generations we call "the future."

Evaluating whether the gains outweigh the losses is tricky business and sometimes beyond our abilities. One of the authors recently attended a conference on health risks and exposure to the environment. Speakers from Canadian and U.S. health agencies explained in detail the risks associated with breastfeeding by mothers consuming fish from Lake Superior. They maintained, however, that the benefits accruing from breastfeeding in terms of mother-child bonding and the nutrition and immunity-transfer of breast milk outweighed the risk associated with the mercury and other chemicals found in the breast milk of mothers living in the Lake Superior Basin. Somewhere in here, however, is a judgment call, as mother-child bonding is not quantifiable and, even if it was, the unit of measure would not be the same as the unit of measure registering the health risk of mercury-contaminated milk.

When evaluating the overall impact of new development, some judgment calls will certainly be required simply because we cannot know what all the effects might be, including a potential array of unintended consequences. The best we can do is to have in place an evaluative process that gives us a credible measure of potential consequences with some degree of certainty before approving a new development. Further, in judging whether a new development is "right" for one's community, there must be indications of the overall integrity of the business. This can be assessed from the existing track record of the business in question, from the business plan (and whether it contains measures for diversification), and, most importantly, whether the business is willing to accommodate the community process aimed at measuring how well the business fits into the overall vision and goals of the community.

Several years ago, a company approached a city government about locating their business in the city's industrial park. This business, which promised 60 local jobs after 5 years of operation, produced pellets created through the incineration of garbage. This high-intensity incineration process burns the organic material in garbage and leaves a residue that is cast into pellets, which are used in the manufacture of lightweight, durable concrete building blocks. In order to make this operation profitable, truckloads of garbage would have to be shipped in daily to add to the waste collected from the city.

Much to the credit of the city, it held a public information session so the company could present its case to the community. The session, although not required by law, was seen as giving the citizens an opportunity to comment on a project that had already raised serious concerns in the community because of the potential environmental consequences of the proposed operation. While there would have been a required state and federal environmental review process for such an operation, as it would be located along the shore of Lake Superior, this early review enabled community values to be aired, which ultimately led to the company going elsewhere.

If a traditional fiscal impact analysis had been done on this project, it is difficult to say what the bottom line would have looked like. But, from a sustainability perspective, this business would have rated poorly because of the necessity of importing garbage from outside the area with the attendant heavy truck traffic, in addition to the air pollution from the high-intensity incineration process.

As a result of this project's having reached the public arena, a neighboring tribe of Indigenous Americans decided to apply for a federal Class A air status, which, if received, would pre-empt any neighboring jurisdiction from allowing development that would require a special permit to operate because of the air pollution it would cause. This action, in turn, created a rift between the city and the tribe, which is still unresolved and unmitigated.

The point of the story in the context of development review is not only to demonstrate the importance of a public review early in the process but also to ensure that the input is received from a cross-section of the community. In this case, because of the regional effects of the manufacturing process, the local community, as well as leaders from adjacent communities, should have been invited to offer their comments, feelings, and values, which brings us back to a question we asked earlier — does a community know what is best for its future?

Did this particular community really know that this industry would be damaging to the environment (a thorough analysis had not been obtained)? Would not the burning of garbage to create another product be consistent with the ecological principle whereby all waste is fuel for other living systems? If the city had had in place a process for evaluating potential new development in the community that itself was a product of community-wide planning, a number of things could have been avoided, such as the rift between two government entities, a certain wariness in the community about the kinds of industry the city might be considering, and lingering concerns about the lack of predictability for citizens and developers alike with respect to how potential new development is evaluated.

Environmental impact analysis

Currently state laws in most states, as well as federal law, require environmental impact assessments if a proposed project is a public utility or if there is potential for negative consequences to the quality of the air and/or water. In some states, such as Florida and California, state law requires environmental review for almost all commercial and industrial developments, as well as residential projects that exceed a certain size.

The review process in California starts with an Environmental Checklist, which is part of an initial study.[137] The checklist poses a series of questions relating to the potential impacts on soils, air, water, plant life, and animal life, as well as those relating to noise pollution, light pollution, land use, natural resources, risk of upset (e.g., risk of explosion or the release of hazardous substances in the event of an accident), population (location, distribution, density, and/or growth rate of the area's population), housing, transportation/circulation, public services, energy, utilities and service systems, human health, aesthetics, recreation, and cultural resources. It also calls for compliance with the community's general plan — a good place to check for consistency with the community's vision. Although local municipalities are free to devise their own format for initial studies, a specific determination must be made regarding whether or not a proposed project may create enough potential negative consequences to require further analysis. While this tool has much merit, it lacks dimensions of the community that could potentially be affected by major new development, which leads us to the notion of a sustainability checklist.

Checklists for sustainability

Checklists for sustainability have emerged primarily from non-government organizations during the last decade because they are, by their nature, non-quantitative and therefore allow too significant room for legal contest. If a decision-making body, whether governmental or nongovernmental, is clear on a community's vision and goals, however, the use of such a checklist is much easier than if the vision and goals are not in place.

While this rather complex review process would discourage some new interests from coming to a community, we maintain that, if a community is desirable enough, this sort of a hurdle would not discourage developers with similar standards who would therefore understand the long-term benefits of such standards to the community as a whole. Let's look at some examples of these lists.

The Minnesota Office of Environmental Assistance has issued a checklist for evaluating the sustainability of community ideas and projects, which it adapted from a similar checklist developed by Sustainable Seattle — a volunteer network and civic forum for sustainability (see Chapter 5).[138] The checklist developed by Sustainable Seattle was designed to help citizens make the best possible choices as they create their own neighborhood plans, as well as to assist individuals and groups in the evaluation of specific neighborhood planning proposals in order to determine which ones do the best job of incorporating the four core values (promoting community, environmental stewardship, economic opportunity, and social equity) while moving the neighborhood toward sustainability.[139]

The checklist of the Minnesota Office of Environmental Assistance presents five categories of statements and a response continuum that ranges from "strongly agree" to "strongly disagree:"

1. *Community development* examines whether the proposal improves the community's sense of security, which means community development evaluates how well a proposal contributes to a sense of community among neighbors and to the critical things that make a community strong; it also probes the "inclusiveness" of the proposal, which encourages the participation of all affected people in the decision-making process.
2. *Ecological health* looks at how well the proposal takes ecological opportunities and limitations into account.
3. *Economic health* examines how well a proposal takes the economic well-being of the community into account by probing the links of economic self-reliance among the area's businesses, products, services, resources, and consumers to increase the recycling of money and other resources within the community.
4. *Social equity* evaluates whether the proposal promotes greater equity within the community and with people outside the community, as well as between present and future generations.
5. *Connections, trade-offs, and the long term* evaluates how well a proposal considers the connections among things, makes balanced trade-offs where necessary, and seeks to understand its consequences on future generations. In other words, this "big picture" consideration must take into account the linkages that a proposal forges among social, economic, environmental, and community issues.

Another checklist, called simply the Sustainable Community Checklist and generated by the Northwest Policy Center at the Graduate School of Public Affairs, University of Washington, is designed to help communities assess their own level of sustainability.[140] It is in workbook format and presents six principles of sustainability to help communities think more holistically about the relationships among economy, community, and environment. Each of the six principles is accompanied by a corresponding set of indicators and examples of projects in the state of Washington that relate to the principle and indicators.

The document offers a caveat that no precise blueprint exists for what sustainable communities will look like. The vision, and the strategies needed to get there, will vary from place to place. What this checklist suggests in the context of development review, is, like the checklist described above, a way of evaluating how well a proposed new development would fit into a community guided by principles of sustainability. The principles offered by this workbook point out that sustainable communities foster commitment to place, promote vitality, build resilience, act as stewards, forge connections, and promote equity.

How might a new business be assessed using these principles? In terms of fostering commitment to place, the first principle poses the question of whether a business offers living-wage jobs and has demonstrated, or at least voiced, its understanding of the community and its vision and goals. The second principle, which addresses community vitality, considers the extent to which a community stresses conscious development over continual growth and encourages local businesses to provide products that are not currently available to keep dollars circulating within the community. The third principle, resilience, might be reflected in a new business by the extent to which it contributes to the diversity of businesses in a community, whether or not diversification is built into its business plan, and its general ability to sustain itself. The fourth principle, which addresses stewardship, posits whether a proposed new business expresses an understanding of efficient use of resources and responsible waste management. The fifth principle, relating to the creation of connections, might be revealed in a new business by the extent to which it proposes to relate to existing businesses for mutual benefit. And, finally, the promotion of equity or fairness, the sixth principle, could be demonstrated by the company's hiring practices or its view of the future and how its products or services or operations consider future generations.

Checklists of the types discussed above can be used by a community in a number of ways. Our above discussion applied them primarily to new business and their use in evaluating the fit of a new business with one's community. These checklists can be adapted, however, for new development in general.

The Traverse City Area Chamber of Commerce New Designs for Growth peer review committee, described earlier, might be one place that such a checklist could be used. Inserting checklists such as these into the government decision-making process would mean revising zoning ordinances in a way that would: (1) base the approval of certain types of development on how well a proposal ranks according to such a checklist, (2) develop findings for permit approval that are tied to components of such a checklist, and (3) combine the checklist with a standard environmental impact checklist to be included as part of the preliminary review of a project. Further, provisions under a zoning ordinance would have to be clear on what sorts of projects merited this relatively stringent review.

Zoning ordinances typically have a set of permitted uses that require only administrative approval, which can typically be carried out by a zoning administrator or planner. Other uses usually fall into a category of either a special-use permit or a conditional-use permit. It is at this level where the public is typically able, officially, to participate in development review through the public hearing process, and it is at this level of review that a checklist, such as we are describing, would naturally fit. On the other hand, there could be a special category of uses that always require this additional review.

While municipalities can propose nearly anything a community desires by way of conditions for approval of development, careful legal scrutiny must be required, of course, in order to avoid lawsuits in the future. Some communities have become such desirable places to live and work, however, that even the most stringent review does not seem to diminish the demand for development. Santa Barbara, CA, is one such place. This town seems to be caught in a self-reinforcing feedback loop in which the more the place works for the people living and working there, the more it works, and as such it is nearly being drowned by its own success, which caused the intensive study underway in Santa Barbara to discover leverage points in the system to control the city's growth and the negative effects, which brings us to monitoring (Chapter 7).

chapter seven

Monitoring progress

Now that we have offered a suggested framework for the creation and implementation of a comprehensive plan, let us look at a framework for monitoring our progress toward achieving our goals and fulfilling the community's vision. We will look at change and our perception of it, progress and how we monitor it, and outputs vs. outcomes.

An important ecological principle to keep in mind during the creative process of both designing and carrying out a plan is diversity. Diversity was highlighted earlier as an important feature of community input during the planning process and then again as an important part of the plan itself. When monitoring the plan and its implementation and gauging progress, a diverse perspective is important. This is not to say that clear indicators of progress cannot be defined; it is to say, however, that we must be certain that the process of defining indicators represents a diverse perspective.

Diversity is related to redundancy in a system. The more diverse a system is, the more stable it is and the greater the built-in redundancy. That is, when one part of the plan does not produce the desired result, another is available to perform the similar, if not the same, function. The greater the diversity of input, the greater the likelihood that redundancy will be part of the plan — redundancy being a natural consequence of the diverse ideas. Diversity suggests both flexibility and adaptability to change and naturally leads us to the question of how we generally respond to change, which in turn depends on how we perceive change.

Change and our perception of it

After designing a plan with a clear vision and clear goals, it is tempting to believe that if we choose the correct measures of success, we will then be able to know if we have succeeded or failed. Here one must keep in mind that success and failure are not events, but rather interpretations of an event.

If you and I both participate in the same event, for example, you may deem the event a smashing success, whereas I may interpret it as a dismal failure — and we are both correct from our own points of view. When, therefore, we have goals and defined ways for achieving the goals through the attainment of set objectives, it is indeed important to define benchmarks or indicators of progress, which we will discuss below, but it is also important to know, short of using indicators and benchmarks, when we are off course.

Responding to the sense of being off course is best done in the collective, where inclusiveness and openness to the opinions and ideas of others are maintained and an indicator of progress is seen as a tool to help us reach a goal rather than becoming the goal itself. For example, a community that has worked together to create a comprehensive plan as well as indicators of progress might allow the process to languish by adopting the products — plan and indicators — as material representations of the desired future. Allowing a product to replace a process is also what happens when humans become too attached to a concept and convert it to something concrete; this is called *reification*. Shifting focus from community values — the intangibles — to measurable indicators of success, could, conceivably erode the values, which brings us to change, how we perceive it and consequently how we respond to it.

How we plan for the future implies being aware of and finding a need to deal with change, which we all know is a universal constant. Whether we are aware of it or not, we all change in response to change. It is inherent and is called *self-organization*.[75] Although a change may be minute and dysfunctional, we nevertheless respond to changes in our environment; in that, we have no choice. Being aware of the change, both external and internal, and seeking to understand the implications of the perceived change as well as the implications of our response indicate a level of awareness that we believe contributes greatly to building and sustaining community.

Some change is so gradual that the period of time after which the change can be viewed as significant might be greater than a typical person's life span. Global climate change, for example, is still viewed by many, both scientists and non-scientists, as a non-issue. And, even for the scientists that are studying and monitoring this phenomenon, the evidence of global climate change may not be extreme enough to warrant the kind of funding required to conduct the necessary research and develop the necessary solutions in time to prevent a crisis. In other words, there may not be the political will to push forward legislation that would result in adequate resources to increase our understanding of this matter. If, however, there was a consensus that enough evidence exists to merit the funneling of tax dollars into the appropriate research in order to get a better handle on this phenomenon, it would most likely happen, with or without overwhelming evidence that a crisis looms on the immediate horizon. Some liken the human experience of gradual change and the inability to sense the need to change to the phenomenon of placing a frog in cool water which is gradually brought to a boil. Apparently a frog will not react to the imminent threat of being boiled alive because it does not detect the inevitable outcome of the gradually heating water and thus dies.

Recently, when speaking with Dr. Anthony Socci of the U.S. Global Climate Change Office in Washington, D.C., one of the authors raised the issue of the gradual nature of global climate change and expressed concern about the lack of attention being paid to this matter, as indicated, in part, by the absence of this issue from the platform of current presidential candidate Al Gore, whose book *Earth in the Balance: Ecology and the Human Spirit*[141] addresses this issue at great length. Dr. Socci's response was that *when* the level of CO_2 is four times greater than it is now — a very dangerous level — or if we can see the imminence of that level being reached, then more attention will be given the problem, which brings us to the notion of the "invisible present." It is therefore necessary to urge communities and individuals to elevate their level of consciousness to a higher one of awareness of cause and effect if they are to be prepared to respond positively, rather than react irrationally, to perceived threats.

Another example of the invisible present is the disappearance of species. In *The Sixth Extinction: How Large, How Soon, and Where?*, a study by Stuart Pimm and Thomas Brooks, we learn that "humanity's impact has increased extinction rates throughout the world to levels rivaling the five mass extinctions of geologic history ... [and] for a wide range of well-studied taxa, the known current extinction rates are several hundred times higher than the background extinction rate demonstrated by fossil records."[84] Based on our knowledge of the extinctions rates of various species of bird, this study reveals that we can predict the potential future losses because they are directly linked to loss of habitat, which, according to Pimm and Brooks, "continues apace." According to author David Quammen, "In the next fifty years, deforestation will doom one half of the world's forest-bird species."[142]

In light of this information, one might ask what can be done to prevent future loss of habitats and thus species or, we add reservedly, the sixth extinction. What will it take for the global society to respond? How many species will be lost before significant actions are taken? Bringing about a significant decrease in CO_2 emissions — significant enough to reverse global warming, according to Dr. Socci — is unlikely. What is the threshold beyond which societies are moved to change or "self-organize" in response to change itself? Or will human society wait until it is struck dead by changes of its own making?

Other questions to ponder include: "How rapidly are we actually capable of understanding physical, cultural, or economic situations that nestle into a complex system that we do *not* fully understood?"[113] Because this question is not asked, there is a massive illusion that we humans are somehow in control of Nature, as evidenced by people, in awe of our having put a man on the moon, who now believe that we are capable of solving all our global problems. "How capable are our social institutions of perceiving the multidimensionality of issues and successfully communicating this information so the public can understand it, and how free is society to respond to this understanding, even if it can be achieved?" Our sluggish response to the continued population growth is due, in part, to strong opposition by some groups against equality for women and family planning. "How quickly can we self-organize or change in response to change?" "How able are humans to perceive their own free will and then, once perceived, under what conditions will they exercise it?" These questions are pivotal in looking at how we respond to changes in the world. We might also consider what types of behavior characterize those humans who are best prepared to deal with this type of gradual change in an effective manner.

Russell Ackoff, in his 1974 book *Redesigning the Future: A Systems Approach to Societal Problems*,[143] describes four types of people and the ways each responds to the world. Donella Meadows, in her article "Chicken Little, Cassandra, and the Real Wolf — So Many Ways To Think about the Future" (*Whole Earth Magazine,* Spring 1999,[143] suggests that one of the four types Ackoff describes — the Interactivist — is the most likely to bring about a sustainable society. Interactivists, unlike Ackoff's Inactivists, Reactivists, and Preactivists, are not willing to settle for the current state, return to the past, or get to the future ahead of everyone else. They want to design a desirable future and invent ways of bringing it about.

Interactivists work to prevent, not merely prepare for, threats and create, not merely exploit, opportunities. Interactivists struggle to achieve self-development, self-realization, self-control, and an increased ability to design their own destinies. They are not satisfiers or optimizers, but rather idealizers. To them, the formulation of ideals and visions is not an empty, imaginary exercise in utopianism, but rather a necessary step toward setting the direction for conscious, sustainable development. Interactivists work to change the foundations, as well as the superstructure, of society, institutions, and organizations. They work to redirect the tide of change, not to resist, ride with, or ride ahead of it.

We agree with Meadows that such a way of approaching the future will help to create a sustainable society. The approach implies being conscious of the fact that we daily live in the intersection between the yesterday and tomorrow, which means being aware of the present moment without losing track of the past and simultaneously inventing possible futures based on past events and current knowledge.

Consistent with the notion of optimal places for leveraging in a system to effect change, the Interactivists seek to make a *structural* change, to alter the very fabric of social consciousness. This type of behavior requires courage and self-knowledge. It requires a fearlessness and deliberate living that accepts not having all the answers and honors the sacred space of ignorance in oneself and others. We can only teach others this way of being by risking living it ourselves.

What, one might ask, does this all mean in the context of having prepared a comprehensive plan with a vision, goals, and objectives to create programs and see the plan implemented through new policies, laws, and citizen initiative? It means continuing to live the identified values of one's community and not believing that any particular product, such as a plan or indicators of progress, can replace the process of continually coming together in the conscious, deliberate creation of a sustainable community.

Thus, while models and paradigms, methodologies and approaches will help us get where we want to go, it is only when each of us strives toward self-realization and development that the collective is most likely to succeed. It is when we can bring a fearless, peaceful, highly conscious view of ourselves and others to the world that we are most effective in our response to change. In so living, we will affect others, whether we see it or not, because this type of behavior is not only contagious but also proffers hope, a rare emotion in today's harried world. Lao Tzu, the sixth-century B.C. Chinese philosopher, said: "Leaders are best when people scarcely know they exist, not so good when people obey and acclaim them. Leaders who fail to honor people are not honored by them. But of good leaders who talk little, when their work is done, their task fulfilled, the people will say, we did this ourselves." Having said this, we must now face the question of creating measures of progress.

Creating measures of progress

There is a good body of literature on indicators of sustainability, sustainable forests, sustainable communities, and so on. Indicators, of course, are bits of information that highlight what is happening in the larger system. Their purpose is to show us how a system is working, whether it is going the way we want it to or not. Indicators tell us which direction a critical aspect of our community, economy, or environment is going in terms of our vision and goals.[144] Indicators are also educational in that those dealing with sustainable community should help communicate what sustainability means.[145] Today, many in the U.S. look to the gross domestic product to determine how well we as a nation are doing economically. We discussed this earlier, and discussed the alternative notion of the genuine progress indicator. Years ago, Robert Kennedy acknowledged the shortcomings of the gross national product, as it was then called, as in indicator of the nation's economic health:[146]

> "The gross national product includes air pollution and advertising for cigarettes and ambulances to clear our highways of carnage. It counts special locks for our doors, and jails for people who break them. The gross national product includes the destruction of the redwoods and the death of Lake Superior. It grows with the production of napalm and missiles with nuclear warheads. ...And if the gross national product includes all this, there is much that it does not comprehend. It does not allow for the health of our families, the quality of their education, or the joy of their play. It is indifferent to the decency of our factories and the

safety of streets alike. It does not include the beauty of our poetry or the strength of our marriage, the intelligence of our public debate or the integrity of our public officials. ...The gross national product measures neither our wit nor our courage, neither our wisdom nor our learning, neither our compassion nor our devotion to country. It measures everything, in short, except that which makes life worthwhile; and it can tell us everything about America — except whether we are proud Americans."

These sage words are a way of introducing how we go about designing indicators that tell us how well we are doing.

Knowing how well we are doing in achieving the goals and objectives of a comprehensive plan can be determined in part from indicators and benchmarks, which are points of reference or standards against which measurements can be compared.[144] However, because the main feature of an indicator is its measurability, what do we do with the immeasurables? Can they be implied by the measurables? Ideally, yes, if the indicators are based on critical issues, identified early in the planning process, that are in turn based on identified community values; in this case, the immeasurables will be "part and parcel" of each indicator. Indicators designed by a community can be very powerful and are intensely democratic, as they are the community's own device for reporting to itself about itself.[144]

Upon reviewing critical issues, sources of data need to be found for the creation of indicators for each goal, objective, and policy. Data can be information in many forms. Access to each type of data identified on an ongoing basis is essential so that progress can be determined — measured — over time. These types of data become the indicators. Examples of sustainability indicators offered by Maureen Hart in her *Guide to Sustainability Indicators* include income disparity, water use per person, hours of work required to meet basic needs, percent of front-line employees who attended employer-sponsored training, ratio of the number of hotel jobs to number of visitors, farm acreage remaining in the county, energy use, and ecological footprint.[145]

Let's say a critical issue defined during a community planning process is that the town is unable to handle the amount of tourism it is experiencing, as revealed in part by the fact that visitors are forced to find lodging elsewhere during a typical summer season. The indicator, in this case, would be the number of motels and hotels (inns) or the number of rooms within a defined area. It is important to examine carefully, however, what constitutes a critical issue before converting it into an indicator.

In our example, it appears that the inability to accommodate the summer tourist trade is limited by the number of rooms available. Another response to this information might be to: (1) make an effort to increase the tourist trade in what is currently seen as the off-season, (2) accept the number of rooms now available and the scale of development this number of rooms represents, and (3) accept the loss in the lodging trade during that one season of the year. This information, in fact, might even bring out other effects of tourism on the city's infrastructure. Thus, an indicator of progress responding to this critical issue — the community's inability to provide adequate lodging during one season of the year — would be the number of additional off-season tourist attractions developed.

Suggested criteria for indicators offered by Sustainable Seattle are that an indicator should be (1) relevant; (2) easily understood by everyone, not just the experts; (3) compelling, illustrating community values; (4) desirable for use by the local media; (5) defensible logically and scientifically; (6) statistically measurable; (7) reliable, so that it can be measured consistently over time in order to produce comparable data; (8) appropriate in scale, suggesting the avoidance of composite indicators; (9) conducive to a proactive rather than reactive response or, worse yet, crisis management; and (10) policy-relevant or of obvious relevance to potential policy formation.[144]

When measuring our progress in achieving the goals of a comprehensive plan, we can do at least three things, from simple to difficult: (1) monitor progress according to the timelines associated with specific objectives intended to carry out the plan, and see if the city or municipality is on target; (2) develop indicators associated with critical issues as described above, which may or may not be tied directly to a definition of sustainability (if sustainable community indicators are preferred, Hart's publication[145] is an excellent resource to guide this process); and (3) work toward having the monitoring of the implementation of vision and goals as well as indicators occur at both the government and community level, which brings us to outputs vs. outcomes.

Outputs vs. outcomes

The initiation and completion of objectives called for in the comprehensive plan are examples of outputs. They are generally quantitative in nature — for example, enlargement of a city's community center. Outcomes are things that follow as a result or consequence.[147] They are more qualitative in nature than outputs and have to do with changed attitudes or higher levels of knowledge in the community or altered human behaviors. Outcomes are, of course, more difficult to measure. For example, one reason for expanding the community center might be to provide space for more community gatherings and to help build a sense of place. How do we know that sense of place, an outcome, has resulted from expanding the community center, an output? An indicator could be devised to measure this or a study could be done. Hart offers a number of indicators for *connectedness*, which is an aspect of a "sense of place." These include: "number of community gardens, percent of people who say they have enough, average distance between residences of extended family members, citizen participation in community projects, neighborhood livability as rated by residents, neighborliness, percent who say most people can be trusted."[145]

A study done in 1995 for Parks Canada sought to establish a protocol for defining the human concept of place in the Lake Superior Basin.[148] The study was conducted through interviews with basin residents. First, the boundaries of each person's "place" were determined, then what sorts of things connected the person to their place: landscape, family connections, type of lifestyle, work-related or social interactions. The interview then sought to get at what deep meanings this sense of place held for the person, especially if there was some spiritual aspect to the connection. Finally, the research attempted to determine whether the person could stretch these "deeper meanings" over a larger area. Thus, it is possible to at least get some idea of the existence of intangibles, such as sense of place, as well as attitudes and other feelings.

Ultimately, progress can be measured and felt in many ways. Some feel that true progress will have happened when we redefine poverty and prosperity to detach them from the measurable things of the material, as so eloquently stated by Robert Kennedy with respect to what the gross national product does not measure — courage, wisdom, learning, compassion, service to others, and so on. It will be a grand day indeed when we can call ourselves the wealthiest nation in the world by looking at the health of our children, our high rate of volunteerism, or the low levels of alcoholism and drug addiction.

So, the beginning of the planning process, when a community determines its core values, is the best time to describe what indicates the presence of that which we value in our community, those features that we work toward keeping alive and well.

chapter eight

Keeping the message alive

When we see land as a community to which we belong, we
may begin to use it with love and respect. —Aldo Leopold

Throughout this book, we have spoken of community building and citizen participation in ways that may require a major shift in values and beliefs. No doubt there will be many cynics, if not disbelievers, when it comes to talk of major shifts in societal attitudes.

The purpose of this chapter is to examine ways of keeping the community engaged in what, until now, we have called a planning process, which is really a process of becoming a community, a process that is ongoing and a way of being. Further, we suggest that this will be a return to something for which we have an inherent ability and a natural affinity because deep inside all of us we know what is right for the Earth and the well-being of all life. Deep inside all of us there is a longing for intimacy — being a part of a greater whole, whether community, family, or even the web of life. Could it be that we have simply been on a detour as part of a greater evolutionary process?

While it may seem to some that we have come dangerously close to being stuck in a rut headed in the other direction, based on the extinction of species, the demise of certain cultures, and other permanent losses, we believe it is not too late for profound changes in ways that we have not yet imagined. In other words, while much of the longing for change seems to represent values associated with a return to ways of more primitive societies and their simpler way of life as humanity's only hope, we think it best to remain open to all the possibilities.

In order to remain open to potential possibilities, we must begin establishing new ways of being a community, ways that retain and celebrate the best features of community as it now is, while remaining open to the need for course corrections, learning how to assess what works and what does not, and doing whatever we can to stimulate and support creativity in ourselves and others. Peter Senge, in a speech to a conference on systems thinking and action, suggested that we simply need to start talking to one another again.[82]

Now, what is it that we need to be communicating? At what scale does this work? What are some of the indicators that a societal "paradigm shift" may be occurring? And, what are the barriers to the continual emergence of a new society?

The message

The message, simply stated, is that we need to discover or rediscover our connection to the rest of life on the planet and know that nurturing it will improve our chances for survival while contributing greatly to our quality of life. In this book, we are suggesting that as we plan for what happens to ourselves and one another (and consequently to the land of which we humans are an inseparable part), we can begin to see, understand, and feel our connection to the Earth, which echoes Aldo Leopold's statement that, "When we see land as a community to which we belong, we may begin to use it with respect and love."

Our message is motivated by perceived risk; that is, we are saying that we humans are at risk, given the way we are currently operating in terms of land management and development. Our practices need to change. How can we communicate this in ways that produce or encourage responsible action? Earlier, we discussed engaging the community in a planning process whereby it should be emphasized that change is imminent, and those changes should be described as they are occurring in the world, in one's region, and particularly in one's own community. And, we suggested that a community can have some "say" over how such changes occur.

We can expect a full range of responses to this message, as with any message proffered to a community at large. It may spark interest; it may not. Communicators often want to "hook" others into involvement through fear, and while fear does indeed draw people into the public arena, fear as a motivator does not usually work well to build a sense of long-term community. This is not to say that emotions and fear will not play a role in the planning process, and, as alluded to earlier, it is important to understand that such emotions are based on psychologically valid factors that are perfectly rational from a psychological perspective.[149]

We know that when people become aware of a risk or a threat, they are inclined to fear the unknown and thus want to control circumstances to their own benefit, or they may be frightened by a perceived dependence on government or industry officials, or they may simply want to protect their belief in a just world. Conflicts that surface from the fear of risk are often polarized between those who trust scientific analysis and believe that the experts "know best" and the general public or an interest group that neither trusts nor accepts these notions — a Modernist-Traditionalist conflict discussed later in this chapter. Understanding this common dynamic is important when seeking to engage the public in meaningful ways.

To engage a community in planning for its future, it is important for the planning staff to: (1) make sure the community recognizes and accepts agency responsibility for making decisions associated with the planning process, (2) state the reasons for planning, (3) describe the planning process and how an individual can become involved, (4) describe what the benefits will be to the community, (5) describe the possible scenarios should no planning be undertaken, (6) provide further information to help citizens evaluate the usefulness of this work, (7) pretest the messages, (8) evaluate the staff's efforts, (9) know the audience or audiences — do not underestimate their intelligence nor overestimate their knowledge, (10) deal directly with uncertainty, and (11) demonstrate the collaborative nature of the endeavor.

Two critical actions are necessary to keep the community engaged. One is to respond promptly to their comments and concerns, and the other is to publicize their meetings and their work. Both are forms of recognition that function to draw citizens into the process.

In a community just outside of Santa Cruz, CA, in a neighborhood called Live Oak, county planners conducted a planning effort in 1992 that was designed to establish the direction for land use, design, and traffic circulation in the area. The neighborhood was first engaged through a series of community meetings, where residents identified what they felt required protection and what needed change. Following the meetings, a workbook was prepared for the community that presented: (1) the ideas gathered at the preliminary meetings; (2) an expression of the citizens' ideas for alternative scenarios regarding land use, transportation, and parks and recreation for ten special areas in the community; and (3) a section that asked for further ideas on criteria for the design and placement of new housing in the community.[150] The community was thus immediately engaged by being asked about neighborhood concerns and requirements. Their responses then formed the foundation for a workbook that was used in the planning process. The workbook provided recognition of the willingness of the residents to participate and express themselves as well as making the ideas of the community more tangible while being a very useful tool in the planning process, which brings us to the question of scale in planning.

At what scale is planning most effective?

In *Pattern Language*,[105] the authors maintain that, "Individuals have no effective voice in any community of more than 5000–10,000 persons. People can only have a genuine effect on local government when the units of local government are autonomous, self-governing, self-budgeting communities, which are small enough to create the possibility of an immediate link between the man in the street and his local officials and elected representatives." They go on to say that this is not a new idea, that it is in fact a model for Athenian democracy, as seen in Thomas Jefferson's plan for democracy in the U.S. and in Confucius' notion of government in China as set forth in *The Great Digest*.[105]

The size of a political community, as well as the visibility of government, either promotes or discourages the sense of connection between citizens and their government. The ideal size of a political community, suggested by the authors of *Pattern Language*, is tied to a rule of thumb offered by author Paul Goodman based on cities such as Athens "in their prime: ...No citizen should be more than two friends away from the highest member of the local unit."[105] Assuming that every citizen knows about 12 people in his local community, and using this notion and Goodman's rule, we can see that an optimal size for a political community is about 12^3, or 1728 households, or 5500 persons. Several other references echo Goodman's rule of thumb (e.g., ECCO, a neighborhood corporation in Columbus, OH; *Blueprint for Survival*, Penguin Books, 1972; a study by Terence Lee, "Urban Neighborhood as a Socio-Spatial Schema," *Ekistics* 177, August 1970) and serve to substantiate the desirability of this size of a community for the best citizen-government relations and, ostensibly, meaningful, functional policy and law.

What must be added to this ideal community size, however, is the need for the decentralization of government. This, according to the authors of *Pattern Language*, should be done using "natural geographic and historical boundaries to mark these communities" where each has the "power to initiate, decide, and execute the affairs that concern it closely," such as land use, housing, maintenance, streets, parks, police, schooling, welfare, and neighborhood services.[105]

Decentralization of government can occur to some extent when government officials go into neighborhoods and help determine future land use. Many municipalities do indeed undertake planning by engaging citizens at the neighborhood level. Because a part of any complete planning process is recognition of land uses and the needs of the larger community — sometimes even the region — planning conducted at the neighborhood level automatically takes these considerations into account, which often leads to conflicts. Because conflicts between adjacent neighborhoods in terms of goals and direction are just as likely to occur as conflicts within a neighborhood, the people leading the process need to be prepared to deal with both, which brings us to the notion of depersonalization.

Is a "paradigm shift" occurring?

Probably the most alarming societal change that seems to follow directly from advances in electronics is our growing independence and perceived lack of need for others because of such technology as e-mail, e-commerce, automated services of all sorts, and so on. Continual advances in electronics have depersonalized our world to a large extent, given us rapid access to information without time to assimilate it, and has enhanced our ability to manipulate information, all of which fosters a heightened illusion of being in control of how the world works. As the perceived control expands, and as our threshold for systems failure lowers as our contact with humans decreases, we become extremely vulnerable.

Some people see a possible "bottoming out" at a societal level as a result of this depersonalization and thus the potential for a major shift in how we view the world — a social transformation, if you will. While the modern age is characterized by individualism, materialism, and the illusion of rationality, the new age or age of sustainability will be characterized by community, spirituality, and intuition.[151] Are the values of mobility, no limits, growth, and anthropocentrism now being replaced with the values of rootedness or sense of place, the acceptance of limits, the notion of less is more, and humans as inseparable part of Nature?

A mass movement is afoot, according to some. Author and sociologist Sally J. Goerner, in her book that discusses how scientific and social movements are meeting in a quest to remake the world, wrote that a "great turning is going on."[152] The "great turning" is difficult to perceive because "in a specialist world, no one has time for integration."[152] Consequently, some major trends go unnoticed. One such trend is based on a 1996 study[153] of the U.S. population by sociologist Paul Ray in which he found that a quarter of the U.S. population fits into a group he calls Cultural Creatives. "Until ten years ago," said Ray, "the U.S. population was composed of two main cultural groups, Modernists and Traditionalists. ...Modernists ground themselves in science, technology, and industry. They tend to disdain older traditions. Traditionalists find their solidity in church and community and have doubts about the course that Modernists set."[153]

Cultural Creatives, most likely without knowing it, are taking counsel from Sitting Bull, the Sioux Chief, who told his warriors, after their victory at the Battle of the Little Big Horn, not to rejoice. He said in essence that the white man was not going to go away, that the Indian peoples must choose the best of their old ways and the best of the white ways and put them together, for that was their path into the future. Likewise, Cultural Creatives must choose the best of the Traditionalists' ways and the best of the Modernists' ways and put them together as they seek a new society that integrates science, spirituality, technology, and community for the health and well-being of the entire Earth.

The new path sought by Cultural Creatives is in response to the deterioration of systems, including education, economics, and politics, which were developed and guided by a way of thinking popularly known as the machine age. Today, Cultural Creatives are understanding that the world is like a waterbed; one cannot touch any single part of it without affecting the whole of it. Put a little differently, one cannot touch a single strand in a spider's web without sending vibrations throughout the entire web complex.

While scientists have known of such interconnectedness for some time, especially physicists, natural historians, and ecologists, it is becoming increasingly apparent that the mechanical notion of how the world works is rapidly falling into unfixable disrepair because scientists finally have the tools not only to explore how interdependent systems work but also to understand what such interdependence really means. "The result [of such knowledge]," says Ray, "is a sudden jolt. We have grossly underestimated the role interdependence plays in shaping *everything*."[153]

Thus, while the many and various applications of our new electronic technology may separate us from one another in the personal sense, this very technology may also be the linchpin to our understanding of the inter-relatedness of all parts to the whole. It may be quite a race, however, between the forces of separation and those of integration. Nevertheless, we feel that, even if science is able to more fully comprehend interdependence, the effective communication of this information to the world will be crucial to the race being won by integration and the emergence of what Goerner calls the "Integral Society."[152]

Barriers to overcome

What evidence do we see today for the appearance of an Integral Society and what barriers can we expect to thwart its development? This is not an idle question because there are always barriers to overcome in any new endeavor; they are simply part of the price of meaningful change. Author Daniel J. Boorstin says it best: "The obstacles to discovery — the illusions of knowledge — are also part of our story. Only against the forgotten backdrop of the received common sense and myths of their time [and ours] can we begin to sense the courage, the rashness, the heroic and imaginative thrusts of the great discoverers. They had to battle against the current 'facts' and dogmas of the learned."[154] Government structure, which precludes authentic community involvement, is surely a barrier, but examples of changing government structure are starting to surface.

The U.S. Forest Service is certainly out in front of other federal agencies in bringing new language and new concepts to the formation realm of policy and law. In 1993, the Northeastern Area of the U.S. Forest Service published *An Ecosystem Approach to Urban and Community Forestry*, wherein the tenets of deep ecology are discussed as a way of guiding a needed shift from an "industrio-scientific paradigm" to a "bioregional paradigm."[155] And, in 1998, the U.S. Forest Service began a new initiative to develop comprehensive monitoring programs to ensure sustainable land management. The agency is working with six national forests that have volunteered to be "pilot forests" in a project aimed at developing criteria and indicators of sustainability which, when implemented, "provide measures of ecological, social and economic well-being."[156]

While the U.S. Forest Service has been edging toward such innovations for a long time, the threats to loggers and other entities with a financial stake in what happens to the nation's forests are now starting to gain attention. An example of such attention has occurred in Minnesota, where a group of independent loggers is suing a group known as the Superior Wilderness Action Network because their comments on timber sales by the U.S. Forest

Service have delayed by several months the awarding of timber harvesting permits.[157]

The plaintiffs claim that the U.S. Forest Service is being influenced by the notion of "deep ecology" and that both the Superior Wilderness Action Network and the New Mexico-based Forest Guardians are pushing this "religion" onto the Service. Attorney for the plaintiffs, Stephen Young, stated that, "If deep ecology bites into the way the Forest Service, the National Park Service, the Department of Natural Resources, and counties manage, then our natural surroundings will be governed by the religious point of view." Young went on to say that, "In a democratic society, the secular point of view is what should prevail."[157]

And so it is that our greatest challenge in fostering a shift in world view or a social transformation will be the fear of loss — most often in the form of lost profits, as represented in this story, and possibly by the fear that somehow separation of church and state is compromised when a spiritual dimension is brought into government policy and law.

But, as Franklin D. Roosevelt and others have admonished, we must not fear this fear. "What is going on at any point in time is not a matter of right versus wrong or good versus evil. It is simply a reflection of where the mainstream of consciousness is at that time," stated Frederick J. Deneke, assistant director of the USDA Forest Service Cooperative Forestry.[158] And, it is precisely this perspective that we believe will disarm our own fear. It will enable us to integrate our minds with our hearts, work collaboratively to find "practical and peaceful solutions, and move forward together to affect the land in a way that benefits all."[158]

At the foundation of all our effort lies our willingness to know ourselves. It is the "engine of our spiritual quest and the real source of power in our lives"[159] — not a new idea, but one that merits constant remembering.

Endnotes

1. Jay Moynihan, Man's efforts pale in comparison to nature, *Ashland Daily Press*, Ashland, WI, October 29, 1997.
2. Chris Maser, *Ecological Diversity in Sustainable Development: The Vital and Forgotten Dimension*, Lewis Publishers, Boca Raton, FL, 1999, 401 pp.
3. Merriam-Webster, Inc., Publishers, *The New Merriam-Webster Dictionary*, Springfield, MA, 1989.
4. Anon., *On Common Ground*, 1(4), cover, 1998.
5. Anon., Almost no trespassing: citizens overwhelmingly give land owner right to choose use, *On Common Ground*, 1(4), 5–8, 1998.
6. This discussion is based on the following: Anon., Eminent domain: the ultimate property right, *On Common Ground*, 1(4), 23, 1998.
7. Nicole Achs, Exurbia, *American City and County*, June, 64–72, 1992.
8. Rutherford H. Platt, *Land Use and Society: Geography, Law, and Public Policy*, Island Press, Washington, D.C., 1996, 505 pp.
9. Jay Moynihan, Information moves faster than market value, *Ashland Daily Press*, Ashland, WI, May 7, 1997.
10. Paul Hawken, Natural capital, *Mother Jones News*, March/April, 40–60, 1997.
11. A.M. Jansson, *Investing in Natural Capital: Ecological Economics Approach to Sustainability*, Island Press, Washington, D.C., 1994, 504 pp.
12. Amory B. Lovins, L. Hunter Lovins, and Paul Hawken, A road map for natural capitalism, *Harvard Business Review*, May/June, 145–158, 1999.
13. The following discussion of the gross domestic product is based on Timothy R. Campbell, Sustainable Public Policy: Its Meaning, History, and Application, paper presented at the annual conference of the Community Development Society in Kansas City, July 19–22, 1998; Nicholas Georgescu-Roegen, *The Entropy Law and the Economic Process*, Harvard University Press, Cambridge, MA, 1971; Clifford Cobb, Ted Halstead, and Jonathan Rowe, If the GDP is up, why is America down?, *Atlantic Monthly*, October, 59–60, 62–66, 1995.
14. Wendell Berry, In distrust of movements, *Resurgence*, 198, 14–16, 2000.

15. The discussion of money as a measure of success is based on Peter Lang, Money as a measure, *Resurgence,* 192, 30–31, 1999; David Boyle, The new alchemists, *Resurgence,* 192, 32–33, 1999.

16. The discussion of eco-efficiency is based on William McDonough and Michael Braungart, The next Industrial Revolution, *Atlantic Monthly,* October, 82, 83–86, 88–90, 91, 1998.

17. The discussion of natural capitalism is based on an interview of Amory Lovins in Satish Kumar, Natural capitalism, *Resurgence,* 198, 8–13, 2000. (Amory Lovins is the co-author, with Paul Hawken and L. Hunter Lovins, of *Natural Capitalism,* Little, Brown, New York, 1999.)

18. Associated Press, Washington to launch new master's program, *Albany (OR) Democrat-Herald, Corvallis (OR) Gazette-Times,* January 24, 1999.

19. The discussion of genuine progress indicators is based on David Orr, Speed, *Resurgence,* 192, 16–20, 1999; William McDonough and Michael Braungart, The next Industrial Revolution, *Atlantic Monthly,* October, 82, 83–86, 88–90, 91, 1998; Timothy R. Campbell, Sustainable Public Policy: Its Meaning, History, and Application, paper presented at the annual conference of the Community Development Society, Kansas City, July 19–22, 1998; Janet N. Abramovitz, Learning to value nature's free services, *Futurist,* 31(4), 39–42, 1997; Gretchen C. Daily, Susan Alexander, Paul R. Ehrlich, Larry Goulder, Jane Lubchenco et al., Ecosystem services: benefits supplied to human societies by natural ecosystems, *Issues in Ecology,* 2, 1–16, 1997; Russell Sadler, We've lost ability to handle growth, *Albany (OR) Democrat-Herald, Corvallis (OR) Gazette-Times,* January 9, 2000.

20. The discussion of urban sprawl is based on Eben V. Fodor, *Better, Not Bigger,* New Society Publishers, Gabriola Island, B.C., 1999, 176 pp.; Donella Meadows, Stopping sprawl, *Resurgence,* 198, 30–31, 2000; Associated Press, Next 25 years to bring huge growth for Oregon, *Corvallis Gazette-Times,* Corvallis, OR, January 3, 2000; Larry Swisher, NW faces issues of growth, *Corvallis Gazette-Times,* Corvallis, OR, January 7, 2000.

21. Janet N. Abramovitz, Learning to value nature's free services, *Futurist,* 31(4), 39–42, 1997.

22. Steve Newman, Earthweek: a diary of the planet, *Albany (OR) Democrat-Herald, Corvallis (OR) Gazette-Times,* June 6, 1999.

23. Kenneth E.F. Watt, Stumbling Blocks to Social Planning, speech presented to Center for Study of Democratic Institutions, Santa Barbara, CA, November 5, 1969.

24. David Ehrenfeld Obsolescence, *Resurgence,* 193, 28–29, 1999.

25. Gregory M. Dunkel, *Whales, Buffaloes, and Overexploitation,* Demopax Tech. Note No. 1, Demopax, Inc., Washington, D.C., 1969, 30 pp.

26. Eben V. Fodor, *Better, Not Bigger,* New Society Publishers, Gabriola Island, B.C., 1999, 175 pp.

27. R. Costanza, R. d'Arge, R. de Groot, S. Farber, M. Grasso, B. Hannon, S. Naeem, K. Limburg, J. Paruelo, R.V. O'Neill, R. Raskin, P. Sutton, and M. van den Belt, The value of the world's ecosystem services and natural capital, *Nature,* 387, 253–260, 1997.

28. Thomas Michael Power, *Environmental Protection and Economic Well-Being: The Economic Pursuit of Quality,* 2nd ed., M.E. Sharpe, Inc., Armonk, NY, 1996, 250 pp.

29. Herman Daly and John Cobb, *For the Common Good,* Beacon Press, Boston, MA, 1989, 534 pp.

30. Wendell Berry, *Home Economics,* North Point Press, San Francisco, CA, 1987, 192 pp.

31. Noam Chomsky, How free is the free market?, *Resurgence,* 173, 6–9, 1995.

32. Francis Hutchinson, We are all economists, *Resurgence,* 173, 57, 1995.

33. Alfred Mayer, The rise of new America, *Mother Earth News,* March/April, 68–72, 1988.

34. The discussion of population growth in the western United States is based on Robert Weller, Western states no longer dependent on California for growth, *Corvallis Gazette-Times,* Corvallis, OR, July 10, 1999.

35. Manfred Max-Neef and Paul Ekins, Eds., *Real Life Economics: Understanding Wealth Creation,* Routledge, New York, 1992, 460 pp.

36. Rahenkampl, Sachs, Wells, and Associates with The American Society of Planning Officials and David Stoloff. *Innovative Zoning: A Local Official's Guidebook,* U.S. Department of Housing and Urban Development Office of Policy Development and Research, Washington, D.C., 1977, 28 pp.

37. Sierra Business Council, *Sierra Nevada Wealth Index,* 1996, 49 pp.

38. Joseph H. Chabourne, *Common Groundwork — A Practical Guide to Protecting Rural and Urban Land: A Handbook for Making Land-Use Decisions,* Institute for Environmental Education, Chagrin Falls, OH, 1994, 223 pp.

39. Congress for New Urbanism, Brochure, 1999.

40. *City Plan,* City of Fort Collins, CO, 1997, 235 pp.

41. *Multimodal Transportation Level of Service Manual,* City of Fort Collins, CO, 1997, 25 pp.

42. Greg Byrne and Tom Vosberg (Community Planning and Environmental Services, City of Fort Collins), Response to City Council Regarding Unintended Consequences of City Plan (memo), 1999, 7 pp.

43. Michael Penn, Taming the suburban wasteland, *On Wisconsin,* Winter, 28–34, 54, 1998..

44. Anon. TNDs and "hybrids:" what's important for sustainability?, *Livable Wisconsin,* 1(2), 1–3, 1997.

45. John G. Neihardt, *Black Elk Speaks,* University of Nebraska, Lincoln, 1961.

46. Wendell Berry, The road and the wheel, *Earth Ethics,* 1, 8–9, 1990.

47. Clyde S. Martin, Forest resources, cutting practices, and utilization problems in the pine region of the Pacific Northwest, *Journal of Forestry,* 38, 681–685, 1940.

48. Geoff Mulgan, Connexity: how to live in a connected world, *Resurgence,* 184, 6–7, 1997.

49. Chris Maser, *Vision and Leadership in Sustainable Development,* Lewis Publishers, Boca Raton, FL, 1998, 235 pp.

50. Geoffrey Hill, The sacredness of space, *Creation Spirituality,* 12, 31–33, 1996.

51. The discussion of forests in the area of Puget Sound, WA, is based on J. Martin McComber, Study shows Puget Sound forests are slowly thinning, *Corvallis Gazette-Times,* Corvallis, OR, July 15, 1998.

52. Phil Williams and Victoria Bruce, Atlanta, an "urban heat island" with higher temperatures than surrounding area, according to a NASA-sponsored study, *University of Georgia Communications News Bureau,* May 20, 1999.

53. Rick Patterson and Jan Aiels, Iowa restoration becomes a community project, *Land and Water,* 42, 43–45, 1998.

54. The discussion of Bill McDonald is based on Arthur H. Rotstein, Genius at home on the range, *Corvallis Gazette-Times*, Corvallis, OR, June 22, 1998.

55. The brief discussion on the scarcity of water is drawn from the author's own experience; Roar Bjonnes, Sweet water and bitter, *Resurgence*, 181, 32–34, 1997; Paul Simon, Excerpt of book *Tapped Out*, *Parade Magazine*, August 23, 4–6, 1998.

56. Associated Press, Residents fume over Tacoma's underwater Hylebos landfill plan, *Corvallis Gazette-Times*, Corvallis, OR, December 9, 1999.

57. Chris Maser, *Forest Primeval: The Natural History of an Ancient Forest*, Sierra Club Books, San Francisco, CA, 1989, 282 pp.

58. Chris Maser, *Sustainable Forestry: Philosophy, Science, and Economics*, St. Lucie Press, Delray Beach, FL, 1994, 371 pp.

59. The discussion about restoring part of the Snake River to a more natural condition is based on Jim Robbins, Engineers plan to send a river flowing back to nature, *The New York Times*, May 12, 1998.

60. Chris Maser and James R. Sedell, *From the Forest to the Sea: The Ecology of Wood in Streams, Rivers, Estuaries, and Oceans*, St. Lucie Press, Delray Beach, FL, 1994, 200 pp.

61. For good examples of how to repair riparian areas, see Steve Apfelbaum and Jack Broughton, Applying an ecological systems approach in urban landscapes, *Land and Water*, 42, 6–9, 1988; David Lee and Jim Lovell, Urban trout stream gets a second chance, *Land and Water*, 42, 16–19, 1998.

62. The discussion of congestion and transportation is based on the following column: Bill Bishop, To reduce congestion, don't build more roads — close 'em, *Corvallis Gazette-Times*, Corvallis, OR, May 20, 1998.

63. Chris Maser, Russ Beaton, and Kevin Smith, *Setting the Stage for Sustainability: A Citizen's Handbook*, Lewis Publishers, Boca Raton, FL, 1998, 275 pp.

64. The discussion of population in Corvallis is based on Patricia Mulder, Time to resume our dialogue on growth, *Corvallis Gazette-Times*, Corvallis, OR, May 10, 1999; Aaron Corvin, Corvallis population hits 50,000, *Corvallis Gazette-Times*, Corvallis, OR, July 7, 1999.

65. The discussion of Seaside, OR, is based on Associated Press, Seaside leaders focus on environment, *Corvallis Gazette-Times*, Corvallis, OR, July 12, 1999.

66. David Skrbina, Convivial communities, *Resurgence*, 196, 16–18, 1999.

67. V.H. Dale et al., *Ecological Principles and Guidelines for Managing the Use of the Land*, a report from the Ecological Society of America, Washington, D.C., 1999, 47 pp.

68. John Hanson, *Shimmer*, Public Television Playhouse, 1993.

69. James L. Creighton, *Citizen Participation/Public Involvement Skills Workbook*, SYNERGY Consultation Services, Cupertino, CA, 1972, 110 pp.

70. The following discussion on Chris Maser's hometown is based on the following articles and public meetings the author has attended: Aaron Corvin, Views of riverbank plan offered, *Corvallis Gazette-Times*, Corvallis, OR, September 23, 1999; Aaron Corvin, Critics ask for riprap halt. *Corvallis Gazette-Times*, Corvallis, OR, September 29, 1999; Wendy Madar, Engineer told his qualms early, *Corvallis Gazette-Times*, Corvallis, OR, October 1, 1999; Aaron Corvin, River plans face rough going, *Corvallis Gazette-Times*, Corvallis, OR. October 5, 1999; Cathy Kessinger, Scientists doubt city's plan, *Corvallis Gazette-Times*, Corvallis, OR, October 6, 1999; Aaron Corvin, Questions dog river project, *Corvallis Gazette-Times*, Corvallis, OR, October 7, 1999; Cathy Kessinger, Voters had faulty data on riverbank, *Corvallis Gazette-Times*, Corvallis, OR.

October 7, 1999; Wendy Madar, Public must be heard accurately, *Corvallis Gazette-Times*, Corvallis, OR, October 8, 1999; Unpublished review of the issues related to the Corvallis riverfront project prepared by scientists from Oregon State University; Tom Peterson, Cut trees so we can see the river, *Corvallis Gazette-Times*, Corvallis, OR, October 8, 1999; Cathy Kessinger, Expert: bank may be fine as is, *Corvallis Gazette-Times*, Corvallis, OR, October 15, 1999; Aaron Corvin, Consultants unveil new plans, *Corvallis Gazette-Times*, Corvallis, OR, October 19, 1999; Aaron Corvin, Council plans another riverfront meeting, *Corvallis Gazette-Times*, Corvallis, OR, October 20, 1999; Aaron Corvin, Competitors kept out of bid, *Corvallis Gazette-Times*, Corvallis, OR, October 21, 1999; Aaron Corvin, Consultant presents compromise river plan, *Corvallis Gazette-Times*, Corvallis, OR, October 22, 1999; No-bid deal weakens trust (editorial), *Corvallis Gazette-Times*, Corvallis, OR, October 27, 1999; Aaron Corvin, Panel questions city's handling of river review, *Corvallis Gazette-Times*, Corvallis, OR, October 27, 2000; Aaron Corvin, Panel questions city's handling of river review, *Corvallis Gazette-Times*, Corvallis, OR, January 20, 2000.

71. John Gray, The myth of progress, *Resurgence*, 196, 11–13, 1999.
72. Tom Peters, *Thriving on Chaos*, Harper & Rowe, New York, 1987, 708 pp.
73. Anon., *Caring for the Soul at Work* (brochure), Open Space Conference, St. Paul, MN, November 9–10, 1997.
74. Congressional Exchange, *Smart Talk for Growing Communities/Meeting the Challenges of Growth and Development*, Congressional Exchange, Washington, D.C., 1998, 40 pp.
75. Donella Meadows, Places to intervene in a system, *Whole Earth*, Winter, 78–84, 1997.
76. Terry Gips, The Natural Step Four Conditions to Sustainability or "System Conditions," workshop handout, Minneapolis, MN, 1998, 2 pp.
77. F. Vivano and K. Howe, Bosnia leaders say nation sits atop oil fields, *San Francisco Chronicle*, August 28, 1995.
78. Paul Wilson, Changing direction: toward sustainable culture, *Northwest Report: A Newsletter of the Northwest Area Foundation*, 19, 6, 1996.
79. Nelson-Ferris Concert Co., *Riding the Wind*, 1994.
80. Anon., Cover, *The Natural Step Newsletter*, 1(6), 6, 1999.
81. John Jackson, Resources, *Not Garbage: Municipal Solid Waste in Ontario*, prepared for the Environmental Agenda for Ontario Project, 1999, 30 pp.
82. Peter Senge, Keynote speech, Systems Thinking and Actions Conference, Atlanta, GA, November 5, 1999.
83. Gary Silberstein, Correspondence to California Senator S.I. Hayakawa, 1974, 1 p.
84. Associated Press. Experts call extinction rates "alarming," *Corvallis Gazette-Times*, Corvallis, OR, November 19, 1995; Stuart L. Pimm and Thomas M. Brooks, *The Sixth Extinction: How Large, How Soon, and Where?*, Department of Ecological and Evolutionary Biology, University of Tennessee, Knoxville, 1999, 29 pp.
85a. Ann Stewart (U.S. Information Officer, Pimicikamak Cree Nation), Personal communication, 1999.
85b. M. Noble et al., Minnesota and Wisconsin groups to form coalition to stop Duluth-Wausau transmission line, press release issued by Minnesotans for an Energy-Efficient Economy, Clean Water Action Alliance, and North American Water Office, December 9, 1999.

86. WOJB-FM, Interview with Wisconsin Public Services Commission staff, Hayward, WI, public radio broadcast, 1999.
87. Electrolux Corp., *Electrolux and the Environment 1994: Policy and Steps Taken,* Stockholm, Sweden, 1994, 19 pp.
88. Beth Wolfensberger-Singer, Housing the soul, *New Age,* January/February, 69–73, 1999.
89. This discussion is based on Jeremy Seabrook, Basic needs, *Resurgence,* 193, 38–39, 1999.
90. Henry L. Diamond and Patrick F. Noonan, *Land Use in America,* Island Press, Washington, D.C., 1996, 351 pp.
91. Terry Gips, Handout prepared for Natural Step training for Lake Superior Binational Forum, Thunder Bay, Ontario, 1999, 36 pp.
92. Jon Magnuson, Personal correspondence from Director of Cedar Tree Institute, Marquette, MI, January 2000.
93. Daniel Kimmis, *Community and Politics of Place,* University of Oklahoma Press, Norman, OK, 1990, 150 pp.
94. Kenneth Margolis, *Paying Attention: An Interview with Barry Lopez,* http://www.environlink.org/enviroar..._and_conversations/Barry Lopez.html.
95. Darrell Morrison, Presentation of proposed campus landscape plan to members of Northland College faculty, staff, and trustees, October 22, 1999.
96. John Friedman, *Retracking America: A Theory of Transactive Planning,* Anchor Press/Doubleday, Garden City, NY, 1973, 278 pp.
97. Ralph Keeny, *Value-Focused Thinking: A Path to Creative Decision Making,* Harvard University Press, Cambridge, MA, 1992, 416 pp.
98. Geoffry Ball, Personal correspondence with Jane Silberstein, 1990.
99. Michael J. Kinsley, *Economic Renewal Guide,* Rocky Mountain Institute, Snow Mass, CO, 1992, 100 pp.
100. Adapted from several lists: *Checklist for Evaluating the Sustainability of Community Ideas and Project Proposals,* Minnesota Office of Environmental Assistance, adapted June 1996 from draft paper by Sustainable Seattle, 2 pp.; Sarah James et al., *American Planning Association Policy Guide on Sustainability,* http://www.planning.org/govt/sustdvpg.htm, 1999, 17 pp.; California State Clearinghouse, *Environmental Checklist Form,* 1990, 4 pp.
101. The following discussion is based on Jay Walljasper, Asphalt rebellion, *Resurgence,* 193, 11, 1999; Peter Headicar, Traffic in towns, *Resurgence,* 197, 22–23, 1999; John Whitelegg, Sorry lorries, *Resurgence,* 197, 28–29, 1999; Calvin Woodward, Commuters face a snarling American road, *Corvallis Gazette-Times,* Corvallis, OR, November 17, 1999; Tara Burghart, Portland tops list of cities with worst congestion, *Corvallis Gazette-Times,* Corvallis, OR, November 17, 1999.
102. William Dietz, Director of Nutrition and Physical Activity, Center for Disease Control, Atlanta, Report heard on National Public Radio, October 27, 1999.
103. James Hillman, Pleasure of walking, *Resurgence,* 197, 10–11, 1999.
104. John Grimshaw, Joy of cycling, *Resurgence,* 197, 12–13, 1999.
105. Christopher Alexander et al., *Pattern Language,* Oxford University Press, New York, 1977, 1171 pp.
106. Karl M. Karlson, Wetland aids sewage solution, *St. Paul Pioneer Press,* September 27, WI section, page 1, 1992.
107. Travis Stansel, Conserving community: Prairie Crossing and Tryon Farms are national role models of green housing, *Conscious Choice,* September, 22–24, 1999.

108. Paul Hawken, *Ecology of Commerce: A Declaration of Sustainability,* Harper Business, New York, 1993.

109. Council of Great Lakes Industries, Correspondence to R. Harding, Director, State of Michigan Dept. of Environmental Quality; Commissioner Karen Studders, Director, Minnesota Pollution Control Agency; Secretary George Meyer, State of Wisconsin Department of Natural Resources; Honorable Tony Clement, Minister of Environment, Ontario, Canada, 1999.

110. *General Plan — 1990–2005,* City of Santa Cruz, CA, 1992, 495 pp.

111. Bill McKibbon, On Livable Communities: Creating Sustainable Urban Environments, presentation to conference on urban sprawl in Boulder, CO, 1998.

112. Amory Lovins, L. Hunter Lovins, and Paul Hawken, A roadmap for natural capitalism, *Harvard Business Review,* May/June, 145–158, 1999.

113. Braden R. Allenby, *Industrial Ecology: Policy Framework and Implementation,* Prentice Hall, Upper Saddle River, NJ, 1999, 308 pp.

114. Chris Maser, *Sustainable Community Development: Principles and Concepts,* St. Lucie Press, Delray Beach, FL, 1997, 257 pp.

115. Chris Maser, *Resolving Environmental Conflicts: Toward Sustainable Community Development,* St. Lucie Press, Delray Beach, FL, 1996, 200 pp.

116. Many of the relationships in this section were drawn from The Conservation Fund, *Conservation Development Evaluation System,* rev. draft, Chicago, IL, 1999, 10 pp.; State of Wisconsin, Natural Resources Code 117, 1990.

117. Angie Wagner, Nevada leads the nation in housing development, *Corvallis Gazette-Times,* Corvallis, OR, December 9, 1999.

118. Rober G. Lee et al., Integrating sustainable development and environmental vitality: a landscape ecology approach, in *New Perspectives in Watershed Management,* Neiman, R.J., Ed., Springer-Verlag, New York, 1992, pp. 499–552.

119. J. Fletcher, Homebuyers are shunning developers' pricey extras, *The Wall Street Journal,* November 21, 1997.

120. Edward T. McMahon, Tourism and the environment: what's the link?, *Forum Journal of the National Trust for Historic Preservation,* Winter, 2–3, 1999.

121. *Design Review Policies,* City of Santa Rosa, CA, 1980, 57 pp.

122. Design guidelines from City of Santa Cruz, CA; City of Capitola, CA; Grand Traverse Bay, MI; Towamencin Village, Montgomery County, PA; Duluth, MN, Downtown Waterfront; State of Vermont; Winona County, MN.

123. *Results of the Visual Preference Survey,* City of Fort Collins, CO, 1995, 61 pp.

124. *Signs and the Small Business — Focus on Facts,* U.S. Small Business Administration, in cooperation with the National Electric Sign Association, [no date], 2 pp.

125. Philip Brasher, Development of farms: open space doubles during 1990s, *Corvallis Gazette-Times,* Corvallis, OR, December 18, 1999.

126. Steve Apfelbaum and Jack Broughton, Applying an ecological systems approach to urban landscapes, *Land and Water,* January/February, 6–9, 1998.

127. The discussion of three tools is based on a publication of the Green Corridor Project and the State of Minnesota, 1998, 126 pp.

128. Virginia Stark, *Yes, You Can! Governmental Authority for Sustainable Policy-Making,* 1999, 98 pp.

129. Telephone conversation with Andrew Jones, systems thinking and environmental management consultant, Asheville, NC, November 1999.

130. *Governor's Design Team Community Manual,* Minnesota Department of Trade and Economic Development, 1991, 74 pp.

131. Telephone conversation with Robert Brander, SmartWood Coordinator, Upper Midwest, 1999.
132. Bill Echlin, Peer site review committee responsible for guiding growth, *Traverse City (MI) Record-Eagle,* January 10, 1999.
133. The discussion on multi-stakeholder groups is based on *Environmental Sustainability Kit,* Environmental Defense Fund, Washington, D.C., 1996, 112 pp.
134. Ed Klophenstein, New land-use law may limit public comment, *Corvallis Gazette-Times,* Corvallis, OR, March 26, 1996.
135. The discussion on "SLAPP" suits is based on John Butterworth, House passes legislation to stop SLAPP suits, *Corvallis Gazette-Times,* Corvallis, OR, May 13, 1999; Anon., Anti-SLAPP legislation defeated, *Corvallis Gazette-Times,* Corvallis, OR, July 7, 1999.
136. Aaron Corvin, Committee seeks to encourage public involvement in local land development process, *Corvallis Gazette-Times,* Corvallis, OR, December 8, 1999.
137. *California State Clearinghouse Handbook: Environmental Checklist Form,* State of California, 1990, pp. 43–46.
138. *Checklist for Evaluating the Sustainability of Community Ideas and Project Proposals,* Minnesota Office of Environmental Assistance, 1996, 2 pp.
139. *Checklist for Neighborhood Sustainability,* Sustainable Seattle, [no date], 6 pp.
140. Rebecca Bauen, Bryan Baker, and Kirk Johnson, *Sustainable Community Checklist,* first ed., Northwest Policy Center, Graduate School of Public Affairs, Seattle, WA, 1996, 44 pp.
141. Al Gore, *Earth in the Balance: Ecology and the Human Spirit,* Houghton-Mifflin Co., New York, 1992, 407 pp.
142. Daniel Quarmman, Planet of weeds, *Harper's Magazine,* October, 57–69, 1998.
143. Paul Moss, Minnesota Office of Environmental Assistance Team biweekly e-mail newsletter [paulmoss@moea.state.mn.us], 1999.
144. *A Primer for Creating New Measurements of Progress,* Sustainable Seattle, 1996, 14 pp.
145. Maureen Hart, *Guide to Sustainable Community Indicators,* 2nd ed., Hart Environmental Data, Andover, MN, 1999, 201 pp.
146. *Indicators of Sustainability,* Sustainable Seattle, 1993, 35 pp.
147. The discussion in this paragraph is based on *Designing Your Town,* American Institute of Architects, Washington, D.C., 1992, 55 pp.
148. Dorothy Lagerroos, Patricia Shifferd, and John Graff, *A Protocol for Defining the Human Concept of Place in the Lake Superior Basin, a Project Funded by Parks Canada,* Ashland, WI, 1995, 48 pp.
149. Michael A. Kamrin, Dolores J. Katz, and Martha L. Walter, *Reporting on Risk: A Journalist's Handbook on Environmental Risk Assessment,* Foundation for American Communications and National Sea Grant College Program, 1995, 113 pp.
150. Brady and Associates, in association with Korve Engineering, *Community Plan Workbook for Live Oak,* Santa Cruz County, CA, 1992, 60 pp.
151. Dorothy Lagerroos, Conflicting Worldviews?, classroom presentation, Northland College, Ashland, WI, 1998.
152. S. J. Goerner, *After the Clockwork Universe: The Emerging Science and Culture of Integral Society,* Foris Books, Edinburgh, 1999, 476 pp.
153. Paul Ray, The rise of integral culture, *Noetic Sciences Review,* 37(Spring), 4–15, 1996.

154. Daniel J. Boorstin, *The Discoverers*, Vintage Books, New York, NY, 1983, 745 pp.
155. *An Ecosystem Approach to Urban and Community Forestry: A Resource Guide*, U.S.D.A. Forest Service, Northeastern Area, U.S. Department of Agriculture, Washington, D.C., 1993, 600 pp.
156. Phyllis Green, Forest Supervisor, Ottawa National Forest, Invitation to stakeholders to participate in indicators project, 1999.
157. Dennis Lien, Suit: religion, logging don't mix, *St. Paul Pioneer Press*, St. Paul, MN, October 2, 1999.
158. Frederick J. Deneke, Forestry: an evolution of consciousness, *Journal of Forestry*, 96(1), 56, 1998.
159. Richard Thieme, *Islands in the Clickstream: Between Transitions*, http://www.thieme works.com, November 30, 1999.